THE NATURE AND SOURCES OF THE LAW

BEACON SERIES IN CLASSICS OF THE LAW

Charles M. Haar, *General Editor*

Commentaries on the Laws of England. Volume IV, *Of Public Wrongs,* by William Blackstone

Selected Historical Essays of F. W. Maitland, chosen and introduced by Helen M. Cam

The Nature and Sources of the Law, by John Chipman Gray

Ancient Law, by Henry Sumner Maine

THE NATURE AND SOURCES OF THE LAW

BY

JOHN CHIPMAN GRAY

LL.D., YALE AND HARVARD

LATE ROYALL PROFESSOR OF LAW IN HARVARD UNIVERSITY

SECOND EDITION

FROM THE AUTHOR'S NOTES, BY

ROLAND GRAY, LL.B.

BEACON PRESS BOSTON

Published 1921 by The Macmillan Company, New York
First published as a Beacon Paperback in 1963
Printed in the United States of America

TO

HIS OLD PUPILS

WHOSE AFFECTIONATE REGARD

HAS BEEN TO HIM

A LIFE-LONG BLESSING

FROM

THEIR GRATEFUL

MASTER

Preface to the Beacon Press Edition

A story of my own experience of Gray as a law teacher may perhaps serve to introduce his book to the student of the science of law.

One morning in the Christmas recess of 1889, during my first year as a student in Harvard Law School, I was in the reading room at work on the first volume of Gray's *Cases on Property.* At the beginning of each section Gray had placed an extract from the *Institutes* of Justinian, in the original Latin. Those were the days when college education was classical and college graduates were expected to read Latin as a matter of course. I was trying to find out what the text of Roman law before me meant and what it had to do with what we were studying; and I thought that I ought to know something about Roman law. So I went to the delivery desk and asked the man in charge for a book on Roman law. He went into the stacks and brought back Lord Mackenzie's *Roman Law,* probably the least useful book for any purpose of an American student that could be conceived. While I was trying unsuccessfully to make something out of it, I heard a gruff voice behind me saying, "Don't read that." I looked up, saw that it was Professor Gray, and asked him, "What should I read?" He asked, "Do you read German?" and on my reply that I could, he took Lord Mackenzie's book away from me, went into the stacks, and came back with Sohm's *Institutionen des römischen Rechts*—in those days the great book on Roman law, which had not then been translated into English—"Read that," he announced and walked off.

This was characteristic of Gray as a teacher. He put the

student in touch with the right material and expected him to put it to good use.

In his study of the nature, forms and sources of law, the American student is handicapped by a deficiency of our English language, which has but one term—"law"—for three ideas of prime importance for the subject. The French can use *ordre juridique, droit* and *loi*. The German can use *Rechtsordnung, Recht* and *Gesetz*. Recently a tendency has grown up to use the English phrase "rule of law" for the idea of a general regime of adjustment of relations and ordering of conduct by reason instead of by force. But that phrase too strongly suggests a further adjustment and ordering by imposed rules laid down by a universal political authority, something which smaller peoples and states, justly suspicious of domination by their more populous and wealthy neighbors, are loath to accept.

Because of the linguistic limitations of English juridical vocabulary, we need an assured distinction between the policing of local communities or even states in their internal activities from the keeping of the peace which must be achieved by force —even if the persons, places, times, and manner in which the force is to be applied are strictly regulated by law. Indeed these aspects of the application of force are commonly regulated by rules. But the administration of justice is not merely a glorified policing. It calls for and employs not force but reason, although in the end its mandates for the solution of particular cases may call for a final disposition of the coercive power of the state. The strength of law is in reason, in the universal appeal of reason to civilized mankind.

Socrates held that a man, in his talks with other men on current topics, ought to know exactly what he is talking about. Definition of terms and precise laying out of the subject of discourse is fundamental. But there is a much needed warning in the maxim of Roman law which states that in law all definition is dangerous. The abstractness and the oracular form of definitions may make them deceptive. Usually they require exposition to make them effective for their purposes. The main point is to grasp the leading idea.

The analytical jurists of the nineteenth century thought of law in terms of policing—the preventing or deterring of wrongs. Philosophical jurists of that time thought of law in terms of metaphysically determined principles of conduct. In ethics, law was held to mean rationally formulated rules of conduct; in philosophy, the leading idea was that of rationally formulated principles of justice. In economics, writers have taken their ideas from political science or from ethics. In political science, the law is commonly thought of in terms of laws. Sociologists are more concerned with the legal order than with law or laws. They commonly use the word "law" to cover all received precepts of conduct. Thus, definition of law has been a battleground of jurisprudence.

Professor Gray did not undertake, much less pretend, to lay down precepts of universal truth to be learned by heart and to guide the student in the study, practicing and teaching of his life work. What Gray sought was to bring out the best and most that wisdom, study and experience have taught us about the nature and sources of law, leaving it to each of his students and readers to make the most and best of it that he can.

1962

ROSCOE POUND
University Professor Emeritus,
formerly *Dean of Harvard Law School*

PREFACE

TO THE FIRST EDITION

Some fifty years ago I came across a copy of Austin's "Province of Jurisprudence Determined," then little read in England, and all but unknown in this country; and since then, although my work has been mainly on other lines, the subject has seldom been for long wholly out of my mind. I put my ideas into substantially their present shape a dozen years ago[1]; I have held them in abeyance more than the prescribed nine years; but I doubt if they would ever have been published had not Columbia University done me the honor of applying the *lene tormentum* of an invitation to give a course of lectures on the Carpentier Foundation.

The lectures were read at Columbia University in the spring of 1908. They have been here divided into thirteen chapters, but no attempt has been made to change the familiar style they bore in delivery. The use of homely expressions and examples helps one to keep a grasp on the facts of daily life, the loss of which is the chief danger in the moral sciences.

There may not be so good a defence for the repetitions in these lectures; readers may be provoked by what they

[1] Professor Gray delivered a brief course of lectures on Comparative Jurisprudence, at the Harvard Law School, in the years 1896 to 1900, and 1901-1902.

will consider damnable iteration; but here, too, it seemed desirable to show how, in approaching the Law from different points of view, the same truths emerge as fundamental.

My wish to keep the lectures within moderate limits has led to the omission of much that might properly have found a place in them. For a fuller and, it may be, a broader treatment of several of the subjects treated, I commend to the reader the books of two of my learned friends, "Studies in History and Jurisprudence," by Mr. James Bryce, now British Ambassador at Washington, and a "First Book of Jurisprudence," by Sir Frederick Pollock, Corpus Christi Professor of Jurisprudence at Oxford.

The student of Jurisprudence is at times troubled by the thought that he is dealing not with things, but with words, that he is busy with the shape and size of counters in a game of logomachy, but when he fully realizes how these words have been passed and are still being passed as money not only by fools and on fools, but by and on some of the acutest minds, he feels that there is work worthy of being done, if only it can be done worthily.

I have endeavored to acknowledge my conscious indebtedness to other writers, but when one has been reading and thinking on a subject for half a century, it is difficult, indeed impossible, to tell what is one's own and what one owes to others. It is best to make no claim to originality; I make none.

It is a pleasure to render my hearty thanks to the authorities of the University, and especially to Dean

Kirchwey and the other members of the Faculty of Law, for their cordial welcome and encouragement.

J. C. G.

JULY 14, 1909.[1]

[1] The author's seventieth birthday. For an account of his life, see 28 Harvard Law Rev. 539; 1 Mass. Law Quart. (No. 2) 29; Proceedings of Mass. Hist. Soc., March, 1915, and May, 1916; and memoir, privately printed, Boston, 1917.

PREFACE

TO THE SECOND EDITION

At the time of Professor Gray's death, in 1915, he had made notes for a second edition of this book. His chief reason for republishing the work was the desire to put it into a form which would reach a larger number of readers. This purpose I have tried to accomplish in several ways, some of which were expressly indicated by the author, others were adopted by me to carry out his intention.

The quotations in Latin, Greek and German have been translated at the foot of the page; and most of the technical legal terms have been explained. Citations have been added to references and quotations, where I could find them. There have been several transpositions, but no omissions except of a few paragraphs at the beginning. The additions to the text, as distinguished from the notes, are all due to the author.

Much has been written, since the publication of the first edition, on the subjects with which this volume deals. As the author did not at all change his views, nor consider it advisable to deal, in the new edition, with what had been written for or against his opinions since their publication, I have not discussed such writings, nor even, in most cases, mentioned them. I have ventured, however, to refer to some passages in recent books and magazines which illustrate statements made in the book. Such references include only a small fraction of the works read in the preparation of this edition; and the material so read is only a part of what has been published, in English alone, since the first appearance of the book. No attempt has been made to cover the ground completely by these annotations, incidental to a revision of which the principal object is an alteration in form.

As the additions to the text and the notes, whether made by the author or myself, are all of an explanatory or illustrative character, or else of no great importance, I have not thought it necessary to distinguish the new portions. I have to thank Russell Gray, Esquire, for various suggestions, and for looking over the proofs.

ROLAND GRAY.

Boston, 1921.

TABLE OF CONTENTS

PART I

NATURE OF THE LAW

CHAPTER III

CHAPTER IV

CHAPTER V

CHAPTER VI

CHAPTER VII

PART II

SOURCES OF THE LAW

CHAPTER VIII

CHAPTER IX

CHAPTER X

CHAPTER XI

CHAPTER XII

CHAPTER XIII

APPENDIX I

APPENDIX II

APPENDIX III

APPENDIX IV

APPENDIX V

PART I

THE NATURE OF THE LAW

INTRODUCTION

Analytic study of legal conceptions

THE Law of a community consists of the general rules which are followed by its judicial department in establishing legal rights and duties.[1] To determine the Law, we have to consider the sources from which that department has drawn it.

In this volume I propose to call your attention to the analysis and relations of some fundamental legal ideas, rather than to tell their history or prophesy their future development. Not that I am insensible to the value of historical studies, nor blind to the fact that legal conceptions are constantly changing, yet, to borrow a figure from the shop, it is well at times to take account of stock, to consider and analyze Law in the stage of development which it has reached, although we believe it neither possible nor desirable that the development should not go on in the future.

Besides, as one should remember, though most legal conceptions alter, and there may be few which are so based on eternal principles that they cannot change while the order of nature continues, yet their change is often exceedingly slow, and many of them go back as far as we have a clear

[1] See pp. 84 *et seq. post.*

knowledge of human affairs, and show to our eyes no signs of decay.

The analytic study of the general conceptions of the Law is not, as experience has shown, without its dangers. It may easily result in a barren scholasticism. "Jurisprudence," as Mr. Dicey says,[1] "is a word which stinks in the nostrils of a practising barrister. A jurist is, they constantly find, a professor whose claim to dogmatise on law in general lies in the fact that he has made himself master of no one legal system in particular, whilst his boasted science consists in the enunciation of platitudes which, if they ought, as he insists, to be law everywhere, cannot in fact be shown to be law anywhere." Yet, as Mr. Dicey in the same article goes on to show, "Prejudice excited by a name which has been monopolised by pedants or impostors" should not blind us to the advantage of having clear and not misty ideals on legal subjects.

Especially valuable is the negative side of analytic study. On the constructive side it may be unfruitful; but there is no better method for the puncture of windbags. Most of us hold in our minds a lot of propositions and distinctions, which are in fact identical, or absurd, or idle, and which we believe, or pretend to ourselves to believe, and which we impart to others, as true and valuable. If our minds and speech can be cleared of these, it is no small gain.

This is the great merit of Austin. His style is inexpressibly wearisome. He himself once expressed a doubt whether his love-letters were not written in the fashion of an equity draughtsman; and certainly his

[1] 5 Law Mag. and Rev. (4th series) 382.

treatise resembles in manner more the charging part of an old bill in equity than any other kind of human composition. The insolence of his language also—though very likely not of his thought—is often offensive, and the theories which he advanced have not remained unshaken. But his unwillingness to let others juggle with words, or to juggle with them himself, or knowingly to leave any dark corner of a subject unexplored, has seldom been equalled, and to many students has made the reading of his crabbed book a lesson never to be forgotten in intellectual honesty.[1]

Classification and definition

The task of an analytic student of the Law is the task of classification, and, included in this, of definition. It has been truly said that he who could perfectly classify the Law would have a perfect knowledge of the Law; but the besetting sin of the analytic jurist is the conviction that his classification and definitions are final. He is often sensitive, over sensitive, to this fault in other writers, but he feels that he himself has said the last word. I cannot hope to escape this failing of all our tribe. But I want to warn my readers of its existence, that they may exercise a judicious scepticism. I shall be more than satisfied if I can interest them enough in the subject to make them think it worth while to question my conclusions.

The Common Law has often been reproached with the lack of precision and certainty in its definitions, but, in truth, it is a great advantage of the Common Law, and of the mode of its development by judicial decision, that its definitions are never the matters resolved by the cases;

[1] The above four paragraphs are reproduced in substance from the author's article, "Some Definitions and Questions in Jurisprudence," in 6 Harvard Law Rev. 21, 23.

they are never anything but *dicta.* If at the end of the sixteenth, or of the seventeenth, or even of the eighteenth century, there had been definitions binding by statute on the Courts; if the meaning of "contract," and "malice," and "possession," and "perpetuities," had been fixed, what fetters would have been imposed on the natural development of the Law. And it is the great disadvantage of a written code, that practising lawyers and jurists alike are hampered by the cast-iron classification and definitions of a former generation, which, in the advancement of legal thought and knowledge, are now felt to be imperfect and inadequate.[1]

But although our attempts at classification are necessarily provisional and temporary, although the one certain prophecy that the legal writer can make is that the classification which approves itself to him at the beginning of the twentieth century will surely *not* be the one which will prevail at its end, yet our imperfect efforts may not be useless; our classification and our definitions, inadequate as they will doubtless prove to be, may yet be stepping-stones to higher things. It may be well to climb up the hill of knowledge, although we feel sure we shall never reach the top.

Value of concrete instances

The danger in dealing with abstract conceptions, whether in the Law or in any other department of human knowledge, is that of losing foothold on the actual earth. The best guard against this is the concrete instance, the example. Much fine-spun speculation has been demolished by showing that it did not fit the facts. I shall, therefore, try to test the soundness of any theories I

[1] Cf. Chalmers, Bills of Exchange (8th ed.) p. liii.

may advance, by applying them to sets of facts and seeing how they work in practice. Nor shall I apologize for the familiar and homely character of my instances—the more familiar the better.

The Common Law is the system whose fundamental conceptions I shall try to analyze, but from time to time I will compare them with the like conceptions in the Civil Law,[1] as exemplified in the Law of Rome, of Germany, of France, and of Scotland. As to the other countries of Europe, I regret to say that I have next to no knowledge of their Law.

[1] *I.e.* the law deriving its origin from ancient Rome.

CHAPTER I

LEGAL RIGHTS AND DUTIES

THE Law is so closely concatenated that it is hard to determine where to approach it; an attack upon any part, to be successful, seems to call for a previous knowledge of other parts. Yet one must begin somewhere. Where shall it be? Man was not made for the Law, but the Law for man. The Law has, for its subject-matter, the legal rights and duties of men. With those rights and duties we will begin. But first, a word or two on rights and duties in general.

Rights and duties in general

Human intercourse in all stages of civilization above the lowest condition of savagery (if even that be an exception) assumes that there is a difference between right and wrong, and that men ought to do right and to refrain from doing wrong. I do not propose to consider the true test of right and wrong,—whether it be the will of God, or living according to Nature, or the dictates of conscience, or the principle of utility, or anything else; nor shall I attempt to analyze the meaning of the word "ought," or to explain the origin of the feeling of obligation; whatever its origin, the members of every society which is far enough advanced to have a Law have acquired it.

The ambiguity of language has been an obstacle in the path of even the physical sciences, but the harm which it has worked in the moral sciences is far greater. These latter deal with the conduct of life, and we are constantly using words, now loosely, as the counters of daily talk, and now with an attempt to pin them down to serve as the exact expressions of the most abstract notions. So it is with the word "right."

Ambiguity of word "right"

In most of the languages of Europe, the same word is used to express "a right" and also "Law." Thus, *jus, recht, droit, diritto, derecho,* etc. This double meaning of the word has worked woeful confusion in the legal philosophy of the Germans. If they have finally grasped the distinction between what they style *objectives recht,* or "Law," and *subjectives recht,* or "a right," the grasp is, on the part of many writers, with a by no means firm hand.

Though in English we are spared this particular ambiguity, the English word "right" furnishes another. It is sometimes a substantive and sometimes an adjective. As an adjective, "right" means "in accordance with what ought to be." But what does "right" mean as a substantive? When we say that John Doe has a right to a farm, what do we mean? I am not speaking, for the moment, of *legal* rights. But, apart from the Law, has a man rights, and if so, what are they? He certainly has, in common parlance. Let us try to get at the meaning of the word a little more precisely.

Right is a correlative to duty; where there is no duty there can be no right. But the converse is not necessarily true. There may be duties without rights. In order for a duty to create a right, it must be a duty *to act or forbear.* Thus, among those duties which have rights corresponding to them do not come the duties, if such there be, which call for an inward state of mind, as distinguished from external acts or forbearances. It is only to acts and forbearances that others have a right. It may be our duty to love our neighbor, but he has no right to our love. *Aime-moi, ou je te tue,* is an extravagance. The utmost to which our neighbor has a right is that we should treat him as if we loved him.

Again, a duty to which a right corresponds must be a duty to act or forbear towards other persons. Among the duties with correlative rights are not included self-regardant duties, those which have no reference whatever to other persons. In our complex state of society, there may be few duties which are absolutely and solely self-regardant; but such duties may be conceived. If a ship, laden with Medford rum, be wrecked on a desert island, although the owner be the sole survivor, and although he have no hope or chance of rescue, it may yet be his duty not to pass his time in drinking up the cargo. But no one has here any right.

Once more, in order to give a man a right, there must be a duty to act or forbear in his interest. There may be a duty to do an act to a person where we cannot say that he has a right to have the act done. Thus, it may be the duty of Jack Ketch to hang Jonathan Wild, but we do not say that Wild has a right to be hanged.

Excluding what ought to be excluded, we have, then, this as a definition of moral right: When one is under a duty to act or forbear in the interest of a person, such a person has a right to that act or forbearance.

Relation of public opinion to rights

Another meaning given to "a right" is to be found adopted and explained in Mr. Holland's "Elements of

Jurisprudence,"[1] as well as anywhere. "What, then," he says, "is 'a legal right'? But first, what is a right generally? It is one man's capacity of influencing the acts of another, by means, not of his own strength, but of the opinion or the force of society. When a man is said to have a right to do anything, or over anything, or to be treated in a particular manner, what is meant is that public opinion would see him do the act, or make use of the thing, or be treated in that particular way, with approbation, or at least with acquiescence; but would reprobate the conduct of any one who should prevent him from doing the act, or making use of the thing, or should fail to treat him in that particular way."

But is this approval by public opinion a necessary element in the idea of a right? In some of the United States,—as, for example, in Texas,—statutes exempt the property of debtors to a very large amount from being taken for their debts, and these statutes, judging from the language of the Courts, meet with the hearty approval of the public opinion of the neighborhood, as designed, they say, "to cherish and support in the bosoms of individuals, those feelings of sublime independence which are so essential to the maintenance of free institutions."[2] Does this give the Texan farmer a right not to pay his debts? Does the fact that he lives in a community where such things are practised and praised affect the question? If a man has to pass upon the rights of himself or of any one else, it is more than probable that his judgment will be affected by the tone of the community in which he lives, but, if he is honest, he does not

[1] Jurisprudence (11th ed.) 81.
[2] *Franklin* v. *Coffee*, 18 Tex. 413, 416.

consciously admit the voice of public opinion as the test of the existence of rights. Public opinion is no more an essential element of rights than it is of morality itself.

It may be said that all this is a question of nomenclature, and that Mr. Holland may give to a word any meaning he pleases, provided his usage is consistent with itself. But it is submitted that, while the need of scientific precision sometimes requires a writer to select and adhere to one of the meanings of a word or phrase between which popular speech varies, he should depart from ordinary usage as little as possible. The failure to observe this rule has two evil results. In the first place, the writer is more likely to be misunderstood by his readers, and secondly, his own attention will sometimes flag, he will unconsciously substitute the common for his own arbitrary meaning, and the ambiguous term will bring his argument to grief.

It is undoubtedly desirable to have a term to express what a man has by virtue of public opinion concerning the duty of others to act or forbear in his interest, but it had best not be "rights" simply; "positive moral rights," though not entirely unobjectionable, seems as unobjectionable as any that has been proposed.

While on this matter of nomenclature, it may be remarked that although "right" and "duty" are used as correlative terms, and in common parlance, as well as in scientific terminology, there can be no right where there is no duty, yet "right" seems to have had its origin in the Law, and "duty" in ethics; that, in spite of each term being now domesticated in the domain of the other, so that they have paired in both places, the expression "moral right" does not come as trippingly from the tongue as "legal right," and, on the other hand, "legal duty" strikes the ear with a less familiar sound than "moral duty"; and that the ideas first evoked by the words "right" and "duty" are of "legal right" and of "moral duty," respectively.

Legal rights and duties

So much as to rights and duties generally: now for legal rights and duties. Human society is organized for the protection and advancement of human interests. The object of its organization is to insure the doing of certain things which individuals could not do, and to protect individuals in the accomplishment of their wishes to an extent to which they could not protect themselves. Sometimes the real purpose of organization is to secure the interests of a very limited number of persons. But yet, such are the blessings of order, that any political organization, however small the number of persons intended to be benefited by it, is better for the rest than anarchy.

To accomplish its purposes, the chief means employed by an organized society is to compel individuals to do or to forbear from doing particular things. Sometimes the society puts this compulsion in force of its own motion; and sometimes it puts it in force only on the motion of the individuals who are interested in having it exercised.

The rights correlative to those duties which the society will enforce of its own motion are the legal rights of that society. The rights correlative to those duties which the society will enforce on the motion of an individual are that individual's legal rights. The acts and forbearances which an organized society will enforce are the legal duties of the persons whose acts and forbearances are enforced.

Legal and moral rights

The poverty of our nomenclature, on which I have

already remarked, has worked a confusion in these fundamental ideas. The word "duty" has been used so preeminently in the sphere of morality that there is attached to it, and, in a less degree, to the correlative word "right," the flavor of "ought," of right as opposed to wrong, which is difficult to remove even by prefixing the word "legal"; and many persons feel a natural repulsion from the statement that, "It is a legal duty to obey a statute commanding an immoral act."

And yet if legal duties are the acts and forbearances which an organized society will compel, it is obvious that many very immoral acts and forbearances have been legal duties.

But some writers, while admitting this, are led by the ethical atmosphere which attends "right" and "duty" to connect law with ethics, not in a legitimate but in an illegitimate way. They recognize "that a positive right is that which is regarded and treated as a right in some system established for the maintenance of rights," and that this positive right may differ from what they call right in fact, or natural right, but they insist that the function of organized society is not to create rights, but to declare them, and that any distinction between legal duties and rights, on the one hand, and duties and rights in fact is due to the imperfection with which society performs its functions; in other words, that the essence of legal duties is that they are moral duties as declared by society, and not simply acts and forbearances which society will enforce; that is, although they do not deny that this last is a correct description, they say that it does not bring out the true nature of legal duties.

Now, it may be granted that an organized society, in

acting through its legislative or judicial organs, is generally purporting to act in accordance with morality, but, on the other hand, many statutes are passed without any question of morality occurring to the legislators, and the real motives of many legislative acts have been undoubtedly selfish and immoral.

Let us take a case which will serve as a test. Suppose some autocrat of absolute power, cynical, utterly selfish or capricious,—a Caligula or a Heliogabalus,—should enact as a whim, that a favored individual should have certain powers of extortion over other citizens. If remonstrated with on the immorality of his edict—"Yes," he would say, "as immoral as you please, but what do I care for morality? It is my will; can't I play the fool if I wish? What are you going to do about it?" Suppose the judges and officers carried out the edict, and the people obeyed. The favorite would have had his legal rights; his victims would have been under a legal duty to obey. The edict did not declare moral rights, it did not purport to declare moral rights, it was issued in defiance of morality; yet, because it was a rule which was enforced by the organized society, it created legal duties and legal rights.

It may be well to be reminded, by the resemblance between names given to legal and moral relations, that organized societies establish many legal duties with a moral purpose, and that they ought not to establish legal duties which are inconsistent with good morals; but it is not well to affirm, simply on similarity in name, that the essence of legal duties is a thing which they sometimes possess and sometimes do not.

The incorrect process of reasoning indicated shows that

it is unfortunate that we have no words for those ideas commonly expressed by "legal duties" and "legal rights" which might be without the ethical coloring which it requires an effort of attention to dissociate from "duties" and "rights" however qualified; but it is a question hardly of the importance given to it by Mr. George H. Smith in his treatise on "The Elements of Right and of the Law," [1] the purpose of which is a strenuous polemic against the use of the expression "legal right." The author insists that there is but one kind of right, that "moral right is a tautology, that a right connotes the idea of moral rightness," and that for "legal right" should be substituted "action" or "legal power." In all the other European languages, as well as the English, the term used to express what Mr. Smith calls "action" or "legal power" is "right," or its equivalent, viz. *recht, droit, diritto, derecho,* etc., and the general usage is too firmly fixed to be changed except by general consent.

"Legal duty"

But though it is unadvisable to banish the term "legal right" from the vocabulary of Jurisprudence, it is not, perhaps, entirely the same with "legal duty." Though the noun substantive "a right" is now become a word familiar in the domain of ethics, it seems, as above remarked, to have been originally a term of the Law,[2] but, on the other hand, the word "duty" had its beginning in the sphere of morality and has never been able to shake off the effect of its surroundings, and while "legal right" is a phrase more familiar than "moral right," "legal duty" is a forced expression.

On the whole, perhaps the best term to express the

[1] 2d ed. Chicago, 1887.
[2] P. 11, *ante*.

correlative of "legal right" would be not "legal duty," but "legal obligation." "Obligation" has a far weaker ethical flavor than "duty," carrying with it the idea of external and not of internal compulsion. And yet it should be remembered that *"obligatio"* in the Civil Law is the regular technical term for the correlative, not of *jura* generally, but of a particular class, *jura in personam;*[1] that, although such a usage cannot be said to have yet established itself in the nomenclature of the Common Law, it is desirable to have a word equivalent to the Roman *obligatio;* and that "obligation" is the most natural to select. In any attempt, therefore, to popularize the conceptions of Jurisprudence to lay readers, it may be best to speak of "legal obligations," there being with them little danger of confusing "obligation" with the *obligatio* of the Roman Law; but in books for more instructed readers there may be less ambiguity in using the expression "legal duty," though, as has been shown, such use has its dangers.

The term "just"

Although usage, *jus et norma loquendi,* allows, indeed requires, us to employ "legal rights" if not "legal duties," without any connotation of moral rightness, the same final judge condemns the use of "just" without that connotation. Hobbes, indeed, affirms that "no law can be unjust,"[2] and Austin, defending him,[3] says: "By the epithet *just,* we meant that a given object, to which we apply the epithet, accords with a given law to which we refer it as to a test. And as that which is *just* conforms

[1] Rights against a person, as distinguished from rights of ownership.
[2] "Leviathan," pt. 2, ch. 30, English Works, vol. 3, p. 335.
[3] 1 Jur. (4th ed.) 276, note.

to a determinate law, *justice* is the conformity of a given object to the same or a similar measure." If by "we" are meant Austin and Hobbes, the statement may be correct, but such is not the common usage. In that usage, justice is indissolubly connected with morality. A debtor in whose favor the period of time prescribed by the statute of limitations has run is under no "legal duty" to pay, his creditor has no "legal right" against him, but if the debtor refuses to pay, his conduct would not be called "just."

Professor Sidgwick puts the matter well: "And hence has arisen a crude definition of Justice, which identifies just conduct with conduct in conformity with Law. But reflection shows that we do not mean by Justice, merely the habit of Law-observance. For, first, we do not always call the violators of law unjust, but only of some laws: not, for example, duellists or gamblers. And secondly, we continually perceive that Law does not completely realize Justice: our notion of Justice furnishes a standard with which we compare actual laws, and pronounce them just or unjust. And, thirdly, there is a part of just conduct which lies outside the sphere of Law: for example, we think that a father may be just or unjust to his children in matters where the Law leaves (and ought to leave) him free." [1]

Protected interests and rights

If it is my interest to receive a hundred dollars from Balbus, or if it is my interest to go out of a room, and if organized society imposes a duty upon Balbus to pay me, or imposes a duty upon everybody not to interfere with my leaving the room, I have a legally protected interest

[1] Sidgwick, Methods of Ethics, Book 3, c. 5, § 1. But see J. S. Mill, Essay on Nature, in Essays on Religion, p. 52.

and I have a legal right. What is the legal right which I have? The full definition of a man's legal right is this: That power which he has to make a person or persons do or refrain from doing a certain act or certain acts, so far as the power arises from society imposing a legal duty upon a person or persons.[1] Therefore, my legal right in the cases supposed is the power to compel Balbus to pay me, or the power to prevent persons from interfering with my leaving the room.

Ihering, in his "Spirit of the Roman Law," defined rights as legally protected interests. This definition was received in Germany with a sort of enthusiasm, and, indeed, it was a great advance on the nonsense that had been talked upon the subject, but it has been strenuously attacked by many German jurists of whom Thon is the protagonist, and there is an extensive literature on the subject.[2] Ihering's adversaries seem on this point to have the better of the argument. The right is not the interest itself; it is the means by which enjoyment of the interest is secured. It is the power to get the money from Balbus, or the power to leave the room, which is the legal right, not the payment of the money or the leaving the room. Common usage, however, permits us to describe this right as the right to be paid, or the right to leave the room, and this usage does not seem likely to lead to any evil results.

By the interests of a man is meant the things which he may desire. I shall not attempt to enumerate or classify the objects of human desire. The object may

[1] *I.e.* compelling at his instance such persons to do such acts. See p. 12, *ante*.

[2] A convenient reference to this literature will be found in 1 Windscheid, Pandekten, § 37.

be the ownership or possession of a corporeal thing, as a book; it may be an act, as eating a dinner; it may be a relation, as marriage; and the desire may be a foolish or hurtful one. The eating of shrimp salad is an interest of mine, and, if I can pay for it, the law will protect that interest, and it is, therefore, a right of mine to eat shrimp salad which I have paid for, although I know that shrimp salad always gives me the colic.

Ways of protecting interests

The legal rights of a man are the rights which are exercisable on his motion.[1] A man has, therefore, no legal right as to those interests in the realizing of which he is protected only by other people exercising their rights. The fact that the State can punish the burglar who breaks into my house does not give *me* any right not to have my house broken into. Not that I am without a right not to have my house broken into. The law can protect my interest not to have a thing done in several ways: as in the first place, by allowing me to withstand the act by force; or secondly, by allowing me to limit the freedom of the person who wishes to do the act by placing obstacles in his way; or thirdly, by appealing to the courts to punish such person. The law may deny to a man this third mode of protecting his interest, but if it allows him the first and second, or either of them, he has a legal right. A system of law may, as the Common Law does, merge the private injury in the crime, and refuse the householder an action against the burglar, but so long as he can withstand the burglar, even to killing, and can draw bolts and bars to keep him out, he has the legal right not to have his house entered. If, when I heard a burglar lifting the latch of my door, the State allowed me to use

[1] See p. 12, *ante*.

neither threats nor force to compel him to desist, and if the State also forbade me to turn any lock or push any bolt, or in any other way interfere to keep him on the outside, and if the only thing to prevent his coming in was the fact that the State could, if it would, hang him or send him to prison, then *I* should have no legal right not to have my house entered, whatever right the State might have.

So the interests of brute animals may have legal protection. Very often, indeed, acts commanded or forbidden towards animals are not commanded or forbidden for the sake of the animals, but for the sake of men; but certain acts of cruelty, for instance, towards beasts, may be forbidden, at least conceivably, for the sake of the creatures themselves. Yet beasts have no legal rights, because it is not on their motion that this protection is called forth.[1]

Right to a defence

The protection which society gives to a man's interests is either *direct* or *indirect*. Sometimes it protects them directly, as when its courts compel a man who is threatening to flood the land of a proprietor upstream to take down his dam; sometimes indirectly, as by giving a man a right to have a wrong-doer compelled to make compensation. And the right to ask the courts for aid is not always a right to sue in them, but is often a right to be protected against suits brought by others. For instance, under a statute of limitations, if a debt remains unpaid for six years, the creditor cannot compel the debtor to pay it; that is, the debtor has a right to interpose the defence of the statute and thereby call upon the court to refuse its assistance to enforce the creditor's demand. So again,

[1] See p. 43, *post*.

a householder has the right to eject by force a trespasser from his "castle." That is, if sued by the trespasser for assault, he can call upon the court to refuse the plaintiff its help. In other words, a man's legal rights include not only the power effectually to call for aid from an organized society against others, but also the power to call effectually upon the society to abstain from aiding others.

We may say that society in these cases limits or qualifies the plaintiff's rights, or that it gives the defendant a right to a defence. The result is the same. To speak of a right to a defence is perhaps not strictly accurate; for it is hard to find a correlative legal duty not to sue. But the phrase is customary, and lends itself to the convenient arrangement of the Law. The Law includes the rules which the courts apply for the determination of the circumstances under which they will refuse to enforce legal rights which would otherwise exist; or, in other words, the circumstances under which they will recognize in the defendant a legal right to a defence.

Let us dwell for a moment more on the nature of the protection which society affords to a man's interests. In the *first* place, it may allow him to protect himself; this is self-help. *Secondly,* it may allow him to appeal to the courts to protect him, as by an injunction forbidding the defendant to do certain acts. *Thirdly,* it may allow him to appeal to the courts for compensation for injuries. In all three of these cases, the actual volition of the man himself is necessary. He must put up his own fists; he must bring his suit for an injunction or for damages in the courts. The State will not double up his fists for him, nor will it bring a suit for him in the courts. The right to these modes of protection is, therefore, his right.

Intervention of administrative officers

But there is a *fourth* method in which the State protects a man's interests, and that is the prevention of injury to them, not by the intervention of the courts, but by the intervention of administrative officers. My interest not to have my windows broken is protected not only by my power of appealing to the courts to prevent or compensate for the breaking, but also by the presence of the policeman on his beat. In this case you may say there is no actual volition on my part. I do not know that the integrity of my windows is threatened. Yet the stopping of the window breaking is really dependent upon my will, for if I tell the police to let the boys go ahead and break my windows, it will cease to interfere. What really happens in this case is that the State assumes a wish on my part (an assumption amply fortified by the ordinary attributes of human nature) that my windows should not be broken. Indeed, after all, in this fourth class of cases is there not an actual volition? Every man undoubtedly actually wishes that his property should be protected, and also that the State, through its administrative officers, should protect it, so that, even in his case, there may be said to be an actual volition and that, therefore, the man has a right. It should be noted that the State may, and probably often does, allow a man to commit to the State a larger power to protect his interests than it would allow him to exercise in his own person.

There is a *fifth* method by which the State protects a man's interests, and that is, by declaring that it will punish criminally acts against certain interests of individuals, and by punishing accordingly. The dread of punishment undoubtedly protects the interests of the individuals, but in this protection the volition of the individuals protected has no place, and it cannot be said that they have any *right* to this form of protection.[1]

Free will and legal rights

To give effect to a man's right, an exercise of free will on his part is necessary. No legal compulsion is laid on any one to enforce his right as such. It is true that one is sometimes under a legal duty to exercise a right, but this is a duty towards B to enforce a right against A, as, for instance, in many cases arising under contracts of indemnity.[2] But the exercise of a legal right against a person is never a legal duty owed to that person. It is of the nature of a man's right as such, that to seek or to abstain from seeking the aid of society for the protection of his interest is a matter of his own free will.

And this leads me to speak of a notion of some writers that the object of organized society in creating rights should be the protection of the freedom of the will. Whether this notion, as is sometimes supposed, originated with Hegel,[3] is a question I do not feel competent to decide. I have no claim to be the one man whom Hegel said understood his philosophy. But, with whomever the notion originated, I conceive it to be erroneous. It might as well be said that the object of creating rights is to restrain the freedom of the will. I wish to have a beautiful watch, but society restrains the exercise of my

[1] In some countries, though this is, I think, not common in the United States, the bringing of certain criminal prosecutions is dependent upon the will of the man injured. In such a case the injured person has a right to have the wrong-doer criminally punished. The form of the enforcement of the right is a mere matter of machinery. Such was the old appeal of death in England. See 4 Bl. Com. 312-316.

[2] B insures X against loss of certain goods; and A negligently destroys the goods. X is under a duty to sue A for the value of the goods in order to relieve B of the payment of the value.

[3] Philosophie des Rechts, §§ 4, 29, *et passim*.

will, because the watch belongs to you. I do not want to pay you a hundred dollars, but society compels me to do it, because I have contracted to pay it. I wish to put you out of the way quietly, but society will not allow me to poison you. In truth, neither proposition is correct.

Rights should be created neither solely to protect the freedom of the will nor solely to restrain it, but to establish and maintain those relations among men which are most for the advantage of society or of its members. This is best obtained sometimes by permitting the will to be exercised, sometimes by restraining it. If one chooses to say that the ideal at which an organized society should aim in creating rights is human perfection, I do not know that there is any objection to it.

Free will and legal duties

An exercise of the will is necessary to give effect to legal rights. What connection with will have legal duties? The legal duties of a person are those acts and forbearances which an organized society will enforce. It is commonly said that legal duties are those acts and forbearances which a society commands. What is a "command," as the word is used by writers on Jurisprudence? Its meaning is well explained by Austin.[1] "If you express or intimate a wish that I shall do or forbear from some act, and if you will visit me with an evil in case I comply not with your wish, the expression or intimation of your wish is a command. A command is distinguished from other significations of desire, not by the style in which the desire is signified, but by the power and the purpose of the party commanding to inflict an evil or pain in case

[1] 1 Jur. (4th ed.) 91.

the desire be disregarded." This conditional evil is called by Austin the sanction of the command.[1]

In order to create a legal duty, it is not necessary that the person subject to the duty should have the will to do it. He may have the will not to do it; it still remains his legal duty. But must he have the potentiality of obeying it? The potential exercise of will is not necessary for the creation of a legal duty. I obtain a judgment against Thomas Dusenbury for a thousand dollars. Dusenbury may not have five dollars in the world; still he is under a legal duty to pay the thousand dollars. Further, must he know of the command? This is not necessary. If there is a statute in a State forbidding the sale of cigarettes, a man who sells a cigarette has violated a legal duty, although he does not know of the statute, and even although he has just arrived from Lithuania, and cannot understand the language in which the statute is written.

A man, therefore, may be bound by a legal duty to do an act, although he cannot possibly do it, and although he does not know that he has been ordered to do it. The exercise of his will, actual or potential, is not necessarily involved in the creation of a legal duty to which he is subject. This emphasizes the point to which I have already referred, the infelicity of the term "legal duty" to signify the burden imposed correlative to legal rights.[2]

That a right should be given effect there must be an

[1] To attribute a desire to society that the persons comprising it should do certain acts, is perhaps to make use of an unnecessary fiction. The legal duties of a person may be defined simply as those acts or forbearances, which if he does not do or forbear, society will inflict an evil upon him.

[2] P. 15, *ante*.

exercise of will by the owner of the right. But an idiot has no will; a fictitious body, like a corporation, has no will. Has an idiot, then, no legal rights? Has a corporation no legal rights? The way the Law meets these questions I will try to show in the next chapter, in which I propose to deal with legal persons, as they have been recognized in different systems of Law.

CHAPTER II

LEGAL PERSONS

The term "person"

In books of the Law, as in other books, and in common speech, "person" is often used as meaning a human being, but the technical legal meaning of a "person" is a subject of legal rights and duties.

One who has rights but not duties, or who has duties but no rights, is, I suppose, a person. An instance which would commonly be given of the former is the King of England; of the latter, a slave. Whether in truth the King of England has no legal duties, or a slave no legal rights, may not be entirely clear. I will not stop to discuss the question. But if there is any one who has rights though no duties, or duties though no rights, he is, I take it, a person in the eye of the Law.

As I showed at the end of the first chapter, a legal duty does not imply any exercise of will on the part of the one subject to the duty, and, therefore, for the existence of a legal duty, the person bound need not have a will; but in order that a legal right be exercised, a will is necessary, and, therefore, so far as the exercise of legal rights is concerned, a person must have a will.

In various systems of Law different kinds of persons are recognized. They may be classified thus: (I) Normal human beings; (II) abnormal human beings, such as idiots; (III) supernatural beings; (IV) animals; (V) inanimate objects, such as ships; (VI) juristic persons, such as corporations. Some of these persons, such as idiots, ships, and corporations, have no real will. How are we to deal with them? That is the most difficult question in the whole domain of Jurisprudence. Let us take these classes in order.

Normal human beings

(I) In the case of normal human beings we are not troubled with any question as to the actual presence of a will. The normal man or woman has a will. Indeed, some German writers make will of the essence of personality. Thus, Hegel defines personality as the subjective possibility of a legal will.[1] So Zitelmann: "Personality . . . is the legal capacity of will. The bodiliness (*Leiblichkeit*) of men, is for their personality, a wholly irrelevant attribute."[2] And again, Meurer: "The juristic conception of the juristic person exhausts itself in the will, and the so-called physical persons are for the law only juristic persons with a physical *superfluum*."[3]

On the other hand, Karlowa,[4] to whom I am indebted for the foregoing quotations, says: "The body is not merely the house in which the human personality dwells; it is, together with the soul, which now for this life is inseparably bound with it, the personality. So, not only as a being which has the possibility of willing, but as a being which can have manifold bodily and spiritual needs and interests, as a human centre of interest, is a man a person."

It is this last definition which American and English jurists impliedly, if not expressly, adopt as the true defini-

[1] See Philosophie des Rechts, §§ 34-39.
[2] Begriff der juristischen Personen, p. 68.
[3] Begriff der heiligen Sachen, § 10, p. 74.
[4] 15 Grünhut, Zeitschr. 381, 383.

tion of a person. It is that which I shall accept. Jurisprudence, in my judgment, need not vex itself about the "abysmal depths of personality." It can assume that a man is a real indivisible entity with body and soul; it need not busy itself with asking whether a man be anything more than a phenomenon, or at best, merely a succession of states of consciousness. It can take him as a reality and work with him, as geometry works with points, lines and planes.

It should be observed, before leaving this class of normal human beings, that they can exercise their rights through agents, such as servants, bailiffs, or attorneys, and they can delegate to their agents the decision of the question whether the rights of the principals shall be exercised or not. But there is no difficulty here; the original spring is a real exercise of will by the owner of the right.

Abnormal human beings

(II) Some human beings have no will; such are new-born babies and idiots. Perhaps it is not correct to say that they are absolutely without wills, but their potentiality of will is so limited that it may be neglected. Yet, though without wills, new-born babies and idiots have rights.

But, further, there are certain human beings who are not destitute of natural wills, but to whom the Law, for one reason or another, denies what may be called a legal will; that is, the Law says their natural wills are inoperative for the exercise of certain classes of rights,—not, generally, for the exercise of all their rights but of certain classes of rights. Such denials vary in different systems of law. Let us take a simple instance from the Common Law. Suppose Doe, a young man of nineteen, owns a house, and Roe, coming along, breaks the windows. Doe has a right to compensation; and yet, if he wills to bring a suit against Roe, either himself or by his agent or attorney, the Law does not regard that will, and the court will refuse in that suit to compel Roe to make compensation, because the right has not been put in motion by a will which the Law regards as operative.

What is to be done? A next friend, or a guardian, exercises his will and brings a suit in the name and behalf of the infant. The will of the guardian is *attributed* to the infant. It is not the guardian, but the infant, who is the subject of the right—the legal person. We usually say this attribution is a fiction.

Fictions in the Law

And here I must make a digression, I fear a rather long digression, on the nature and use of fictions in the Law. There is a strong feeling against the use at the present day of fictions in the Law. This feeling is justifiable or not, according as the fictions belong to the one or the other of two classes, the distinction between which was clearly brought out, for the first time, so far as I am aware, by Ihering,[1]—one of the many services which he has rendered to the science of Jurisprudence.

The first class of fictions is called by Ihering "historic fictions." These historic fictions are devices for adding new law to old without changing the form of the old law. Such fictions have had their field of operation largely in the domain of procedure, and have consisted in pretending that a person or thing was other than that which he or it was in truth (or that an event had occurred which had not in fact occurred) for the purpose of thereby giv-

[1] 3 Geist d. röm. R. (4th ed.) § 58, pp. 301-308.

ing an action at law to or against a person who did not really come within the class to or against which the old action was confined.

The prætors employed such fictions in aiding them to build up the towering fabric of the Roman Law on the narrow basis of the Twelve Tables.[1] Thus, persons to whom the prætor thought it just that a man's property should go on his death,—relations, for instance, on the mother's side, who were not heirs,—were, by a fiction, considered heirs and were allowed to use actions such as heirs could use. *"Heredes quidem non sunt, sed heredis loco constituuntur beneficio prætoris. Ideoque seu ipsi agant, seu cum his agatur, ficticiis actionibus opus est, in quibus heredes esse finguntur."* [2]

So when it was thought just that an action which was given by the Civil Law only to or against a Roman citizen should be extended to or against a foreigner; *"Civitas Romana peregrino fingitur, si eo nomine agat aut cum eo agatur, quo nomine nostris legibus actio constituta est, si modo justum sit eam actionem etiam ad peregrinum extendi."* [3]

In the Common Law

Fictions have played an important part in the administration of the Law in England, and it is characteristic of the two peoples that the use of fictions in England

[1] The prætors were high officers charged with the administration of justice in the earlier days of Roman law. The Twelve Tables were a codification of the ancient customary law, made about the year 450 B. C. and inscribed upon bronze tablets.

[2] "Heirs indeed they are not, but they are put in the place of heirs by favor of the prætor. And therefore whether they sue, or are sued, there must be fictitious suits in which they are feigned to be heirs." Ulp. Fragm. 28, 12.

[3] "Roman Citizenship is fictitiously given to a foreigner, if he sue or be sued under a head under which by our laws an action lies, if only it be just that that action be extended also to a foreigner." Gai. 4, 37.

was bolder and, if one may say so, more brutal in England than it was in Rome.

Thus, for instance, in Rome the fiction that a foreigner was to be considered as a citizen was applied in this way. It was not directly alleged that the foreigner was a citizen, but the mandate by the prætor to the judge who tried the case was put in the following form: "If, in case Aulus had been a Roman citizen, such a judgment ought to have been rendered, then render such a judgment." In England the plaintiff alleged a fact which was false, and the courts did not allow the defendant to contradict it.

One of the purposes for which the English courts allowed fictions was to extend their jurisdiction. A maxim says that to extend jurisdiction is the part of a good judge. When judges and their officers were paid largely by fees, there was a somewhat less exalted motive. The modes in which the courts employed fictions for this end are familiar to all readers of Blackstone.

Of the three superior Courts of Law, the King's Bench, the Common Pleas and the Exchequer, the Court of Common Pleas alone had original jurisdiction of causes between subject and subject not involving violence or fraud; but, as an exception, when a man was in the custody of the Marshal or prison-keeper of the Court of King's Bench, he could be sued also in the latter court. Now a plaintiff, wishing to sue in the King's Bench for an ordinary debt, would allege that the defendant was in the custody of the Marshal, and that therefore the case was within the jurisdiction of that court. The allegation was false, but the court did not allow the defendant to contradict it.

By a like fiction, the Court of Exchequer extended its

jurisdiction. It was properly a court of revenue only, but a debtor of the King was allowed to sue another subject in that court, on the ground that the defendant, by withholding from the plaintiff his due, made the plaintiff less able to discharge his debt to the King. Now a plaintiff, desiring to sue in the Exchequer to collect money or damages to which he was entitled, brought a writ called *quo minus,* in which, after stating his claim against the defendant, he alleged that by reason of the withholding by the defendant of the plaintiff's due, the plaintiff was the *less able* to discharge his debt to the King. The allegation that the plaintiff was indebted to the King was false, but the court did not allow it to be contradicted.[1]

These devices, however, were not applicable to suits for the recovery of a freehold interest,—that is, of an interest in fee or for life in land. Of such suits the Court of Common Pleas had sole jurisdiction. But suits to recover interests less than freehold—*i.e.* terms for years—could be brought in the King's Bench. Thomas Plowden, then, desiring to sue in the King's Bench to recover a freehold interest from Henry Moore, who was in possession, caused a suit to be brought in that court by one John Doe, in which it was alleged that Plowden had leased the land to Doe for a term of years, that Doe entered upon the premises leased, that one William Stiles, known as the casual ejector, entered upon the premises leased, and with swords, knives, and staves ousted Doe from the land. At the same time Plowden sent to Moore a letter purporting to be written to Moore by his "loving friend" Stiles, the casual ejector, saying that unless

[1] 3 Blackstone, Com. 43, 45.

Moore appeared as defendant, Stiles would suffer judgment to be entered against him. Doe and his lease, Stiles and his swords, knives, and staves, were the creatures of fiction, but the court would not let Moore in to defend the suit unless he would confess lease, entry, and ouster.[1] The fictitious proceeding was brought over to this country, and prevailed everywhere in the Colonies, except in Massachusetts and New Hampshire. The fictitious Doe changed his name to Jackson in New York and to Den in New Jersey. I do not know if even now the old fiction has entirely disappeared in the United States.[2]

There was no lack of other fictions in the English Law, in the shape of allegations which one of the parties made and the other was not allowed to deny, in order that the wine of new law might be put into the bottles of old procedure. Thus, in an action of trover to recover damages for the detention of goods to which the plaintiff was entitled, he alleged that he casually lost the goods and that they came to the possession of the defendant by finding. The most grotesque of these fictions was that by which, for the purpose of giving a remedy in England for a wrong done in the Mediterranean, it was alleged that the Island of Minorca was at London, in the parish of St. Mary Le Bow in the Ward of Cheap;[3] and yet, perhaps, the palm must be given to that fiction of the United States Federal Courts that all the stockholders in a corporation are citizens of the State which incorporates it. This fiction is remarkable for the late date

[1] 3 Bl. Com. 203.

[2] The common law action of ejectment still exists in Alabama. See Civil Code (1907), sec. 3838; *Perolio* v. *Doe*, 197 Ala. 560.

[3] *Mostyn* v. *Fabrigas*, Cowper, 161.

of its origin and for its absurd results. I shall return to it in another connection.[1]

Disuse of fictions

As Maine says, in his "Ancient Law," [2] fictions of the historical kind are almost a necessity of the Law at a certain stage of human development. "They satisfy the desire for improvement, which is not quite wanting, at the same time that they do not offend the superstitious disrelish for change which is always present." But as a system of Law becomes more perfect, and its development is carried on by more scientific methods, the creation of such fictions ceases, and better definitions and rules are laid down which enable us to dispense with the historic fictions which have been already created. Such fictions are scaffolding,—useful, almost necessary, in construction,—but, after the building is erected, serving only to obscure it. A chief objection to their continuance,—to quote again from Maine,[3]—is that they are "the greatest of obstacles to symmetrical classification. . . . There is at once a difficulty in knowing whether the rule which is actually operative should be classed in its true or in its apparent place."

Thus, to take an instance from the practice as to the jurisdiction of the Court of Exchequer, of which I have spoken, should we say: The Court of Exchequer has jurisdiction only over matters concerning revenue, but as the ability of the King's debtor to pay the Sovereign may depend upon his collecting money due him from other subjects, the King's debtors may sue in the Exchequer to recover their debts, and if any one alleges that he is a

[1] P. 184, *post*.
[2] Pollock's ed. p. 31.
[3] *Ib.*, p. 32.

debtor of the King's, the Court of Exchequer will hold it to be an uncontradictable truth? Or should we say, all persons can sue in the Court of Exchequer to recover money due them, if they allege in their declaration—truly or falsely is immaterial—that they are debtors to the King?

Dogmatic fictions

The second class of fictions, according to Ihering's division, which he calls dogmatic fictions, instead of being obstacles to symmetrical classification, have been introduced and used as aids to it. These dogmatic fictions are not employed to bring in new law under cover of the old, as are the historic fictions, but to arrange recognized and established doctrines under the most convenient forms.

Thus, there is a legal doctrine of unimpeachable soundness that a purchaser or mortgagee cannot be deprived of his interest in the land by any dealings by the seller or mortgagor, subsequent to the sale or mortgage, with one who knows of it. Thus, if A. mortgages land to B., and afterwards makes a deed of it to C., who knows of the mortgage to B., C. can hold nothing as against B. Further, it is desirable that a purchaser or mortgagee should be able to protect himself by recording his title. Thus, to take the example just given, if A. mortgages to B. and B. records his mortgage, a deed from A. to C. will pass nothing as against B., whether C. knows of the mortgage or not. Now, C. is excluded in both the cases suggested, but really on distinct technical grounds. In the first case, he is excluded because he knows of the mortgage to B.; in the second, because B. has recorded his mortgage; and yet, because it is convenient to treat the whole subject together as the results in both cases are the same, we put it under the head of notice, and say that the registration is constructive notice—that is, notice by fiction—to all the world.

Fictions of the dogmatic kind are compatible with the most refined and most highly developed systems of Law. Instead of being blameworthy, they are to be praised when skilfully and wisely used. Yet, though handy, they are dangerous, tools. They should never be used, as the historic fictions were used, to change the Law, but only for the purpose of classifying established rules, and one should always be ready to recognize that the fictions are fictions, and be able to state the real doctrine for which they stand.

Attribution of will to abnormal human beings

Let us return, now, to the particular occasion for the application of a dogmatic fiction which we have to consider,—the case of a human being who is either naturally destitute of will, or to whose will the Law, for one reason or another, has denied the power of putting in motion his rights in certain matters. We have defined a man's legal rights as those rights which society will enforce on his motion,[1] but with more entire accuracy it may be said that a man's legal rights are the rights which society will enforce on the motion of some one authorized by society to put his rights in motion. In the case of a normal human being, the only one authorized by society to put a man's rights in motion is the man himself; but in the case of an abnormal human being, the person authorized to do so is not the man himself, but some one else. Who such person is, is a matter to be determined by the rules of each particular system. The fiction comes in when we say that what is, in truth, the will of some one

[1] P. 18, *ante*.

else exercised on his behalf, is the will of the possessor of the right,—when we attribute another's will to him. It is convenient to bring together, by means of this attribution, the rights of normal and abnormal persons, for the interests which the rights are given to protect are the same in both classes, and in both classes the same results follow from the exercise of the rights.

Where action on behalf of an abnormal human being is taken in the courts, the will attributed to him is that of some other definite person. How about cases where the administrative officers of the State protect him or his property?[1] Where the inability to will is not natural, but imposed by Law, as in the case of a young man just under age, the imposed inability does not extend to these cases. The young man may request the police to protect him or his property. Where the ability to will is really absent—as in the case of a new-born child or of an idiot—the will which the Law attributes to the abnormal human being is not that of any definite individual, but that which is common to all, or the vast majority, of normal human beings. In the case of juristic persons, as we shall see, the application of dogmatic fictions is more complicated.

Unborn children

Included in human beings, normal and abnormal, as legal persons, are all living beings having a human form. But they must be *living* beings; corpses have no legal rights. Has a child begotten, but not born, rights? There is no difficulty in giving them to it. A child, five minutes before it is born, has as much real will as a child five minutes after it is born; that is, none at all. It is just as easy to attribute the will of a guardian, tutor, or

[1] See p. 22, *ante*.

curator to the one as to the other. Whether this attribution should be allowed, or whether the embryo should be denied the exercise of legal rights, is a matter which each legal system must settle for itself. In neither the Roman nor the Common Law can a child in the womb exercise any legal rights.[1]

But putting an end to the life of an unborn child is generally in this country an offence by statute against the State; and in our Law a child once born is considered for many purposes as having been alive from the time it was begotten.[2]

Supernatural beings

(III) We have hitherto been considering as persons, human beings. We have now to pass to beings who, though not human, are intelligent, that is, *supernatural* beings. There is no difficulty in giving legal rights to a supernatural being and thus making him or her a legal person. Supernatural beings—Gods, angels, devils, saints—if they deal in earthly business and appear before earthly tribunals, must do so through priests or other human beings, but the relation which obtains between a God and his priests is like that which obtains between a

[1] See 1 Windscheid, Pand. § 52.

[2] The history of the development of the Common Law on this subject is curious. Originally, a child does not seem to have been considered for any purpose as living before his birth. The House of Lords, at the end of the seventeenth century, misunderstanding the existing law, and to the great disgust of the Judges, allowed a child who was begotten but not born at the end of a life estate to take the property as if he had been born at that date. Then the doctrine was extended to cover all cases where it was for the benefit of the child to be considered as having been born. Is the doctrine to be extended to cases where such extension benefits, not the child, but others? It is well settled that it does so extend in cases arising under the Rule against Perpetuities; whether it should be extended to other cases is yet *sub judice*. The leading authorities are collected in 5 Gray, Cases on Property (2d ed.) 47-54, 718-720 (1908).

normal man and his agents or attorneys, and not like that which exists between an infant and his guardian, where, as we have seen, the will of the latter is attributed to the former. There is no need of fiction here. In the society which recognizes the legal rights of a God, the existence of the God is a fact of revealed religion, and that authority to represent him has been given by the God to the priests, is also a fact of revealed religion. The society is dealing with what it believes to be a reality, just as much as when it deals with human beings; it is not pretending that that is true which it knows or believes not to be true.

In several systems of Law, supernatural beings have been recognized as legal persons. This was true, to a limited extent, in ancient Rome.[1] The temples were, perhaps, owned by the Gods. The Romans held very different views from those of Mr. Malthus. He who had the most children served the State best, and so, a privilege to take by will was given to those women who had had at least three children,—*jus trium liberorum*. In the course of time, the same privileges were given as a reward to persons who had not had three children, or indeed, any children at all, but the same name was retained, and so, oddly enough, to Diana, of all persons in the world, or rather out of the world, was given the *jus trium liberorum*.[2]

When, under Constantine, Christianity took the place, as the State Church, of the older religions, it might have

[1] 3 Gierke, Deutsche Genossenschaftsrecht, 62-65.

[2] Dion Cassius, 55, 2; Ulp. Fragm. 22, 6; 1 Pernice, Labeo, 260-263. It should be observed that it is to *Diana Ephesiaca* that Ulpian allows testamentary privilege, and it is perhaps not clear that the Ephesian Artemis did not have children.

been supposed that the Christian God and his saints would have become legal persons; but this does not seem to have been the case. The early Christians were wary of imitating the religious establishments of the Empire; in their own organizations they had recourse more readily to the analogies and precedents of the civil administration. The Church buildings and charitable institutions were owned by corporations, or were like the modern German *stiftungen,*[1] and Justinian [2] enacted that if any one should make Christ his heir, the church of the testator's domicil should be the heir, and, if any archangel or martyr was named as heir, his oratory should be deemed the heir. I will return later to this law of Justinian's, in connection with juristic persons.[3]

Though the sound view undoubtedly is that in the Civil Law of the present day there are no supernatural persons, yet the opposing view has not been without defenders. Thus Uhrig says: "Since the Church (*Kirchengemeinde*) is the bride of Christ, she dwells with him in this house of God, and the property of the Church (*Kirchenvermögen*) belongs as dowry to her, but the Lord has *durante matrimonio* the property in her dowry."[4]

But in the Germany of the Middle Ages, God and the saints seem to have been often regarded as true legal persons.[5] Sometimes the expression is odd enough: Thus, a donor declares, "*Dat unse leve frauwe Maria die moder Christi Jesu und der ritter Sanctus Georgius disses*

[1] P. 58, *post.*
[2] 1 Cod. 1, 2, 25 (26).
[3] Pp. 293-297, *post.*
[4] See 1 Meurer, Der Begriff der heiligen Sachen, § 57, p. 282, note 1.
[5] 2 Gierke, Deutsche Genossenschaftsrecht, 527 *et seq.*, quoting the following instances, with many others.

kirspels gruntherrn sein"; or *"Domini genetrici beatæ Mariæ in perpetuum possidendum perdono"*; or to Saint Widon *"in perpetuam hereditatem,"* or *"Deo omnipotenti ejusque prænominatis apostolis hereditario jure conceditur."* [1] Sometimes the supernatural person is charged with a legal duty. Thus, *"Sanctus Spiritus tenetur* 40 *sol. pro duabus mansis quas habuit in domo laterali." "Sanctus Spiritus in Travemunde dat* 5 *marcas annuatim de molendino et pratis et agris."* [2]

In the Common Law, neither the Deity nor any other supernatural being has ever been recognized as a legal person.[3] Blasphemy has been dealt with as a crime, but the legal person who has a legal right, and who alone can put it in motion, is, as in all crimes, the State. Very probably the motive of the State in giving itself this right to sue for blasphemy was, originally, because it was deemed that such prosecution was pleasant to the Almighty or would avert his wrath. Now such prosecutions are usually defended on the ground that the utterance is offensive to many of the community.

Animals as having rights

(IV) Thus far we have been considering human beings and supernatural beings, but animals may conceivably

[1] "That our dear lady Mary the mother of Jesus Christ and the knight Saint George be the feudal lords of this parish." "To Our Lord's mother, the blessed Mary, I grant to be possessed for ever." "For a perpetual inheritance." "It is granted to Almighty God and his aforesaid apostles to be held by hereditary right."

[2] "The Holy Ghost is bound to pay 40 shillings for the two fields which it has had in the side farm." "The Holy Ghost in Travemunde gives 5 marks annually as rent of a mill and meadows and fields."

[3] There is on record, however, in the registry of deeds for Sullivan County, Pennsylvania, a deed of land in the town of Celestia, by which Peter Armstrong and his wife grant said land "to Almighty God, who inhabiteth Eternity, and to his heirs in Jesus Messiah." Armstrong was a member of a religious community that flourished in that place for many years.

be legal persons. *First,* legal persons because possessing legal rights.[1] In the systems of modern civilized societies, beasts have no legal rights. It is true there are everywhere statutes for their protection, but these have generally been made, not for the beast's sake, but to protect the interests of men, their masters. Such statutes have sometimes, however, been enacted for the sake of the animals themselves. It has, indeed, been said that statutes passed to prevent cruelty to animals are passed for the sake of men in order to preserve them from the moral degradation which results from the practice of cruelty, but this seems artificial and unreal; the true reason of the statutes is to preserve the dumb creatures from suffering. Yet even when the statutes have been enacted for the sake of the beasts themselves, the beasts have no rights. The persons calling upon the State for the enforcement of the statutes are regarded by the Law as exercising their own wills, or the will of the State or of some other organized body of human beings. The Law of modern civilized societies does not recognize animals as the subjects of legal rights.

It is quite conceivable, however, that there may have been, or indeed, may still be, systems of Law in which animals have legal rights,—for instance, cats in ancient Egypt, or white elephants in Siam. When, if ever, this is the case, the wills of human beings must be attributed to the animals. There seems no essential difference between the fiction in such cases and in those where, to a human being wanting in legal will, the will of another is attributed.

[1] P. 20, *ante.*

Animals as subject to duties

Secondly, animals as legal persons, because subject to legal duties. In modern systems of law, beasts are not subject to legal duties. As we have seen, the power of obeying or of understanding a command is not necessary for the creation of a duty. And, if a dog is unable to understand the words of a statute, so is an idiot or a new-born child. But in order that any being may become a legal person by virtue of a command issued by organized society, the command must be directed to that being. Now, the State does not give commands to dogs. If there is an ordinance that the town constable may kill all dogs without collars, the constable may have a legal right to kill such dogs, but the dogs are not under a legal duty to wear collars. A legal duty to put collars on the dogs is imposed on their masters.[1]

In modern Jurisprudence, animals have no legal duties, but in early stages of the Law, they seem to have been regarded for some purposes as having legal duties, for a breach of which they were liable to be punished. The fiction here, if fiction there was, did not consist, as would be the case if legal rights were given to beasts, in attributing to them the will of human beings, but in attributing to them a capacity to receive commands directed to them. It is likely, however, that there was often no conscious use of fiction at all. It was genuinely believed that the animals really knew that they were disobeying the Law. Moreover, it is highly probable that in primitive times such dealings with beasts originated in a crude notion of vengeance, without any distinct attribution of intelligence or will to the animal, and when such practices survived. they often, it is likely, took on the form

[1] Pp. 24, 25, *ante.*

of religious expiation, rather than of punishment for breach of legal duty.[1]

This idea of regarding an animal as the subject of a legal duty prevailed among the Jews and the Greeks. Thus, "And surely your blood of your lives will I require; at the hand of every beast will I require it, and at the hand of man";[2] "If an ox gore a man or a woman that they die; then the ox shall be surely stoned and his flesh shall not be eaten."[3] So in Plato, "'Εὰν δ' ἄρα ὑποζύγιον ἢ ζῶον ἄλλο τι φονεύσῃ τινά . . . ἐπεξίτωσαν μὲν οἱ προσήκοντες τοῦ φόνου τῷ κτείναντι, διαδικαζόντων δὲ τῶν ἀγρονόμων οἷσιν ἂν καὶ ὁπόσοις προστάξῃ ὁ προσήκων, τὸ δὲ ὄφλον ἔξω τῶν ὅρων τῆς χώρας ἀποκτείναντας διορίσαι."[4]

The most remarkable instances of the treatment of beasts as having legal duties are to be found in the judicial proceedings against them which were had in the Middle Ages. They were summoned, arrested, and imprisoned, had counsel assigned them for their defence, were defended, sometimes successfully, were sentenced and executed. I should like to dwell on this curious development of manners and belief, which is little known, but it is so foreign not only to any actual but to any rational jurisprudence that I do not feel as if I ought to linger on it longer.[5]

[1] See Holmes, Com. Law, 7-24.

[2] Gen. ix. 5.

[3] Ex. xxi. 28.

[4] "And if a beast of burden or other animal cause the death of any one, the kinsmen of the deceased shall prosecute the slayer for murder, and the wardens of the country, such, and so many as the kinsmen shall appoint, shall try the cause, and let the beast when condemned be slain by them, and cast beyond the borders." Plato, De Legibus, IX, 12. Trans. by Jowett (1871), vol. 4, 385.

[5] See Amira, Thierstrafen, especially p. 6 and p. 15, note 5; A. Franklin, La vie Privée d'autrefois, Les Animaux, Tom. 2, p. 255; Osenbrüggen, Rechtsgeschichtliche Studien, 139-149; Farmer Car-

Inanimate things as having rights

(V) Now to go a step outside the domain of living beings. Inanimate things may conceivably be legal persons. *First,* legal persons as possessing legal rights. Inanimate things may be regarded as the subject of legal rights, and, as such, entitled to sue in the courts. Such, perhaps, were some of the temples in pagan Rome,[1] and such seem often to have been church buildings and the relics of the saints in the early Middle Ages. Thus, we find gifts *"ad sanctum locum ubi ego jacere cupio, i.e. apud sanctum Albanum"; "locis sanctorum conferimus"; "locis venerabilibus"; "tradidi ad reliquias Sancti Salvatoris et Sanctæ Mariæ et in manus Liudgeri presbiteri, qui easdem reliquias procurabat, portionem hereditatis meæ"; "trado ad monasterium quod dicitur Scaphusa et est exstructum . . . ubi,"* [2] etc. These and many like examples will be found in Gierke.[3] If an inanimate thing is regarded as the subject of a legal right, the will of a human being must, as in the case of an animal, be attributed to it, in order that the right may be exercised.

Inanimate things as subject to duties

Secondly, inanimate things as legal persons, because subjects of legal duties. As is the case with animals, inanimate things have been regarded as the subjects of legal duties,—I was about to add in primitive times,

ter's Dog Porter, 2 Hone, Every Day Book, 198; *Quoniam Attachiamenta,* c. 48, pl. 10-13, in *Regiam Majestatem* (Ancient Laws of Scotland), ed. Skene (1609), fol. 86.

Since writing the above I have seen the Criminal Prosecution and Capital Punishment of Animals, by E. P. Evans, New York, 1906. It is of great value as a book of reference.

[1] But see 2 Puchta, Inst. § 191, p. 7; 1 Meurer, § 53.

[2] "To the holy place where I wish to be buried, that is, at Saint Albans"; "we offer to the abodes of the saints"; "to the revered places"; "I have transferred to the relics of the Blessed Savior and the Blessed Mary and into the hands of Liudger the priest, who has charge of the said relics, a portion of my inheritance"; "I transfer to the monastery called Scaphusa, built where," etc.

[3] 2 Deutsche Genossenschaftsrecht, 542-546.

but, as we shall see, the notion has persisted even to our own days. If there was a fiction here, it was not in attributing the real will of a human being to the thing, but in assuming that the thing had an intelligence of its own. It would seem, however, that there was often no conscious fiction, but some vaguely realized belief that the thing had a true intelligence and will; and very often, as in the case of animals, the idea of religious expiation had a great, if not a chief, part in the proceedings against inanimate things.

In Greece, proceedings against inanimate things were not, it would seem, infrequent.[1]

In the Common Law, this attribution of guilt to inanimate things, and this mixture of the idea of punishment with that of expiation, appears in the form of deodands. When a man had been convicted of homicide, the weapon or other article with which the deed was done, the thing itself or its value, was called a deodand, and, as its name imports, was at first forfeited to the Church, but afterwards to the Crown. This is the reason for the allegation of the value of the lethal weapon which appears in the old indictments. Thus, on an indictment for murder or manslaughter by stabbing, the indictment alleged that the prisoner then and there struck the deceased with a certain knife of the value of one shilling, which he then and there in his right hand held. And in England the doctrine was applied as late as 1842,[2] in the case of a locomotive engine. It should be added that anything which had killed a man was liable to be forfeited as a

[1] Besides the citations in Holmes, Com. Law, 7, 8, see Demosthenes, Κατὰ Ἀριστοκράτους, § 18.

[2] *Queen* v. *Eastern Counties R. Co.*, 10 M. & W. 58.

deodand, though there had been no homicidal intent on the part of a human being; and in that form there have been precedents in the early history of this country. In the records of the Colonies of Plymouth and Massachusetts, there are instances of the forfeiture of a boat or a gun as having caused the death of a man.[1]

Judge Holmes, in his book on the Common Law, has shown how the imagination that there must be life in a moving object affected the law of deodands, and, as he justly remarks, this notion appears most conspicuously and persistently in the Admiralty. In the Admiralty, proceedings *in rem* are brought against ships. This, however, at the present day, is a mere form. But a most remarkable instance of application in the substantive law of this barbarous notion of a ship's intelligence occurred only some forty years ago. On land, when a man's vehicle, say his automobile, is taken by the Law out of his custody, law and justice, alike, in all civilized countries, impose on him no liability for accidents that the vehicle may cause while in the hands of the official. A sheriff takes my horse and wagon on legal process against me; his bailiff in charge of them runs over a woman; I am not liable. An officer is appointed to take charge of carriages and drive them over a bridge; he takes possession, by virtue of his authority, of your carriage, and an accident occurs; you are not responsible. Suppose, now, a ship is in the hands and under the orders of a pilot, whom the owner and master have been compelled to take against their will, and, by the pilot's negligence, a collision ensues. The Supreme Court of the United States, in 1868,[2]

[1] *E.g.* a boat. Plymouth Colony Records, vol. I, p. *157. (1638)
[2] *The China*, 7 Wall. 53.

held that in such a case the ship was guilty. Judge Holmes [1] speaks of this decision with more tenderness than it deserves.

Juristic persons

(VI) Thus far we have been dealing with cases where a legal person, the subject of a legal right or a legal duty, is, or is believed to be, some one or something real. Where there has been a fiction, it has consisted in attributing to or assuming for such real entity a will which he, she, or it does not, in truth, possess; but this is the only fiction. The being or thing to which this will is by fiction given is a reality,—a man, a dog, a ship. We have now to consider juristic persons, so called.

The power of conceiving an abstraction which is imperceptible to any of the senses, which yet has men for its visible organs, and which, although not having a will and passions, may yet have the will and passions of men attributed to it,—this power is one of the most wonderful capacities of human nature. If not a necessity of their nature, it is a power which the races of men seem to find no difficulty in exercising. If there was a time when man was without the personifying faculty, it is found in full play in the early history of civilization. Among no people has the conception of the personality of the State been more highly developed than among the Greeks, and the idea of the corporation was recognized by the Romans.

One dislikes to call such an entity "fictitious," because "fictitious" is what Bentham would call a "dyslogistic epithet," and the same objection applies, though in a less degree, to the use of "artificial." Perhaps, "juristic"

[1] Com. Law, 28.

is best. But, after all, there is no objection to calling such abstract entities fictitious, if we bear in mind Ihering's distinction between historical and dogmatic fictions. This fiction of an abstract entity is not an historical fiction, like that of the casual finder in trover, or of the casual ejector, invented to bring in new law or to extend remedies, but it is used to classify and arrange old and acknowledged law.[1]

Corporations

The usual form of a juristic person is a corporation. Indeed, corporations are the only juristic persons known to the Common Law.[2] What is a corporation? In *the first* place, there must be a body of human beings united for the purpose of forwarding certain of their interests. *Secondly,* this body must have organs through which it acts; it must be an organized body of men; neighbors turning out to hunt down a robber do not form a corporation. The interests of an organized body of men cannot be effectually forwarded unless these interests are protected by the State; and to give this protection, legal rights must be created, and the organization through which the body is to act must be recognized by the State. If a body of men acts through an organization which the State does not recognize, the Law will not give effect to the act as the act of the organization, though it may be the act of some or all of its members.[3]

[1] It may be called a "rational fiction." See 14 Columbia Law Rev. 469, 471.

[2] Except the State.

[3] *Corporations de facto.* A statute has enacted that an organized body of men shall become a corporation upon performing certain acts. Sometimes in such a case although the body has failed to perform the acts, the Law will yet accord certain of the rights and impose certain of the duties which would have been created had the acts been performed. This means that the body is recognized by the State as a corporation for certain purposes, but not for all.

As I have said, to effect the purposes of a corporation, its interests must be protected by the creation of rights. To whom shall these rights be given? Whom shall the State recognize as the person or persons on whose motion the rights are to be exercised? That is, *whose* are the rights?

Putting all fictions aside, let us get down to the "hard pan" of fact. A corporation is an organized body of men to which the State has given powers to protect its interests, and the wills which put these powers in motion are the wills of certain men determined according to the organization of the corporation.

How is this state of things to be brought within the scheme of rights and duties upon which the superstructure of the Law rests? In this way. The powers granted by the State are not the rights of the men whose wills put them in motion, for it is not the interests of those individual men that are protected; but, by a dogmatic fiction, their wills are attributed to the corporation, and it is the corporation that has the rights.

Now it is to be observed, that thus far there is nothing peculiar to juristic persons. The attribution of another's will is of exactly the same nature as that which takes place when the will, for instance, of a guardian is attributed to an infant. How far this attribution is allowed to occur in the one or the other class of cases is a question of positive law, but, so far as the process takes place, and by whatever name it is called, it is of essentially the same

Such bodies are called corporations *de facto*. They are discussed by my colleague in the Harvard Law School, Professor E. H. Warren, in two valuable articles in the Harvard Law Review, 20 H.L.R. 456; 21 H.L.R. 305.

character. With all legal persons, except normal human beings,[1] there is the same fiction of attributing the will of a man to some one or something other than himself—it matters not who or what that some one or something else is. The step is as hard to take and no harder, whether he, she, or it be an idiot, a horse, a steam tug, or a corporation. Neither the idiot, the horse, the steam tug, nor the corporation has a real will; the first three no more than the latter. But with the juristic person we have an additional fiction. That additional fiction consists in forming an abstract entity to which the wills of men may be attributed.

Is a corporation a real thing?

This is the common view, but it has been contended that there is no fiction here, that the corporation is a real thing. Is the corporation to which these wills of individual men are attributed a real thing, or only a thing by fiction, a fictitious entity? If it is a fictitious entity, we have a double fiction; first by fiction we create an entity, and then by a second fiction we attribute to it the wills of individual men. If the corporation is a real entity, then we have need only of this second fiction.

Whether a corporation is a real or only a fictitious entity is a question which I shall not undertake to solve. I fear I should find no end in wandering mazes lost. According to an old saying, everybody is born either a nominalist or a realist. And what is true of all the world is true probably of my readers. I shall not undertake to supply any of them with a new set of innate ideas. And I shall not attempt to answer the question whether corporations are realities or fictions, because to

[1] Excepting also supernatural beings. See p. 39, *ante*.

do so is unnecessary for my purposes. The facts are beyond dispute; the State imposes duties upon people for the protection of the interests of the organized bodies of men called corporations, and the rights correlative to these duties it allows to be set in motion by the wills of individual men determined by the organization of the corporation, which wills it attributes to the corporation. Whether the corporation be real or fictitious, the duties of other people towards it and the wills which enforce the rights correlative to those duties are the same. The Law is administered, and society is carried on in precisely the same way on either theory.

It should be observed that even if a corporation be a real *thing,* it is yet a fictitious *person,* for it has no real will, but it would be a fictitious person only as an idiot or a ship is a fictitious person. The reason why idiots and ships have not been called juristic persons, and classed with corporations, is that in the Roman and the Common Law the prevalent idea seems to have been that corporations were fictitious entities, were things only by fiction, and that, therefore, in their case, in distinction from the case of idiots and ships, there was need, as I have said, of a double fiction, and they ought to be put under a separate head and distinguished by a different name, viz. juristic persons.

Under the Roman Law there was little discussion as to the nature of corporations, and under the Common Law there has been little. Such discussion is alien to the eminently practical character of both systems. The prevailing notion has undoubtedly been that a corporation was not a real thing, but I do not think there can be said to be any settled opinion to that effect.[1]

Has a corporation a real will?

Before leaving the subject I ought to notice a theory which of late years has grown up in Germany, and which holds not only that a corporation is a real thing, but that it has a real will. Gierke, who is the chief expounder of this theory, declares that it is not original with him, but was first taught by Beseler. He confines the doctrine to the old German Law and admits that in the Roman system the corporation was a fictitious person; indeed, he maintains that view with no little warmth against some writers who had attempted to give real personality to the Roman corporation.[2] He believes that in Germany the old national view and the Roman have been struggling for the mastery, and that the former is getting the better of the contest. His view will be found set forth briefly in the article by him on Juristische Person in Holtzendorff's Lexicon.

Assuming that a corporation is a real thing, the question whether it can have a real will or not depends on whether there is such a thing as a general will. I do not believe that there is. There may be agreeing wills, but not a collective will; a will belongs to an individual. When we speak of the will of the majority on a point, we mean that on that point the wills of the majority agree. A collective will is a figment. To get rid of the fiction of an attributed will, by saying that a corporation

[1] See a discussion of "Corporate Personality" by A. W. Machen, in 24 Harvard Law Rev. 253, 347, and an article by T. Baty in 33 Harvard Law Rev. 358.

[2] 3 Gierke, Deutsche Genossenschaftsrecht, 131.

has a real general will, is to drive out one fiction by another.[1]

On and about this question there has been an enormous number of pages written. But difference in practical results from adopting this theory there seems to be none. Under it acts and forbearances are imposed on men as duties for the purpose of protecting the interests of corporations; the rights corresponding to these duties are given to the corporation; the actual wills by which in fact these rights are exercised are the wills of men designated in accordance with the organization of the corporation and the positive Law of the State; and this is just what happens under the theory of the Roman and the Common Law. In short, whether the corporation is a fictitious entity, or whether it is a real entity with no real will, or whether, according to Gierke's theory, it is a real entity with a real will, seems to be a matter of no practical importance or interest. On each theory the duties imposed by the State are the same, and the persons on whose actual wills those duties are enforced are the same.[2]

I have spoken of the rights of corporations. As to their duties, a word will suffice. The State imposes legal duties upon corporations, to protect the rights of other persons, including the rights of individual members of the corporation. How the State will enforce these duties

[1] 1 Windscheid, Pand. (9th ed.) § 49, *n.* 8.

[2] I ought to add that the lamented Professor F. W. Meitland was a convert to Gierke's views. See the introduction to his translation of a portion of Gierke's Genossenschaftsrecht, under the title of Political Theories of the Middle Ages; also essay in 3 Collected Papers, 304. No one holds Maitland's memory in more respect or affection than I, but it must be remembered that his greatness lay in historic investigation, not in dogmatic speculation.

is matter for the positive Law of the State. It makes no difference whether the corporation is a fictitious person, or a real person with a fictitious will, or a real person with a real will. For instance, take the question of the liability of a corporation for a tort, say for slander. The corporation's liability or non-liability may be held on either theory. The existence of the liability or non-liability depends upon the positive prescriptions of the Law.

Creation of corporations

Who creates the abstraction known as a corporation? It is sometimes said that all corporations are creatures of the State. This is not literally accurate. Whenever men come together for a common purpose, it is the course of human nature for them or their leaders to personify an abstraction, to name it, and to provide it with organs. Such organized bodies may be of every degree of importance, from the Roman Catholic Church down to the poker club that meets at a village tavern.

To say that all such organizations are in truth creatures of the State, because they exist only by its sufferance, might be unobjectionable, if the control of the State over its citizens was absolute. If it had the power of preventing any communication of thought on religious subjects by words or signs, no church could exist in the territory of that State; but it has no such power; and organized societies which a State has forbidden to exist have often continued in spite of its efforts. The Catholic Church existed in England in the reign of Queen Elizabeth; the Carbonari existed in Italy under the Austrian and Bourbon rules; the Knights of the Golden Circle existed in the Northern United States during the Civil War.

But that over which a State has the sole authority is the making of a corporation into a juristic person. The State may not have created a corporation, but unless it recognizes it and protects its interests, such corporation is not a juristic person, for such a corporation has no legal rights.

Corporations sole

The term "corporation sole" is used in the Common Law. When a man who has rights and duties by virtue of holding an office or exercising a function, dies, one of three things may happen—the rights and duties may come to an end, or they may pass to his heirs, or they may pass to his successors. Rights and duties enjoyed or imposed by virtue of an office, passing to heirs, or hereditary offices, are hardly ever created at the present day, but in England a few have come down from early times.

In some cases where like rights are enjoyed by successive occupants of an office, a corporation sole is created. In some cases, but not in all. Successive clerks of a city council may have the same right, as, for instance, to a salary, but the succession of such clerks does not usually form a corporation sole. Among the qualities of a corporation sole, which distinguish it from a mere succession of officers or persons exercising the same rights, the most important, apart from matters of procedure, seem to be, that if a corporation sole exists, an occupant of an office can generally acquire property for the benefit of his successors as well as himself; that he can generally recover for injury inflicted on property pertaining to the office while such property was in the hands of his predecessor; and that he can sometimes enter into a contract which will bind or inure to the advantage of his successors.

Whether a corporation sole is in any case created is a

matter for the positive Law of any particular jurisdiction. They are not uncommon. A bishop of the English Church is a corporation sole; so is the minister of a Congregational parish in Massachusetts.

A corporation sole does not seem to be a fictitious or juristic person; it is simply a series of natural persons some of whose rights are different and devolve in a different way from those of natural persons in general.

Corporations are, as I have said, the only juristic persons known to the Common Law. Property is never made into a juristic person. If property is given in England or in the United States for charitable uses, it is always vested in some man or corporation which holds it for the charitable uses, and is the subject of the rights and duties concerning it. If a testator devotes property to a charitable purpose, but names no one to carry out the purpose, the title to the property vests in the heir or executor until some other trustee is appointed to take it. The notion of a subjectless right or duty is utterly alien to the Common Law.[1]

Stiftungen

But in Germany there are juristic persons which are not corporations and which have no members. These are known as *Stiftungen* (foundations). They consist of property devoted to charitable uses, the title to which is not vested in individuals or corporations. As this legal concept is interesting and unfamiliar, I may be excused for dwelling on it a moment.

In pagan Rome, eleemosynary institutions for the relief of the poor and suffering, so far as they existed at all, were institutions of the State, and their administra-

[1] But cf. p. 46, *ante*.

tion was part of the functions of the State. They were simply portions of the machinery of government. It was only upon the establishment of the Christian Church that institutions of the kind independent of the State came into existence. They were probably regarded as corporations.[1]

All fiction apart, what actually takes place in case of a *stiftung?* Persons are subjected to duties with reference to property which has been devoted to charitable purposes. These duties are enforced on the motion of certain persons, but these persons have no rights, for it is not their interests which are protected, nor are there any other persons to whom their wills can be attributed; they exercise their wills not for the sake of any definite persons, but for the sake of certain objects; that is, in the case of a *stiftung* (which, as I have said, is a conception unknown to the Common Law) there are duties, to which there are no correspondent rights residing in definite men or corporations. By a dogmatic fiction the property in question is constituted a juristic person, and the fiction is a justifiable and beneficent one, because the duties which exist when a *stiftung* is created are of the same kind as those which exist as between natural persons, and the employment of the fiction enables them to be classified and treated together.

The view taken in the preceding section *as to the actual state of facts* in the case of a *stiftung* agrees, I think, in substance with the theory advanced by Brinz in his *Lehr-*

[1] See Appendix I. There may, however, have been gifts for such purposes to *collegia*, or guilds, under the pagan emperors. S. Dill, Roman Society from Nero to Marcus Aurelius, pp. 254-255, 282. For such gifts to municipalities, see *ib.* pp. 193-195, 224.

buch der Pandekten.[1] But Brinz denied that a *stiftung* was a juristic person. He maintained that there could be legal duties without legal rights, and that the *stiftung* was an instance of it. This theory has excited a hot, and, *more Germanico,* a voluminous controversy. Brinz's opponents declare that a legal duty without a legal right is unthinkable, and that a legal right without a subject is equally unthinkable, and that therefore the allowance of a *stiftung* necessarily carries with it the allowance of a juristic person. We may congratulate ourselves that in the Common Law no such controversy can arise, for the conception of *stiftungen* finds no place in our system.

A word with regard to two entities which are found in the Roman Law, and which, perhaps, should be included among juristic persons, *Fiscus* and *Hereditas jacens.*

The *Fiscus*

Originally a basket of woven twigs used for keeping money, the term *fiscus* came to mean the imperial treasury, in distinction from the *ærarium* or public treasury, but in course of time the fisc absorbed the *ærarium* and became the treasury of the State. The fisc is never called a person, but passages in the Digest and the Code show it to us as a creditor and a debtor and a party to a suit; that is, as a subject of legal rights and duties. The Romans do not seem to have thought much on the personality of the fisc, or to have compared it with that of a corporation. They appear to have considered it distinct from the State. In modern times, the term continues to be used in some systems of Law derived from the Roman, and in them the fisc is now defined as the State in its relation to property. If the term is to be retained, this is a good defini-

[1] Vol. 2, § 228, and elsewhere.

tion, but in this sense it seems superfluous, and that it is best to do away with the word as a legal term altogether, and to speak of the State as the subject of those rights and duties which have been attached to the fisc.[1]

Hereditas jacens

In the interval between the death of the ancestor and the moment when the heir accepted the inheritance, the Romans placed the *hereditas,* commonly known by the civilians as the *hereditas jacens.* This *hereditas* was an abstraction, and probably, to a limited extent at least, a juristic person. There is nothing corresponding to the *hereditas jacens* in the Common Law.[2]

Ihering's doctrine of passive rights

One point more as to legal rights may be noticed. Ihering, who is always worth listening to, even if one does not agree with him, while, in opposition to Brinz, he denies most strenuously the conceivability of a right without a subject, has a view of his own on rights not only of juristic persons but of all legal persons, which he has elaborated at great length.[3] He divides a right into two sides,—its active side, "the legal position which the right has as a result for the one to whom it belongs"; and the passive side, "the position of legal obligation or limitation in which a person or thing is placed through the right." He admits that as a permanent situation one side cannot exist without the other, but he insists that temporarily the passive side can exist without the active, and that this temporary divorce may take place, either in the interval between the disappearance of one subject and the appearance of another, or, in the case of a right on a

[1] On the fisc and its character, see 3 Gierke, Deutsche Genossenschaftsrecht, 58-61; 1 Karlowa, Röm. Rechtsgeschichte, § 64; 1 Holtzendorff, Rechtslex. *sub. voc.*

[2] On the *hereditas jacens,* see Appendix II.

[3] *Passive Wirkungen der Rechte,* 10 Jahrb. f. Dogm. 387-580.

condition precedent, before the condition is fulfilled. He compares such a right to a bed which has been made up, but which is yet empty; and he puts a case like this: A. owns land and, as such owner, has a right of way over land of B.; A. abandons the land, so that it is without an owner, which state of things can occur in the Civil Law, though with us a man who has become owner of land cannot renounce ownership. Here, Ihering says, there is no longer any one to whom the right of way belongs, but the right still exists on its passive side, and when the property which was abandoned is again occupied, say by C., then the right comes again into full existence on both sides. The case of the *hereditas jacens* furnishes him with another instance.

One criticises a writer of Ihering's ability with diffidence, but has he not been deceived here by a form of words? Certain facts have given A., the former occupier, a right to deal with B.'s land in a certain way, to put it to a certain use, to walk over it; and certain facts give C., the present occupier of the premises abandoned by A., a similar right to deal with B.'s land,—a *similar* right, but not the same right. The first right has ended; a new one has begun.

Even if we regard the right of C. as the *same* thing as the right of A., yet, in the interval between A.'s occupation and C.'s occupation, if there is a suspension of the right, it is of the whole right,—not only of the active side but of the passive side as well. Both active and passive sides of the right must come into existence together; indeed, the separation between the two sides which Ihering maintains, and the possibility of one existing without the other, is unthinkable. Ihering himself admits that it is unthinkable as a permanent condition, and, in truth, it is just as unthinkable as a temporary condition. There cannot, even temporarily, be an inside without an outside, a front without a back.

But, it may be said, in the case supposed, let us assume that after A. has abandoned his land, and before C. has come into occupation, B. has obstructed the way. Cannot C., after he has come into occupation, compel B. to take down the obstruction, or to pay damages for having put it up? I am not sufficiently familiar with the Civil Law to know whether this is the case, but certainly there might be a system of law in which it was so. But what would this prove? Only that B. may be under a legal duty; that is, may be commanded by the State to do certain acts which C. has a right to have done, and this legal duty may arise from certain facts (including acts by B.) having happened before C. acquired any right. But this does not show that B. was under a legal duty to C. before C. had any right, but only that among the acts, forbearances, and events which cause a right to spring into existence, past acts and forbearances are often included, a proposition obvious enough.

Although Ihering is careful to indicate that he is speaking of *rechte* in the subjective sense, or, as we say, rights, it seems possible that he has been misled by the ambiguous meaning of "*recht*."[1] *Recht*, he says, does not exist for itself, but to forward certain purposes,—that the purpose is often a continuing one, intended, for instance, to last beyond the life of any particular individual. True of *recht* in the objective sense, or, as we say, Law. Rules

[1] P. 8, *ante*.

of Law may be established for continuing purposes; and to give effect to these purposes, rights (*rechte im subjectiven sinne*) are given to successive individuals, but there is no need that these rights themselves be continuous.

CHAPTER III

THE STATE

In theology it may be that the chief artificial person is the Church; but in Jurisprudence the chief artificial person is the State. The State is an artificial person created in order that, by assuming it as the entity whose organs are the men engaged in protecting a mass of human beings from external and internal fraud and violence, a unity of operation may be given to those organs.

The State an artificial person

Austin, in his "Province of Jurisprudence Determined," as one might suppose from his hatred of mysticism and unreality, will have nothing to do with artificial persons.[1] "*The* State," according to him, "is usually synonymous with '*the* sovereign.' It denotes the individual person, or the body of individual persons, which bears the supreme powers in an independent political society." I should be glad if I could follow Austin here, and get rid of the State altogether as a fictitious entity; if we could take "State" as simply an equivalent for the whole number of men whose commands are obeyed in a given community; but it seems to me this cannot be done, and that scientific Jurisprudence will be right in following the popular feeling and seeing, behind the individual man or men who "bear the supreme powers" in any commu-

[1] 1 Jur. (4th ed.) 249, note.

nity, the abstract conception of the State of whom those men are to be deemed the organs.

I will try to explain what I mean. It is conceivable that a number of men may obey the commands of an individual simply as being that individual. Not only is it conceivable, but in the history of the world there is reason to suppose that this has actually happened. But in the present generation, in all civilized and half-civilized countries, and in many barbarous communities, even when all the functions of government are in the hands or under the control of one man, yet he is obeyed not simply as Abdul-Aziz, or as Crazy Horse, but as Sultan of Turkey, or as Chief of the Pottawottamies. At any rate, when there is any binding rule for the succession to absolute power upon the death of the present holder, we have an entity other and greater than the individual Sultan or Chief, we have the State; as, in the most primitive of organizations, the family, the individuals who compose it are under the rule of one person, not because he is Noah or Abraham, but because he is the father; and on his death the organization does not come to an end, but the power over the family passes to another person, often in accordance with rules of great complexity.

But let us take a case where it is even clearer that there is some recognized power behind that of the mere sum of the so-called sovereign individuals. If we assume, with Austin, that Parliament is the sovereign of England, that does not mean that the individuals who happen to be King, Peers, and Representatives of the Commons, as an unorganized horde, or even a majority of them, are the sovereigns of England, but that the King, the House of Lords, and the House of Commons, acting separately and in accordance with highly artificial rules, is the sovereign. The abstract entity of the State which creates those rules lies behind the sovereign, who is only its organ.

Creators of the State

Who creates the State, and on what basis does its continuous existence rest? In every aggregation of men there are some of the number who impress their wills upon the others, who are habitually obeyed by the others, and who are, in truth, the rulers of the society. The sources from which their authority flows are of the most diverse character. They may be, or may pretend to be, divinely inspired. It may be their physical strength, their wisdom, their cunning, their virtues, their vices,—oftenest, perhaps, their assiduity and persistence,—that have given them their power. The sources of this power are, indeed, so various, and its mode of action so subtle and often unknown even by those who exercise it, that it is impossible to define or closely trace it.

Such rulers may have official position, but often they are without it. A king-maker or president-maker, the favorite of a monarch, the boss of State politics, may pride himself on his private station. Nor does the machinery of government make any great difference. The real rulers of a country are probably not much more numerous in a democracy than in a monarchy. In a government carried on by parties, which seems the only means yet discovered by which, in republics or limited monarchies, government can be carried on with tolerable success, the subjection of thought and will to party leaders is extreme. The mistakes and disasters that have occurred, by attempting to carry into practice the theory that the persons in whom is vested the machinery of government are the real rulers of a country, would be ludicrous, if the subject was not so serious. The condition of affairs, in many of the cities of the United States, is a good example of the evil.[1]

These rulers, sometimes suddenly and obviously, as, for instance, in the establishment, by a successful rebellion, of an independent State, but oftener by degrees and obscurely, create or uphold, by personification, an abstract entity and impose a belief in it on the mass of which they form a part; and they bring this abstract personality to play a part in real life by giving it as organs real human beings, bound together in their action by artificial rules.

It is sometimes said that the State is the creature of the people. This is untrue, if it is meant that, as a fact, the people uphold it. The people, in that, as in other things, exercise no power against those to whom they have subjected their wills. The people no more have created and uphold the State because they have the physical strength to kill their rulers, than the horses of a regiment of cavalry have created and uphold the regiment because they have the physical strength to demolish their riders.

It must be borne in mind, however, that the creation and upholding of the personified abstraction of the State, and the furnishing it with organs, react powerfully on the rulers of the people. The fact that a person is an official of the State has some tendency to make him not only a formal but a real ruler; the existence of the machinery furnishes an obstacle to change; and the leaders have their own desires and imaginations profoundly af-

[1] See A. M. Kales, Unpopular Government in the U. S., Chap. II.

fected by the existence, especially the long-continued existence, of the belief in the organized personality of the State.

To satisfy their social instincts or desires, to accomplish objects which they could not singly achieve, these ruling spirits make this abstraction and personify it. In no other way could a body of rulers so changing, so indeterminable, effect their object. This personification of an abstraction, the naming of it,—family, village, tribe, city, state,—and the giving to it human beings as organs, seems a necessity of human existence. It is, at any rate, the way in which the world has developed. The Law of an organized society assumes the existence of that society; to deny it would be to commit suicide.

This use of a personified abstraction to give coherence and continuance to the efforts of the rulers is, as I have said, almost, if not quite, a necessity of human existence, but, like other necessary things, it has its good and its evil side. On the one hand, it has enormously fortified altruism under the guise of patriotism. That one should sacrifice his life for the greatest good of the greatest number, has always been a hard saying both to the head and heart, but many have found it sweet to die for the personified *patria*. Yet, on the other hand, the idea of the State is merely a device by which certain men—kings, governors, voters, judges, tax-gatherers, hangmen—are brought into concerted action for the benefit of human beings, and the notion that the State has a value apart from the men and women who compose it and will compose it, is a superstition.

Power of the State

Whether the power of the State is subject to any legal limitation, is a matter which has been much discussed.

The true view seems to be that the power of the State is unlimited, so far as is consistent with the abstract idea, which is the State; its organs—legislative, judicial, and administrative—exist only to express its will, and they cannot contradict it; but, after all, the State is but a personified abstraction,—it is an idol, a dumb idol, whose use is to give a title to its law-making and judgment-giving priests; and the real rulers of the congeries of men, who are the members of the State, can limit the attribution to it of will.

I believe that the State is an abstraction created and furnished with organs by the real rulers of society. But it may tend to bring out the true idea of the State to consider some of the theories that have at various times prevailed as to its origin and the source of its authority.

Theory of divine origin of the State

First. That the organization of the State rests on the will of God. Of course, in a sense, every believer in a personal God must believe that all things which exist, including the organs of the State, exist by His will. But this is not what is meant. Nor, again, is it meant that the revealed word of God or the dictates of natural religion prescribe an obedience to the commands of the organized body called the State. This may well be. This duty to obey the commands of an existing organized body calls for obedience to any new government which has *de facto* established itself in place of an old,—for instance, in turn to the kingdoms, republics, and empires which have succeeded each other in France. While the revolutionary change is going on, there is room for no little casuistry, but when the change is completed, the duty to obey an existing government calls for allegiance to the new government.

The proposition that the organization of the State rests on the will of God calls for the belief that a special form of organization—monarchical, for instance, or federal—is commanded by the Deity, and cannot be altered without sin. But if the will of God is the origin of the form of State organization, it must be His revealed will, for certainly that Parliament shall consist of King, Lords, and Commons, or that the President's veto can be overridden by a two-thirds vote of both Houses, are doctrines not derivable from the light of natural religion; and as to revealed religion, no one, at the present day, is likely to seek and find in the divine oracles a rule in favor of a single Chamber or of an hereditary nobility. The true doctrine has been well expressed thus: "The command of God does not appear as a ground of law, but only raises the legal duty towards the lawful government into a religious duty."

Undoubtedly the ruling spirits of society in forming a government have often claimed to act under divine guidance, and this claim has been believed in, not only by the mass of the community, but often by the rulers themselves; and further, it is this belief that has given them their power; but in such cases it has been the will of the rulers that has really organized the State. The organization of the State was the same whether the rulers who created it had or had not a revelation from above. Some of those who have most confidently asserted the divine origin of a State which they liked would be the first to deny the inspiration of Numa or Joseph Smith.

"Might is right"

Second. That might is right. The objection felt to this proposition rests on the ambiguity of the word "right." If by "right" is meant what is morally right, or in accordance with justice, then the proposition is false. If, on the other hand, it is meant that a man's legal rights depend upon the power of the State to protect them, the expression is well enough, and yet, even in this latter sense, it is in danger of being misunderstood. This might which creates the State is not the might exercised by its organs; it is the might of the rulers who have created and uphold it.

The social contract

That the State is founded on contract. If by "contract" anything more is meant than the recognition of a state of fact by present opinion, it can hardly nowadays be necessary to labor on the refutation of such a notion. The theory of the original social contract has been the lay figure set up by recent writers on political subjects only that they might have the satisfaction of knocking it over. Austin's laborious demolition of it has done the work, if at wearisome length, yet effectually and once for all.[1] For us who are considering not what fancies may be dreamed in order to tabulate the facts in accordance with a preconceived system, but what the facts really were and are, it is enough to say that no one of the defenders of the theory of the original social contract pretends that there ever, in truth, was such a contract.[2]

Indeed, since Kant's time, few have been willing to put forth the notion of an original social contract in an undisguised form, and its adherents have clothed it in the garb which Kant gave it. He defined the original social contract as "properly only an outward mode of representing the idea by which the rightfulness of the process

[1] 1 Jur. (4th ed.) 309-335.
[2] But see 16 Jour. Comp. Leg. (n. s.) 322.

of organizing the Constitution may be made conceivable." [1] The phrase is not clear, but the line of his reasoning seems to be this: "The organization of the State was rightful." "I deny it." "I will make you understand it. I say that the ancestors of the present members of every organized political society made a contract with each other by which each released certain rights and created the present organization of the State: that being so, you must admit, must you not, that the organization of the State was rightful?" "Perhaps so, if what you say as to the original contract is true; but is it true?" "No, it is not in the least true, but I have told it to you in order that you might conceive the rightfulness of the organization of the State." Austin certainly has a better excuse for his roughness than he sometimes has when he attacks "the conceit of an original covenant which never was made anywhere, but which is the necessary basis of political government and society." [2]

Perhaps what Kant means is that no organization of a political society can be regarded as good if not such as it may reasonably be supposed the original members of society would have agreed with each other to make, had they been so asked, or, in other words, that the test for the goodness of an organization of society is its conformity with such a contract concerning it as it may be assumed the original members of the society would have made, had they made any. If this be his meaning, his expression of it is not felicitous. He cannot mean to say that no organized political body, no State, can exist

[1] Kant, Rechtslehre, (Philosophy of Law) sec. 47. Hastie's Trans. p. 169.

[2] P. 334, note.

unless it is one which its members, as wise men, would have contracted to create, and it would seem, therefore, that his meaning must be that all forms of government are pernicious which are not such as would originally have been entered into by wise men; and this does appear to be what he means. "This [the original social contract], however," he says, "is but a mere idea of the reason; possessing, nevertheless, an indubitable (practical) reality in this respect, that it obliges every legislator to enact his laws in such a manner as they might have originated in the united will of the people."[1] This may or may not be the duty of a legislator, but there seems no need of invoking the fiction of an original compact to enforce it. It would be simpler to say (and quite as true) that the organization of a State is bad, for which its present members cannot be imagined as entering into a contract.

Sovereignty

Much has been said and written about sovereignty. I do not deny the interest of the topic, nor, from some points of view, its importance; but from the point of view of Law and Jurisprudence, I think its importance has been exaggerated.

Putting aside the cases where a number of people habitually subject themselves to one man simply as an individual, there are two forms of political organization. *First.* All political power is formally collected into the hands of one man, considered as King or Chief, determined by artificial rules of succession, a man clothed with a *persona*, like what is called in the Common Law a corporation sole.[2] *Second.* All political powers are given

[1] Ueber den Gemeinspruch, Das mag in der Theorie richtig sein, II, Folgerung.

[2] P. 57, *ante*.

to a body of men organized in a particular way. In the first case, there is a sovereign and subjects; in the second, a commonwealth and citizens.

Of the second type were the Greek cities and are most of the political organizations which have been created in modern times, but in many of the countries of Europe, the first was the condition of things which existed, or, in the opinion of the person calling himself Lord or King, existed,—the Prince of the "Leviathan"[1] is the ideal of such a ruler; and we find in so-called limited monarchies a nomenclature continuing which is derived from the first condition of things, although in truth the political organizations now have the second shape. Thus, in the Kingdom of Great Britain and Ireland, the King is not, and does not believe himself to be, the sole holder of political power; yet he is styled the Sovereign; the Army and Navy are called His Army and Navy. So in international matters, treaties between nations profess to be made between His Catholic Majesty and His Britannic Majesty.

But this, though a popular use, is not the scientific use of the term "sovereign." Austin "with great concision," as Sir Henry Maine says, defines "sovereign" thus: "If a determinate human superior, not in a habit of obedience to a like superior, receive habitual obedience from the bulk of a given society, that determinate superior is sovereign in that society, and the society (including the superior) is a society political and independent. To that determinate superior, the other members of the society are subject; or on that determinate superior, the other members of the society are dependent. The position of

[1] "Leviathan, or the Matter, Form and Power of a Commonwealth," by Thomas Hobbes (1651).

its other members towards that determinate superior, is a state of subjection, or a state of dependence. The mutual relation which subsists between that superior and them, may be styled the relation of sovereign and subject, or the relation of sovereignty and subjection."[1] And he goes on to point out that it is only in an absolute monarchy that the sovereignty is vested in one person, and that in all others, be they called limited monarchies, oligarchies, aristocracies, or democracies, the sovereignty is held by a number of persons.

But Austin fails to bring into prominence the fact that whenever the power is not vested in one person, but is held by a number of persons, that number are always combined for action in accordance with artificial rules, and will have the obedience of the community only when they act in accordance with those rules. Parliament, for instance, is said by Austin to be the Sovereign of England; but suppose King, Lords, and Commons should meet in one chamber and vote together, an order passed by them would not be obeyed by the English people.

And when political power is vested in a number of persons, not only may their mode of action be limited, but the objects to which their action can be directed may also be limited. Certain matters may be excluded from those upon which they can issue commands that will be obeyed.

Sovereignty in the United States

This is seen most clearly in federal governments. Austin is of the opinion that in the United States "the sovereignty of each of the states, and also of the larger state arising from the federal union, resides in the states' governments, *as forming one aggregate body:* meaning by

[1] 1 Jur. (4th ed.) 226, 227.

a state's government, not its ordinary legislature, but the body of its citizens which appoints its ordinary legislature, and which, the union apart, is properly sovereign therein."[1] But the powers of the United States—that is, of all the States' governments "as forming an aggregate body" over the individual citizens of a particular State—are very limited in character; they are defined by the Constitution, and commands by such aggregate body on matters outside of the Constitution would not be obeyed by the individual citizens.

Austin attempts to surmount this difficulty with the aid of the Fifth Article of the United States Constitution, which provides for amendments to be effected by a ratification by three-fourths of the States. But this hardly solves the difficulty. Suppose Congress recommends to the States the passage of an amendment to the Constitution authorizing an income tax to be levied without regard to population, and suppose this is ratified by a majority, but not by three-fourths, of the States, and Congress thereupon passes an Act imposing such a tax. The Act would not be obeyed.

Who, then, would be sovereign in the United States? The States as an aggregate body? But the majority of them cannot on this point enforce their will. Can we say that the dissenting minority of the States are the sovereign of the United States? They have certainly had their way upon the supposed occasion. They have commanded that the law by which an income tax shall be apportioned according to population shall not be changed, and their commands will be obeyed; yet, surely, this

[1] 1 Jur. (4th ed.) 268.

minority cannot be called sovereign; except as an obstacle to amending the Constitution, it is powerless.

Take an even stronger instance: The power of amending the Constitution of the United States is limited by the exception that "No State, without its consent, shall be deprived of its equal suffrage in the Senate." Suppose all the States except Utah have agreed that Utah shall have only one senator, such agreement would have no effect, and yet that hardly makes the State of Utah the Sovereign of the United States.

It may be said that if all the other States were unanimous in the opinion that Utah should have only one senator, they would force the result, and it is possible that if the States continue with very different populations, the majority in number of the States may be opposed by an overwhelming majority of the population, and in that case the Constitutional safeguard to secure the position of the smaller states in the Senate may give way; but that will be a revolution, a change of sovereign.

The truth is that the ideal or fictitious entity, the State, can manifest itself only through organs, and these organs may be so limited that there are certain acts they cannot perform, and therefore there may be no one sovereign in Austin's sense, with complete powers. Such is the case in the United States of America.[1]

An independent State is a legal unit, but to divide the members of a State into rulers and ruled, and call the former sovereign and the latter subjects, furnishes no

[1] The essay on Sovereignty by Professor Bliss of the University of Missouri, published in 1885, clearly expounds this view. Unfortunately, the unsatisfactory character of the discussion on the nature of Law, with which the Essay opens, repels students from reading further.

aid to the understanding of the Law of the State. To determine who are the real rulers of a political society is well-nigh an impossible task,—for Jurisprudence a well-nigh insoluble problem. To estimate, even approximately, the power that a certain statesman or demagogue has or had in a political society is a problem whose elements are too conflicting and too obscure for human judgment.

Idea of a sovereign unnecessary

To attempt to draw a precise line within any political society between sovereign and subjects, is to introduce a needless difficulty into Jurisprudence. The idea of the State is fundamental in Jurisprudence; but having postulated the State, we can turn at once to see what are its organs, legislative, judicial, and administrative, and to consider the rules in accordance with which they act. Austin's method would be to attempt to discover the sovereign from the society, and then to refer the organs of government to the sovereign, but this intermediate step, which it is very difficult to take rightly, is superfluous. The organs of government can be as directly referred to the State as they can be to the sovereign.

The real rulers of a political society are undiscoverable. They are the persons who dominate over the wills of their fellows. In every political society we find the machinery of government, king or president, parliament or assembly, judge or chancellor. We have to postulate one ideal entity to which to attach this machinery, but why insist on interposing another entity, that of a sovereign? Nothing seems gained by it, and to introduce it is to place at the threshold of Jurisprudence a very difficult, a purely academic, and an irrelevant question.

Legal rights of the State

Legal rights have been defined as the rights correlative to the duties which the State will enforce, either on its own motion, or on the motion of individuals; the former are the rights of the State, the latter are the rights of the individuals.[1] But it has been denied by some that the State can have any legal rights against any of its members.

The expression of the idea that a State has no rights against its members cannot be traced, that I am aware of, farther back than Austin. Omitting some of his amplifications, his doctrine is this: A sovereign government has no legal rights against its own subjects. Every legal right is the creature of a positive law; and it answers to a relative duty imposed by that positive law and incumbent on a person or persons other than the person or person in whom the right resides. To every legal right, there are therefore three parties: The sovereign government which sets the positive law, and which through the positive law confers the legal right, and imposes the relative duty; the person or persons on whom the right is conferred; the person or persons on whom the duty is imposed, or to whom the positive law is set or directed. . . . A sovereign government cannot acquire rights through laws set by itself to its own subjects. A man is no more able to confer a right on himself, than he is able to impose on himself a law or duty. Every party bearing a right has necessarily acquired the right through the might or power of another; that is to say, through a law and a duty laid by that party on a further and distinct party. Consequently, if a sovereign government had legal rights against its own subjects, those rights would be the creatures of positive laws set to its own subjects by a third person or body. And, as every positive law is laid by a

[1] P. 12, *ante*.

sovereign government on a person or persons in a state of subjection to itself, that third person or body would be sovereign in that community whose own sovereign government bore the legal rights; that is to say, the community would be subject to its own sovereign, and would be also subject to a sovereign conferring rights upon its own. Which is impossible and absurd.[1]

Partial exercise of power to create rights

But I do not go along with Austin. There are some objects desired by individuals which the State will protect, and some which it will not protect. It is an interest of mine, an object of my desire, that my neighbor does not drive across my land. That is an interest which the State will protect; I have a legal right. It is an interest of mine, an object of my desire, to drive across my neighbor's land. This interest of mine the State will not protect; I have no legal right to drive over my neighbor's land. So with the interests of the State. It is for the interest of the State that robbery should be prevented. It protects this interest by issuing a command and imposing a duty; it creates for itself a legal right. It may be its interest, an object of its desire, that the citizens of the State should not have dirty hands, that they should wash their hands at least once a day; but if it does not enforce this interest by imposing a duty, then it has no legal right to the diurnal ablution.

There is, of course, this difference between the State and the individual: The State can create legal rights, the individual cannot. There are innumerable interests of the State, conditions in the life of its citizens, which, if they existed, would be greatly to the advantage of the State; but the State does not protect these interests by imposing

[1] 1 Jur. (4th ed.) 290-292.

duties, because to do so would injuriously affect greater interests. It is desirable that people should wash their hands; the State would be better and happier if they did, and it may wish that they did; but it does not enforce this, its interest, because its enforcement would mean an amount of domestic espionage which would be a greater injury to the State than the unwashed hands. Yet the State might, if it would, enforce this interest.

But the distinction between all those interests, on the one hand, which the State in fact protects, through its judicial and administrative organs, whether at its own instance or at the instance of individuals, and all those interests, on the other hand, which it does not in fact so protect, either at its own instance or at the instance of individuals, although it might do so if it would, is important and desirable to make, and the name which analogy suggests and usage has given for the power to invoke such protection for the former is "legal right." Certain interests of Watkins will, on his motion, be protected by the State, and, if the question arises which of his interests the State will protect, it will be determined by the courts of the State according to rules which form the Law of the State; and the interests which the Law says are to be protected are the objects of Watkins's legal rights. So certain interests of the State will, on the motion of the State, through its officers, be protected by the State, and, if the question arises what interests of the State the State will protect, the question will be determined by the courts of the State according to its Law; and interests which the Law says will be protected are the objects of the legal rights of the State.

And this nomenclature is not only adapted to the true

theory of human relations, but it is suited to any practical view of affairs. What we want for the conduct of life is to know what are the acts and forbearances which the State protects, and what are the acts and forbearances which it compels; in other words, what are legal rights and duties? At whose instance these acts and forbearances are protected and enforced, though important, is yet of secondary importance.

Or the matter may be put in this way: Every State has judicial organs whose function is, by aid of certain rules called the Law, to determine what interests are now entitled to be protected, and what acts and forbearances the State will now, on its own motion or on the motion of individuals, enforce If an officer of the State, on its behalf, demands the performance of a certain act, for instance, that a woman who has worn a high hat at the theatre shall be hanged, and the Law does not provide for her execution, then the State has now no right to have her hanged. It is true that the State may prescribe a different rule for the judges; that is, it may cause the Law to be changed, and the court will sentence the woman to be hanged; but the State has then a legal right which it did not have before. The State has an indefinite power to create legal rights for itself, but the only legal rights which the State has at any moment are those interests which are then protected by the Law,—that is, by the rules in accordance with which the judicial organs of the State are then acting.

CHAPTER IV

THE LAW

Definition of the Law

THE Law of the State or of any organized body of men is composed of the rules which the courts, that is, the judicial organs of that body, lay down for the determination of legal rights and duties. The difference in this matter between contending schools of Jurisprudence arises largely from not distinguishing between the Law and the Sources of the Law. On the one hand, to affirm the existence of *nicht positivisches Recht*, that is, of Law which the courts do not follow, is declared to be an absurdity; and on the other hand, it is declared to be an absurdity to say that the Law of a great nation means the opinions of half-a-dozen old gentlemen, some of them, conceivably, of very limited intelligence.

The truth is, each party is looking at but one side of the shield. If those half-a-dozen old gentlemen form the highest judicial tribunal of a country, then no rule or principle which they refuse to follow is Law in that country. However desirable, for instance, it may be that a man should be obliged to make gifts which he has promised to make, yet if the courts of a country will not compel him to keep his promise, it is not the Law of that country that promises to make a gift are binding. On the other hand, those six men seek the rules which they follow not in their own whims, but they derive them from sources often of the most general and permanent character, to which they are directed, by the organized body to which they belong, to apply themselves. I believe the definition of Law that I have given to be correct; but let us consider some other definitions of the Law which have prevailed and which still prevail.

Of the many definitions of the Law which have been given at various times and places, some are absolutely meaningless, and in others a spark of truth is distorted by a mist of rhetoric. But there are three theories which have commended themselves to accurate thinkers, which have had and which still have great acceptance, and which deserve examination. In all of them it is denied that the courts are the real authors of the Law, and it is contended that they are merely the mouthpieces which give it expression.

Law as the command of the Sovereign

The *first* of these theories is that Law is made up of the commands [1] of the sovereign. This is Austin's view. "Every Positive Law," he says, "obtaining in any community, is a creature of the Sovereign or State; having been established immediately by the monarch or supreme body, as exercising legislative or judicial functions; or having been established immediately by a subject individual or body, as exercising rights or powers of direct or judicial legislation, which the monarch or supreme body has expressly or tacitly conferred." [2]

In a sense, this is true; the State can restrain its courts from following this or that rule; but it often leaves them free to follow what they think right; and it is certainly a forced expression to say that one commands things to be

[1] See p. 24, *ante*.
[2] 2 Jur. (4th ed.) 550, 551.

done, because he has power (which he does not exercise) to forbid their being done.

Mr. A. B., who wants a house, employs an architect, Mr. Y. Z., to build it for him. Mr. Y. Z. puts up a staircase in a certain way; in such a case, nine times out of ten, he puts it up in that way, because he always puts up staircases in that way, or because the books on construction say they ought to be so put up, or because his professional brethren put up their staircases in that fashion, or because he thinks to put it up so would be good building, or in good taste, or because it costs him less trouble than to put it up in some other way; he seldom thinks whether Mr. A. B. would like it in that way or not; and probably Mr. A. B. never thinks whether it could have been put up in any other fashion. Here it certainly seems strained to speak, as Austin would do, of the staircase as being the "creature" of Mr. A. B.; and yet Mr. A. B. need not have had his staircase put up in that way, and indeed need never have had any staircase or any house at all.

When an agent, servant, or official does acts as to which he has received no express orders from his principal, he may aim, or may be expected to aim, *directly* at the satisfaction of the principal, or he may not. Take an instance of the first,—a cook, in roasting meat or boiling eggs, has, or at any rate the ideal cook is expected to have, *directly* in view the wishes and tastes of her master. On the other hand, when a great painter is employed to cover a church wall with a picture, he is not expected to keep constantly in mind what will please the wardens and vestry; they are not to be in all his thoughts; if they are men of ordinary sense, they will not wish to be; he is to seek his inspiration elsewhere, and the picture when done is not the "creature" of the wardens and vestry; whereas, if the painter had adopted an opposite course, and had bent his whole energies to divining what he thought would please them best, he would have been their "tool," and the picture might not unfairly be described as their creature.

Now it is clear into which of these classes a judge falls. Where he has not received direct commands from the State, he does not consider, he is not expected to consider, *directly* what would please the State; his thoughts are directed to the questions—What have other judges held? What does Ulpian or Lord Coke say about the matter? What decision does *elegantia juris* or sound morals require?

It is often said by hedonistic moralists that, while happiness is the end of human life, it is best attained by not aiming directly at it; so it may be the end of a court, as of any other organ of a body, to carry out the wishes of that body, but it best reaches that object by not directly considering those wishes.

Austin's statement that the Law is entirely made up of commands directly or indirectly imposed by the State is correct, therefore, only on the theory that everything which the State does not forbid its judges to do, and which they in fact do, the State commands, although the judges are not animated by a direct desire to carry out the State's wishes, but by entirely different ones.

"A Law" and "The Law"

In this connection, the meaning of "Law," when preceded by the indefinite, is to be distinguished from that which it bears when preceded by the definite, article. Austin, indeed, defines the Law as being the aggregate of the rules established by political superiors;[1] and Bentham says, "*Law,* or *the Law,* taken indefinitely, is an abstract and collective term; which, when it means anything, can mean neither more nor less than the sum total of a number of individual laws taken together."[2] But this is not, I think, the ordinary meaning given to "the Law." *A* law ordinarily means a statute passed by the legislature of a State. "*The* Law" is the whole system of rules applied by the courts. The resemblance of the terms suggests the inference that the body of rules applied by the courts is composed wholly of the commands of the State; but to erect this suggestion into a demonstration, and say:—The system administered by the courts is "the Law," "the Law" consists of nothing but an aggregate of single laws, and all single laws are commands of the State,—is not justifiable.

It is to Sir Henry Maine that we owe the distinct pointing out that Austin's theory "is founded on a mere artifice of speech, and that it assumes courts of justice to act in a way and from motives of which they are quite unconscious. . . . Let it be understood that it is quite possible to make the theory fit in with such cases, but the process is a mere straining of language. It is carried on by taking words and propositions altogether out of the sphere of the ideas habitually associated with them."[3]

Austin's theory was a natural reaction against the views which he found in possession of the field. Law had been defined as "the art of what is good and equitable"; "that which reason in such sort defines to be good

[1] 1 Jur. (4th ed.) 89.
[2] 1 Benth. Works, 148.
[3] Maine, Early Hist. of Inst. 364, 365.

that it must be done"; "the abstract expression of the general will existing in and for itself"; "the organic whole of the external conditions of the intellectual life." [1] If Austin went too far in considering the Law as always proceeding from the State, he conferred a great benefit on Jurisprudence by bringing out clearly that the Law is at the mercy of the State.

Law in the consciousness of the people

The *second* theory on the nature of Law is that the courts, in deciding cases, are, in truth, applying what has previously existed in the common consciousness of the people. Savigny is the ablest expounder of this theory. At the beginning of the *System des heutigen römischen Rechts,* he has set it forth thus: "It is in the common consciousness of the people that the positive law lives, and hence we have to call it *Volksrecht*. . . . It is the *Volksgeist*, living and working in all the individuals in common, which begets the positive law, so that for the consciousness of each individual there is, not by chance but necessarily, one and the same law. . . . The form, in which the Law lives in the common consciousness of the people, is not that of abstract rule, but the living intuition of the institute of the Law in its organic connection. . . . When I say that the exercise of the *Volksrecht* in single cases must be considered as a means to become acquainted with it, an indirect acquaintance must be understood, necessary for those who look at it from the outside, without being themselves members of the community in which the *Volksrecht* has arisen and leads its continuous life. For the members of the community, no such inference from

[1] Celsus; Hooker; Hegel; Krause. See Holland, Jur. (11th ed.) 20.

single cases of exercise is necessary, since their knowledge of it is direct and based on intuition." [1]

Savigny is careful to discriminate between the common consciousness of the people and custom: "The foundation of the Law," he says, "has its existence, its reality, in the common consciousness of the people. This existence is invisible. How can we become acquainted with it? We become acquainted with it as it manifests itself in external acts, as it appears in practice, manners, and custom: by the uniformity of a continuous and continuing mode of action, we recognize that the belief of the people is its common root, and not mere chance. Thus, custom is the sign of positive law, not its foundation." [2]

Opinions of jurists

Savigny is confronted by a difficulty of the same kind as confronted Austin. The great bulk of the Law as it exists in any community is unknown to its rulers, and it is only by aid of the doctrine that what the sovereign permits he commands, that the Law can be considered as emanating from him; but equally, the great bulk of the Law is unknown to the people; how, then, can it be the product of their "common consciousness"? How can it be that of which they "feel the necessity as law"?

Take a simple instance, one out of thousands. By the law of Massachusetts, a contract by letter is not complete until the answer of acceptance is received.[3] By the law of New York, it is complete when the answer is mailed. Is the common consciousness of the people of Massa-

[1] 1 Savigny, Heut. röm. Recht, § 7, pp. 14, 16; § 12, p. 38.
[2] Heut. röm. Recht, § 12, p. 35.
[3] This used to be the Law in Massachusetts. I am not so sure that it is now. (See 1 Williston, Contracts, § 81.)

chusetts different on this point from that of the people of New York? Do the people of Massachusetts feel the necessity of one thing as law, and the people of New York feel the necessity of the precise opposite? In truth, not one in a hundred of the people of either State has the dimmest notion on the matter. If one of them has a notion, it is as likely as not to be contrary to the law of his State.

Savigny meets the difficulty thus: "The Law, originally the common property of the collected people, in consequence of the ramifying relations of real life, is so developed in its details that it can no more be mastered by the people generally. Then a separate class of legal experts is formed which, itself an element of the people, represents the community in this domain of thought. In the special consciousness of this class, the Law is only a continuation and peculiar development of the *Volksrecht*. The last leads, henceforth, a double life. In its fundamental principles it continues to live in the common consciousness of the people; the exact determination and the application to details is the special calling of the class of jurisconsults." [1]

But the notion that the opinions of the jurisconsults are the developed opinions of the people is groundless. In the countries of the English Common Law, where the judges are the jurists whose opinions go to make up the Law, there would be less absurdity in considering them as expressing the opinions of the people; but on the Continent of Europe, in Germany for instance, it is difficult to think of the unofficial and undeterminate class of jurists,

[1] 1 Heut. röm. Recht, § 14, p. 45.

past and present, from whose writings so great a part of the Law has been derived, as expressing the opinions of the people. In their reasonings, it is not the opinions of the people of their respective countries, Prussia, or Schwartzburg-Sonderhausen, which guide their judgment. They may bow to the authority of statutes, but in the domain of Law which lies outside of statute, the notions on Law, if they exist and are discoverable, which they are mostly not, of the persons among whom they live, are the last things which they take into account. What they look to are the opinions of foreign lawyers, of Papinian, of Accursius, of Cujacius, or at the *elegantia juris*, or at "juristic necessity." [1]

The jurists set forth the opinions of the people no more and no less than any other specially educated or trained class in a community set forth the opinions of that community, each in its own sphere. They in no other way set forth the *Volksgeist* in the domain of Law than educated physicians set forth the *Volksgeist* in the matter of medicine. It might be very desirable that the conceptions of the *Volksgeist* should be those of the most skilful of the community, but however desirable this might be, it is not the case. The *Volksgeist* carries a piece of sulphur in its waistcoat pocket to keep off rheumatism, and thinks that butchers cannot sit on juries.

Not only is popular opinion apart from professional opinion in Law as in other matters, but it has been at times positively hostile. Those who hold that jurists are the mouthpieces of the popular convictions in matters of law have never been able to deal satisfactorily with the

[1] See an article by Professor Pound, in 31 Harvard Law Rev. 1047.

reception of the Roman law in Germany, for that Law was brought in not only without the wishes, but against the wishes, of the great mass of the people.[1]

Judges as discoverers of the Law

A *third* theory of the Law remains to consider. That theory is to this effect: The rules followed by the courts in deciding questions are not the expression of the State's commands, nor are they the expression of the common consciousness of the people, but, although what the judges rule is the Law, it is putting the cart before the horse to say that the Law is what the judges rule. The Law, indeed, is identical with the rules laid down by the judges, but those rules are laid down by the judges because they are the law, they are not the Law because they are laid down by the judges; or, as the late Mr. James C. Carter puts it, the judges are the discoverers, not the creators, of the Law. And this is the way that judges themselves are apt to speak of their functions.[2]

Only what the Judges lay down is Law

This theory concedes that the rules laid down by the judges correctly state the Law, but it denies that it is Law because they state it. Before considering the denial, let us look a moment at the concession. It is a proposition with which I think most Common-Law lawyers would agree. But we ought to be sure that our ideas are not colored by the theories or practice of the particular system of law with which we are familiar. In the Common Law, it is now generally recognized that the judges have had a main part in erecting the Law; that, as it now stands, it is largely based on the opinions of past generations of judges; but in the Civil Law, as we shall see hereafter, this has been true to a very limited extent. In

[1] See Appendix III.
[2] See pp. 218-240, *post*.

other words, judicial precedents have been the chief material for building up the Common Law, but this has been far otherwise in the systems of the Continent of Europe.[1] But granting all that is said by the Continental writers on the lack of influence of judicial precedents in their countries to be true, yet, although a past decision may not be a source of Law, a present decision is certainly an expression of what the Law now is. The courts of France to-day may, on the question whether a blank indorsement of a bill of exchange passes title, care little or nothing for the opinions formerly expressed by French judges on the point, but, nevertheless, the opinion of those courts to-day upon the question is the expression of the present Law of France, for it is in accordance with such opinion that the State will compel the inhabitants of France to regulate their conduct. To say that any doctrine which the courts of a country refuse to adopt is Law in that country, is to set up the idol of *nicht positivisches Recht*;[2] and, therefore, it is true, in the Civil as well as in the Common Law, that the rules laid down by the courts of a country state the present Law correctly.

The great gain in its fundamental conceptions which Jurisprudence made during the last century was the recognition of the truth that the Law of a State or other organized body is not an ideal, but something which actually exists. It is not that which is in accordance with religion, or nature, or morality; it is not that which ought to be, but that which is. To fix this definitely in the Jurisprudence of the Common Law, is the feat that Austin accomplished. He may have been wrong in treating

[1] P. 205, *et seq. post*.
[2] P. 84, *ante*.

the Law of the State as being the command of the sovereign, but he was right in teaching that the rules for conduct laid down by the persons acting as judicial organs of the State, are the Law of the State, and that no rules not so laid down are the Law of the State.

The Germans have been singularly inappreciative of Bentham and Austin, and, as so often happens, the arrival at a sound result has been greatly hampered by nomenclature. Ethics is, in Continental thought, divided into two parts, one dealing with matters which can be enforced by external compulsion, and the other with those which cannot. The former of these is called *Rechtslehre.* According to Kant, Moral philosophy (*Metaphysik der Sitten*) is divisible into two parts: (1) the metaphysical principles of Jurisprudence (*Rechtslehre*), and (2) the metaphysical principles of ethics (*Tugendlehre*).[1] Jurisprudence has for its subject-matter the aggregate of all the laws which it is possible to promulgate by external legislation.[2] All duties are either duties of justice (*Rechtspflicht*) or duties of virtue (*Tugendpflicht*). The former are such as *admit* of external legislation; the latter are those for which such legislation is not possible.[3] *Rechtslehre*, that is, deals not only with the rules which the State has actually imposed upon conduct, but also with all conduct which can be *potentially subjected* to such

[1] Kant, Rechtslehre, (Philosophy of Law), Preface, at beginning. Hastie's trans. p. 3.

[2] *Ib.* Introduction to Jurisprudence, A, What is Jurisprudence?, at beginning. Hastie, p. 43.

[3] *Ib.* Introduction to Moral Philosophy, III, Divisions of the Metaphysic of Morals, at beginning. Hastie, p. 24. I owe the reference to these passages of Kant to an article by John W. Salmon, in 11 Law Quarterly Rev., 121, 140, on the Law of Nature. See also Willoughby, Nature of the State, 113, note.

rules; and this has tended to obscure the distinction between the rules which have actually been laid down from those which might have been laid down. But of late years, the Germans, in their own way, have been coming round to Austin's view; and now the abler ones are abjuring all "*nicht positivisches Recht.*" [1]

Questions not previously decided

To come, then, to the question whether the judges discover preëxisting Law, or whether the body of rules that they lay down is not the expression of preëxisting Law, but the Law itself. Let us take a concrete instance: On many matters which have come in question in various jurisdictions, there is no doctrine received *semper, ubique, et ab omnibus.* For instance, Henry Pitt has built a reservoir on his land, and has filled it with water; and, without any negligence on his part, either in the care or construction of his reservoir, it bursts, and the water, pouring forth, floods and damages the land of Pitt's neighbor, Thomas Underhill. Has Underhill a right to recover compensation from Pitt? In England, in the leading case of *Rylands* v. *Fletcher,*[2] it was held that he could recover, and this decision has been followed in some of the United States—for instance, in Massachusetts; but in others, as, I believe, in New Jersey, the contrary is held.[3]

Now, suppose that Pitt's reservoir is in one of the newer States, say Utah, and suppose, further, that the question has never arisen there before; that there is no statute, no decision, no custom on the subject; the court has to decide the case somehow; suppose it should follow *Rylands*

[1] See Bergbohm, Jurisprudenz et Rechtsphilosophie, *passim.*
[2] L. R. 3 H. L. 330.
[3] *Wilson* v. *New Bedford,* 108 Mass. 261; *Marshall* v. *Welwood,* 38 N. J. Law, 339.

v. *Fletcher* and should rule that in such cases the party injured can recover. The State, then, through its judicial organ, backed by the executive power of the State, would be recognizing the rights of persons injured by such accidents, and, therefore, the doctrine of *Rylands* v. *Fletcher* would be undoubtedly the present Law in Utah.

Suppose, again, that a similar state of facts arises in the adjoining State of Nevada, and that there also the question is presented for the first time, and that there is no statute, decision, or custom on the point; the Nevada court has to decide the case somehow; suppose it should decline to follow *Rylands* v. *Fletcher*, and should rule that in such cases the party injured is without remedy. Here the State of Nevada would refuse to recognize any right in the injured party and, therefore, it would unquestionably be the present Law in Nevada that persons injured by such an accident would have no right to compensation.

Let us now assume that the conditions and habits of life are the same in these two adjoining States; that being so, these contradictory doctrines cannot both conform to an ideal rule of Law, and let us, therefore, assume that an all-wise and all-good intelligence, considering the question, would think that one of these doctrines was right and the other wrong, according to the true standard of morality, whatever that may be. It matters not, for the purposes of the discussion, which of the two doctrines it is, but let us suppose that the intelligence aforesaid would approve *Rylands* v. *Fletcher*; that is, it would think the Law as established in Nevada by the decision of its court did not conform to the eternal principles of right.

The fact that the ideal theory of Law disapproved the

Law as established in Nevada would not affect the present existence of that Law. However wrong intellectually or morally it might be, it would be the Law of that State to-day. But what was the Law in Nevada a week before a rule for decision of such questions was adopted by the courts of that State? Three views seem possible: *first*, that the Law was then ideally right, and contrary to the rule now declared and practised on; *second*, that the Law was then the same as is now declared practised; *third*, that there was then no Law on the matter.

The first theory seems untenable on any notion of discovery. A discoverer is a discoverer of that which is, —not of that which is not. The result of such a theory would be that when Underhill received the injury and brought his suit, he had an interest which would be protected by the State, and that it now turns out that he did not have it,—a contradiction in terms.

No Law previous to decision

We have thus to choose between the theory that the Law was at that time what it now is, and the theory that there was then no law at all on the subject. The latter is certainly the view of reason and common sense alike. There was, at the time in question, *ex hypothesi*, no statute, no precedent, no custom on the subject; of the inhabitants of the State not one out of a hundred had an opinion on the matter or had ever thought of it; of the few, if any, to whom the question had ever occurred, the opinions were, as likely as not, conflicting. To say that on this subject there was really Law existing in Nevada, seems only to show how strong a root legal fictions can strike into our mental processes.

When the element of long time is introduced, the absurdity of the view of Law preëxistent to its declaration is obvious. What was the Law in the time of Richard Cœur de Lion on the liability of a telegraph company to the persons to whom a message was sent? It may be said that though the Law can preëxist its declaration, it is conceded that the Law with regard to a natural force cannot exist before the discovery of the force. Let us take, then, a transaction which might have occurred in the eleventh century: A sale of chattels, a sending to the vendee, his insolvency, and an order by the vendor to the carrier not to deliver. What was the Law on stoppage *in transitu* in the time of William the Conqueror?

The difficulty of believing in preëxisting Law is still greater when there is a change in the decision of the courts. In Massachusetts it was held in 1849, by the Supreme Judicial Court, that if a man hired a horse in Boston on a Sunday to drive to Nahant, and drove instead to Nantasket, the keeper of the livery stable had no right to sue him in trover for the conversion of the horse. But in 1871 this decision was overruled, and the right was given to the stable-keeper.[1] Now, did stable-keepers have such rights, say, in 1845? If they did, then the court in 1849 did not discover the Law. If they did not, then the court in 1871 did not discover the Law.

Courts make *ex post facto* Law

And this brings us to the reason why courts and jurists have so struggled to maintain the preëxistence of the Law, why the common run of writers speak of the judges as merely stating the Law, and why Mr. Carter, in an advance towards the truth, says of the judges that they are discoverers of the Law. That reason is the unwillingness to recognize the fact that the courts, with the consent

[1] *Gregg* v. *Wyman*, 4 Cush. 322; *Hall* v. *Corcoran*, 107 Mass. 251.

of the State, have been constantly in the practice of applying in the decision of controversies, rules which were not in existence and were, therefore, not knowable by the parties when the causes of controversy occurred. It is the unwillingness to face the certain fact that courts are constantly making *ex post facto* Law.[1]

The unwillingness is natural, particularly on the part of the courts, who do not desire to call attention to the fact that they are exercising a power which bears so unpopular a name, but it is not reasonable. Practically in its application to actual affairs, for most of the laity, the Law, except for a few crude notions of the equity involved in some of its general principles, is all *ex post facto*. When a man marries, or enters into a partnership, or buys a piece of land, or engages in any other transaction, he has the vaguest possible idea of the Law governing the situation, and with our complicated system of Jurisprudence, it is impossible it should be otherwise. If he delayed to make a contract or do an act until he understood exactly all the legal consequences it involved, the contract would never be made or the act done. Now the Law of which a man has no knowledge is the same to him as if it did not exist.

Again, the function of a judge is not mainly to declare the Law, but to maintain the peace by deciding controversies. Suppose a question comes up which has never been decided,—and such questions are more frequent than persons not lawyers generally suppose,—the judge must decide the case somehow; he will properly wish to de-

[1] Technically the term "*ex post facto* Law" is confined with us to statutes creating crimes or punishments. I use the term here in its broader sense of retroactive Law.

cide it not on whim, but on principle, and he lays down some rule which meets acceptance with the courts, and future cases are decided in the same way. That rule is the Law, and yet the rights and duties of the parties were not known and were not knowable by them. That is the way parties are treated and have to be treated by the courts; it is solemn juggling to say that the Law, undiscovered and undiscoverable, and which is finally determined in opposite ways in two communities separated only by an artificial boundary, has existed in both communities from all eternity. I shall recur to this matter when we come to consider the topic of Judicial Precedents.

Law and the Natural Sciences

It may be said that there are reasons, based on the highest welfare of the human race, why the Law should be so or otherwise, and that it is one of the functions and duties of a judge to investigate those reasons; that he is an investigator as much as, in his sphere, was Sir Isaac Newton; that he may make mistakes, just as Newton did; and yet that truth is largely discovered by his means. But the difference between the judges and Sir Isaac is that a mistake by Sir Isaac in calculating the orbit of the earth would not send it spinning round the sun with an increased velocity; his answer to the problem would be simply wrong; while if the judges, in investigating the reasons on which the Law should be based, come to a wrong result, and give forth a rule which is discordant with the eternal verities, it is none the less Law. The planet can safely neglect Sir Isaac Newton, but the inhabitants thereof have got to obey the assumed pernicious and immoral rules which the courts are laying down, or they will be handed over to the sheriff.

Decisions as conclusive evidence of the Law

It is possible to state the facts in the terms of discovery by use of a device familiar enough in the Common Law. We may say that the rule has always existed, and that the opinions and consequent action of the judges are only conclusive evidence that such is the rule; but this is merely a form of words to hide the truth. Conclusive evidence is not evidence at all; it is something which takes the place of evidence and of the thing to be proved, as well. When we say that men are conclusively presumed to know the Criminal Law, we mean that men are to be punished for certain acts without regard to whether they know them to be against the Law or not; when we say that the registration of a deed is conclusive evidence against all the world, we mean that all the world are bound by a registered deed whether they know or not of its existence.[1]

Rules of conduct laid down and applied by the courts of a country are coterminous with the Law of that country, and as the first change, so does the latter along with them. Bishop Hoadly has said: "Whoever hath an *absolute authority* to *interpret* any written or spoken laws, it is *he* who is truly the *Law-giver* to all intents and purposes, and not the person who first wrote or spoke them";[2] *a fortiori*, whoever hath an absolute authority not only to interpret the Law, but to say what the Law is, is truly the Law-giver. *Entia non multiplicanda.* There seems to be nothing gained by seeking to discover the sources, purposes, and relations of a mysterious entity called "The Law," and then to say this Law is exactly expressed in the rules by which the courts decide cases. It is better to consider directly the sources, purposes, and relations

[1] Cf. p. 36, *ante*.

[2] Benjamin Hoadly, Bishop of Bangor, Sermon preached before the King, 1717, p. 12.

of the rules themselves, and to call the rules "The Law."

There is a feeling that makes one hesitate to accept the theory that the rules followed by the courts constitute the Law, in that it seems to be approaching the Law from the clinical or therapeutic side; that it is as if one were to define medicine as the science of the rules by which physicians diagnose and treat diseases; but the difference lies in this, that the physicians have not received from the ruler of the world any commission to decide what diseases are, to kill or to cure according to their opinion whether a sickness is mortal; whereas, this is exactly what the judges do with regard to the cases brought before them. If the judges of a country decide that it is Law that a man whose reservoir bursts must pay the damage, Law it is; but all the doctors in town may declare that a man has the yellow fever, and yet he may have only the German measles. If when a board of physicians pronounced that Titius had the colic, *ipso facto* Titius did have the colic, then I conceive the suggested definition of medicine would be unobjectionable.

To sum up. The State exists for the protection and forwarding of human interests, mainly through the medium of rights and duties. If every member of the State knew perfectly his own rights and duties, and the rights and duties of everybody else, the State would need no judicial organs; administrative organs would suffice. But there is no such universal knowledge. To determine, in actual life, what are the rights and duties of the State and of its citizens, the State needs and establishes judicial organs, the judges. To determine rights and duties, the judges settle what facts exist, and also lay down rules according to which they deduce legal consequences from facts. These rules are the Law.[1]

Law distinguished from other rules for conduct

There are one or two other matters connected with the Law which remain for consideration: *First*, The rules which constitute the Law of a community are distinguished from the other rules by which members of the community govern their conduct by the fact that the former are the rules laid down by the courts of the community in accordance with which they make their decrees. Very often these rules are overridden in the mind of a member of a community by other rules, of supposed morality, for instance, or of fashion, as where a man aids a runaway slave, or fights a duel. And again, when the conduct prescribed by the rules of Law is followed, the fact that those rules are laid down by the courts is not always, nor generally, the chief or predominant motive in the minds of those who follow them. The motive that restrains Titius from killing Balbus, or deters John Doe from taking Richard Roe's handkerchief out of his pocket, is not primarily that the one fears being hanged or the other fears being sent to jail; it is some other reason, religious, moral, social, sentimental, or æsthetic, which moves him. There is generally no occasion for the courts to apply their rules, but the fact that the courts will apply them, if necessary, makes them the Law.

[1] The Law has sometimes been said to be the rules which the courts *will* follow. See Judge Holmes's article, 10 Harvard Law Rev. 457; Collected Legal Papers, 167; and his opinion in *American Banana Co.* v. *United Fruit Co.*, 213 U. S. 347, 356. When this form of expression is used, we must not say in reference to a case like that suggested at p. 96, *ante*, that there was then no law on the subject in Nevada, but we must say that it was not then known what the Law *would* be.

Further, when persons do not voluntarily act in accordance with the rules laid down by the courts, but are compelled thereto by force, the force is often applied, not in consequence of a judicial order, but by the persons directly interested in having the rules followed or by some administrative officer not acting under judicial authority,—as when Stiles expels Batkins as a trespasser from his domestic castle, or policeman X. arrests Watkins for being drunk and disorderly.[1] But in all such cases, the rules are Law, because, in the ultimate resort, the judges will apply them in protecting Stiles and the policeman against any violent acts or any prosecution in the courts by the intrusive Batkins or the vagabond Watkins.

The Law not always obeyed

Second. Suppose, however, that the bulk of the community habitually act contrary to certain rules laid down by the courts,—will you call such rules Law? The question is the same when asked with regard to those rules which the judges lay down in compliance with statutes passed by the legislative organ of the State, as in regard to those which they frame of their own motion. Suppose the Legislature enacts a statute which is so odious to the inhabitants of the State that the bulk of the community disobey it from the start, and yet the judges declare that it has been duly and constitutionally enacted. In countries where statutes can be abrogated by disuse (a matter which we shall afterwards consider [2]), the courts may, after a space of time, declare that such a statute is no longer to be considered binding, but we are here considering a case where the courts lay down a rule in accordance with the statute. Is such a rule Law? I submit

[1] See p. 21, *ante.*
[2] Pp. 189, *et seq. post.*

that it is most in accordance with usage, and most convenient in practice, to consider the declaration of the courts following the action of the Legislature as being "the Law." If there is a statute recognized by the courts forbidding the sale of wine, and yet wine is sold publicly and with impunity, it seems best to say, not that the Law allows the sale of wine, but that the Law against the sale of wine is disregarded. And it must be the same, as I have said, whether the declaration of the court is founded on a statute or is derived from any of the other sources of the Law.[1]

In certain of these cases, an unnecessary difficulty arises from misunderstanding what the Law is. Let us take such a case as I have suggested: Suppose that in one of the United States there is a statute providing that whoever sells wine shall be punished by fine or imprisonment, and suppose, further, that the statute is so hated that juries will not convict. This statute, being followed by the courts, is an element of the Law in the State, but it is not the whole of the Law. It is also doubtless Law in the State that no one shall be punished for crime except after being found guilty by a jury. The whole Law must be taken together. We say the Law is that a man selling wine shall be punished, but in truth the Law is, that a man selling wine *and convicted thereof by a jury* shall be punished. If there has been no conviction by a jury, one of the elements which the Law declares necessary for the infliction of the punishment does not exist. In old statutes this essential element is often expressed, *e.g.* St. 14 Eliz. *c.* 3: "If any person or persons" shall counterfeit coin,

[1] See, however, what is said on the limits of judicial power pp. 121 *et seq. post.*

"the offenders therein, being convict according to the laws of this realm of such offenses, shall be imprisoned," etc.

The Law consists of rules made by the State

Third. To say that the Law of an organized body is composed of the rules *acted on* by its courts would be too broad. It is only the rules which the courts lay down of their own motion, or which they follow as being prescribed for them by the body of which they are the courts, that, according to the ordinary usage of language, can be called the Law of that body.

Take, for instance, the courts of a political society. They have constantly, in the causes brought before them, to apply general rules of conduct which are yet not laws. Thus, A. and B. may enter into an agreement by which A., for a consideration, expressly or impliedly promises to obey the commands of B. on certain matters; those commands may take the form of general rules; and the existence and validity of such a rule may be brought in question in a court of law. In most cases where the legal relation of master and servant is established there are such general rules. Gladys, who has hired Norah for a housemaid, dismisses her for misconduct; Norah sues for her wages; the alleged misconduct is the not wearing of a cap; the existence of a rule requiring the wearing of a cap, its legality and scope, may all have to be determined by the court, yet Gladys's household ordinance is not the Law of the land.

It may be said that such rules are made by agreement of the parties, and are given by them to the court as rules by which, in controversies between them, it is to decide. But such rules do not always spring from contract. In many communities, the relations between master and slave have formed an important topic in the Law; and at the present day, in all countries, a father has authority to make rules on many subjects for his children, *e.g.* that they are to live in such a place, or are to go to bed at a certain hour. But these rules are no part of the Law, as commonly understood, though they can conceivably come before a court, and the court must pass in its decision upon their existence and validity.

A class of these rules forming no part of the Law of a country, and yet daily discussed and applied by its courts, are the by-laws of corporations. It would seem as if Austin [1] counted the by-laws of corporations as part of the Law of the land existing as Law by the express or tacit authority of the supreme legislature. He makes them a part of the Law in the same manner in which he brings judicial precedents under that head. He considers both by-laws and judicial precedents to be commands of the sovereign, by virtue of the doctrine that what the sovereign permits he commands.

But there seems to be no distinction between the valid regulations of a corporation and the valid regulations of a *paterfamilias.* I should suppose Austin would hardly make these last part of the Law of the land. To do so would amount to saying that all commands not directed to particular acts which the State allows to be made and enforced by any reward or punishment are part of the Law of the land,—a nomenclature, to say the least, very inconvenient, and a wide departure from usage, both popular and professional.

Laws of bodies other than the State

It should be borne in mind that rules, although not

[1] 2 Jur. c. 28 (4th ed.) p. 538.

the Law of the State, may yet be the Law of another organized body. Thus, the by-laws of a private corporation may be part of the Law of the organized body which that corporation is, and yet not be part of the Law of the land. So the rules by which Titius governs his children are no part of the Law of Titius's State, but they may all the same be part of the Law of Titius's family.

Such organizations may be the creatures of the State, as insurance or other business corporations; or they may be independent of the State, as the Roman Catholic Church; or even hostile to it, as a Nihilist club; but that is immaterial on the question whether such an organization has its own Law. It is true that an interest which a member of a club, for instance, may have that another member of the club itself should do or forbear, may be protected by the State by virtue of some rule which the courts of the State follow,—say, with regard to contracts generally,—or may be denied protection by the State by virtue of some rule which the courts of the State follow,—say with regard to gambling,—but apart from its relations with the State, if any organized body of men has persons or bodies appointed to decide questions, then that body has judges or courts, and if those judges or courts in their determinations follow general rules, then the body has Law and the members of the body may have rights under that Law. Thus, the Roman Catholic Church has courts and a Law, and by virtue of its power in inflicting excommunication and other spiritual censures, it gives rights to itself and its members.[1]

[1] The peculiar history of the Church of England, the compromise between temporal and spiritual interests which was effected at the Reformation, and the fundamental differences among its members

The Church of England

General administrative rules are laws

Fourth. One question more presents itself: Are all the general rules for conduct made by the administrative organs of a political (or other) organization to be called "laws"? Or is there a class of such rules to which the name of "laws" is to be denied?

We must bear in mind the distinction to which I have referred between *a* law and *the* Law, as those terms are generally employed.[1] *A* law is a formal general command of the State or other organized body; *the* Law is the body of rules which the courts of that body apply in deciding cases. So there are really two questions: First, is a general order of an administrative organ of an organ-

as to the grounds on which its frame of government rests, make it difficult to say whether that frame, in the opinion of its judges, has its foundation in the revealed will of God or in Acts of Parliament. The range of opinion within it extends from those dwellers in an ecclesiastical Tooley Street, who regard themselves as the remnant from which all other Christian bodies, Greek, Roman, and Protestant, are parted by schism, to that keeper of the King's conscience who said to a delegation of Presbyterians, "Gentlemen, I am against you and for the Established Church. Not that I like the Established Church a bit better than any other church, but because it *is* established. And whenever you get your damned religion established, I'll be for that too." (Lord Thurlow. See Campbell's Lives of the Chancellors (5th ed.), vol. 7, p. 319). Sir Robert Phillimore and Lord Westbury were both judges in the English Church, but it is likely that they held very different theories as to the grounds on which the hierarchy of that Church is based. But it is not easy to believe that a religious organization, whose highest court is the Judicial Committee of His Majesty's Privy Council, was ever revealed directly or impliedly from Heaven; and the true doctrine would seem to be that the English Church owes its constitution to the State, and that although, in the opinion of many of its members, it would be sinful in the State to give it any other constitution, yet the judges of the Church must look to the Law of the land, to the King's Ecclesiastical Law, to determine the nature of the organization whose judges they are, and that so long as the Church is established, it is practically impossible that it should be otherwise. The report of the Hampden Case (11 Queen's Bench Reports, 483 (1848); and full report by R. Jebb) will be found instructive on this point.

[1] P. 87, *ante*.

ized body *a* law of that body? Secondly, is such an order a source of *the* Law of that body?

Such an order certainly seems to be a command of the organized body and, therefore, a law of that body. To take cases like those which Mr. Frederic Harrison suggests as showing that there are rules of the State which are not laws; a regulation by the proper authority (or, indeed, by the supreme legislature) that all recruits for the army shall be five feet six inches high, or a direction in the infantry tactics that the goose step shall be twenty-eight inches, or an order by the commandant of a fort that a sentry shall always be posted before a certain cellar.[1] Are such regulations, directions, and orders laws? They are unquestionably commands with sanctions; they are of a general and permanent character; they are formally issued by a person empowered by the State to issue them and they are issued on behalf of and for the supposed advantage of the State. They seem to be as much laws of the State as statutes passed by its legislative organ.

Are these regulations and orders sources of the Law? It is hard to imagine any of them which may not be brought before a court for application and whose ultimate sanction is not that the courts will apply to them. Let us take one of Mr. Harrison's instances,—a regulation from the British War Office that no recruit shall be enlisted who is not five feet six inches high. Suppose a recruiting officer musters in a man who is five feet five inches only in height, and pays him the King's shilling; afterwards the officer is sued by the Government for being

[1] 30 Fortnightly Rev., 690; Jurisprudence and the Conflict of Laws, p. 49.

short in his accounts; among other items he claims to be allowed the shilling paid to the undersized recruit. The court has to consider and apply this regulation and, whatever its effect may be, that effect will be given to it by the court exactly as effect will be given to a statute providing that murderers shall be hanged, or that last wills must have two witnesses.

It is, therefore, on the best consideration I can give the subject, impossible to say that any general rule of conduct laid down by an administrative organ of a political (or other) organized body, and applied, if necessary, by its courts, is not a source of Law.

CHAPTER V

THE COURTS

The Law of an organized body, political or other, being the rules laid down by the judicial department of that body, it is now necessary to consider courts or judges; I use the terms as synonymous.

Office of a Judge

It is, of course, not necessary that a judge be called by that name; it is the functions which he exercises, and not the name by which he is called, that mark his essential character. Thus, the Lord High Chancellor of England is a judge. And, further, persons having judicial functions may have also functions which are not judicial. Thus, the Lord Chancellor, again, is not only a judge, he presides over the House of Lords and dispenses much of the ecclesiastical patronage of the Crown. In some primitive communities, the legislative, judicial, and administrative powers are united in the same persons or in a single individual.[1]

[1] The distinction between administrative and judicial functions, when exercised by the same person, is happily illustrated in the case of the visitor of a college. Visitors have two functions. The first is to visit the college, *proprio motu*, without being called thereto by any one. Such visitations were originally liable to great abuses. When the visitor, who was generally a bishop, wanted to go on a junket, he visited a college, with a great train of chaplains and retainers, and lived at free quarters, to the great oppression and impoverishment of the college. The founders of the colleges in Oxford and Cambridge, therefore, perceiving that visitations were not unmixed blessings, often provided, in establishing the

A judge of an organized body is a man appointed by that body to determine duties and the corresponding rights *upon the application of persons claiming those rights.* It is the fact that such application must be made to him, which distinguishes a judge from an administrative officer.

The essence of a judge's office is that he shall be impartial, that he is to sit apart, is not to interfere voluntarily in affairs, is not to act *sua sponte,* but is to determine cases which are presented to him. To use the phrase

statutes of their foundations, that a visitation should not be held more frequently than once in three or five years. The college was liable to support the bishop and to have every corner and nook poked into at his will in every third or fifth year; but that once over, there was to be rest and recuperation during another three or five years. Visitations of this kind were called general visitations. But besides this function of making a general visitation, a visitor of a college has another, a judicial, function. It is his duty to hear complaints of members of the college against the Master and Fellows, or other governing body, of the Master and Fellows against any member, and of one member against another. These complaints can be made at any time, and the visitor can hear them at once. In hearing them he is acting in a judicial capacity, and his court is always open; while at a general visitation he is acting in an administrative capacity. The difference between these two functions of a visitor of a college was pointed out by Lord Chief Justice Holt in the classical passage of his opinion in *Philips* v. *Bury,* 2 T.R. 346, 348. "Now though the visitor be restrained by the constitutions of the college from visiting *ex officio* more than once in five years, yet as visitor he has a standing constant authority at all times to hear the complaints and redress the grievances of the particular members. . . . For visiting is one act, in which he is limited in time; but hearing appeals and redressing grievances is his proper office and work at all times."

The same learned Chief Justice's strong opinion on the immutable distinction between administrative and judicial functions was shown by his answer to one who declared himself sent by the Holy Ghost to bid the Chief Justice enter a *nolle prosequi* in the case of a prisoner: "Thou art a lying knave; if the Holy Ghost had sent thee, he would have sent thee to His Majesty's Attorney General and not to me, for the Holy Ghost knows well I have no power to enter a *nolle prosequi.*" ("I do not wish to prosecute," the form used in discontinuing a criminal prosecution.) For varying versions of the anecdote, see 3 Campbell's Lives of the Chief Justices, 3d ed., p. 9; Dict. of National Biography, "Holt," near end.

of the English Ecclesiastical courts, the office of the judge must be promoted by some one.

A judge's usual function is to determine controversies between parties, of which parties the State, or other organized body, whose judge he is, may be one. Even if in non-contentious proceedings a judge cannot be said to determine an actual controversy, application must be made to him by some one interested in having a matter determined, in order to fix rights and prevent a controversy arising. Thus, in granting probate of an undisputed last will, which is an extreme case of a non-contentious proceeding, the judge is determining a question, —viz., whether a certain paper is the last will of a deceased person,—in order to prevent controversies between people interested, or claiming to be interested, in the succession to the estate of the deceased; and he grants probate, not of his own motion, but on the application of the executor. If no application is made to him, the testamentary paper remains without probate; so also in voluntary insolvency proceedings.

A judge is to determine rights. He may be, and often is, given authority to enforce his decision, but this is not necessary. The function of determination is the essential element in the judicial position. The power to enforce the decision is accidental.

Power to enforce decisions not essential

Sometimes, even, the decision of the court of an organized body other than the State is enforced, not by that body, but by the State. Thus, in other days, after a Church court had adjudged a person to be a heretic, and "*foro Seculari relinquendum esse decrevit . . . ac Sancta Mater Ecclesia non habet ulterius quid faciat in præmissis*"; it was the State which issued the writ *De hæretico comburendo;* [1] and in the United States, at the present day, the judgment of a Church court has often to be enforced by an action of ejectment or of tort in the civil courts.[2]

Even when the organized body in question is the State, the function of some of its courts may be only that of determination. Thus, a court of probate decides whether a person had died testate or intestate, and thereby fixes the rights of persons claiming to be legatees or next of kin; but it may have no machinery for enforcing these rights.

Although power to enforce his decrees is not necessary to constitute a man a judge, yet there is a means somewhere of enforcing them. Take the case just suggested: The judge of a probate court may have no power to enforce his decrees, yet if one who is named executor in a testamentary paper obtains probate of it, he can enforce his claim as executor in the Common Law courts, which he could not do in the absence of probate.

Difference of opinion between courts

There may sometimes be a difference of opinion between the courts of the same political or other organization. They may apply different rules. What, in that case, is the Law of such organization? It is the rule generally followed. If the courts generally of a country follow certain rules, those rules do not cease to be the Law because of a sporadic departure from them by a particular judge. A judge once decided in Massachusetts

[1] "Shall have decreed that he must be relinquished to the Secular tribunal, . . . and Holy Mother Church has nothing further to do in the premises." 1 Gibson, Codex (2d ed.) 338, note.

[2] *E.g.* in *Watson* v. *Jones*, 13 Wall. 679.

that payment on Sunday was no discharge of a debt, but that has never been the Law of Massachusetts.[1]

A permanent difference of opinion between courts of the same organized body is usually prevented by the fact that, in most organizations having several courts or judges, there is a supreme appellate tribunal, to which all the other courts are subordinate. When such is the case, the rules followed by the supreme tribunal are the Law of the organization. It is true, as we shall see later, when we come to consider the subject of Judicial Precedents, that on the modern theory, if not in the practice, of the Germans, decisions of appellate courts are not sources of Law to the lower courts;[2] but although, in determining what is the Law *now,* that is, what are the rules which the courts will now apply, a court of first instance may not now be bound by a past decision of an appellate court, as a precedent, yet even assuming this to be so, still upon a question as to what *was* the Law of the organization at that past time, it would seem as if the rule which was followed by the court that then had the final power of determination was the Law at that time.

Sometimes, however, perhaps (1) there may be coördinate courts of one political body, with the same powers, and no common superior; or (2) there may be independent courts for different matters, each of which is supreme in its sphere, as is probably the case with the House of Lords and the Judicial Committee of the Privy Council in England;[3] or, (3) what is a very common

[1] See *Johnson* v. *Willis,* 7 Gray, 164.

[2] P. 209, *post.*

[3] *Dulieu* v. *White & Sons,* [1901] 2 K. B. 669, 677, 683; *Smith* v. *Brown,* L. R. 6 Q. B. 729, 736.

arrangement in the United States, cases involving an amount above a certain sum may be carried to an appellate court, while those involving a less amount cannot be.

Independent coördinate courts

(1) In the case where there are two or more coördinate courts of the same organization, having no common superior, and yet having the same territorial jurisdiction, the same jurisdiction of persons and causes, and the same powers, and these courts habitually follow different rules on any point, I do not see how we can avoid saying that the organization has no Law on that point. It is to be observed that the existence of such an anarchic condition of things is vastly improbable.

Independent courts for different matters

(2) Let us now consider the case where different classes of action are brought, or different remedies applied, in courts above which there is no common appellate tribunal. For instance, suppose a suit against Edwin by one who has supplied goods to Angelina, and also a libel for divorce by Angelina against Edwin. On the same undisputed facts, the court of Common Law might, as a matter of Law, rule that Edwin and Angelina were never married, while the Divorce Court might rule that they were. So again, when a seaman, on the one hand, files a libel for his wages against his ship in the Admiralty, or, on the other, sues the ship's owners for them in a court of Common Law, the Admiralty and the Common Law might follow different rules. In these cases, we could not say that on such facts the Law was that a marriage had or had not taken place, or that a sailor had or had not earned his wages. We should have to say that on such facts the Law was that a man could not be made liable for the debts of a woman, but that he could obtain a divorce from her as his wife; and that on such other facts, the Law was

that a sailor could sue a ship, but not the owners, or *vice versa.*

It should be observed that, in the case of two courts having different machineries, the rules which one follows may be said to be the Law of the land, though they are different from those followed by the other. Thus, it would not be incorrect to say that it was the Law of England that, if land was devised to A. and his heirs, in trust for B. and his heirs, A. could not turn B. out of possession of the land, although A. could, before the introduction of equitable pleas, turn B. out by an action of ejectment at Common Law, for as Equity would enjoin A. from bringing ejectment, the rules on this subject in the courts of Equity might be said to be the Law of the land.

Courts with limited right of appeal

(3) Let us now take the case suggested where the right of appeal is limited by the amount involved. In countries where the doctrines of the English Common Law prevail, there is no difficulty. The rules laid down by the higher court in those cases which, being above the money limit, have been brought up by appeal, would be binding on the lower courts, and would be followed by them, as well in those cases in which the amount involved was too small to allow an appeal, as in those cases which could be carried up. But in Germany, apparently, it would open to a court of first instance, if its judge disagreed with the opinion of the appellate court, to continue to decide finally cases below the limit of appeal in one and the same way, although his decisions in cases above the limit were being constantly reversed.

Suppose, to take a particular instance, that in a country where the German doctrine prevails, all the courts of first instance persist in deciding that the holder of an overdue coupon cut from a bond is not entitled to interest upon it, while the supreme tribunal rules that such holder is entitled to interest; and suppose, also, that no appeal is allowed when the subject-matter in dispute is of a value less than twenty-five marks. Hans has a coupon for twenty marks which has been a year overdue, and Fritz has a coupon due at the same time, but which is for the sum of thirty marks. It seems absurd to say that the Law in that country is that Hans cannot get interest on his coupon and that Fritz can on his; and even more absurd to say that if Hans has two coupons of twenty marks each, or, if he waits until a second coupon on the same bond has become overdue, and then sues on both, he can recover interest on both. But yet, such is the fact. The holder of a single coupon will not be helped by the State to the interest; he has nothing which it will protect; he has no right to the interest. As to it, he stands as in any other matter where, though he may have a moral right, he has no legal right. It is absurd, but the absurdity lies in a theory of judicial organizations and judicial duty which allows an inferior court to disregard a rule for decision which a higher court has adopted.

This is not the place to discuss the topic of conflict between the Federal and State courts in the United States, for that conflict is not between courts of the same political organization, but between courts which, although they may have the same territorial jurisdiction, are yet the courts of different political organizations. The matter will be discussed in the chapter on Judicial Precedents in the United States.[1]

Limits of judicial power

Thus far we have seen that the Law is made up of the rules for decision which the courts lay down; that all such rules are Law; that rules for conduct which the courts do not apply are not Law; that the fact that the courts apply rules is what makes them Law; that there is no mysterious entity "The Law" apart from these rules; and that the judges are rather the creators than the discoverers of the Law.

Is the power of the judges, then, absolute? Can the comparatively few individuals who fill judicial position in the State, for instance, lay down rules for the government of human intercourse at their bare pleasure or whim? Not so; the judges are but organs of the State; they have only such power as the organization of the State gives them; and what that organization is, is determined by the wills of the real rulers of the State.

Who are the rulers of a State, is a question of fact and not of form. In a nominal autocracy, the real rulers may be a number of court favorites or the priests of a religion; and in a democracy, the real ruler may be a demagogue or political boss.[2]

It is conceivable that a body of judges may be the ruling wills of a community, and then they hold their powers by virtue of dominating other wills, but this, except in a very primitive community, can hardly ever be the case. The half-a-dozen elderly men sitting on a plat-

[1] Pp. 248, *et seq. post.*
[2] Pp. 67-68, *ante.*

form behind a green or red cloth, with very probably not commanding wills or powerful physique, can exercise their functions only within those limits which the real rulers of the State allow for the exercise; for the State and the court as an organ thereof are the product of the wills of those rulers.

Who is to determine whether the judges are acting within those limits? In all the less important matters, the rulers intrust the determination of this question to the judges themselves; thus the judges are allowed to say what are the details of the organization of a State and the distribution of its powers among its organs; but, on the most vital matters, the rulers themselves determine what the organization of the body is and within what limits its organs shall work; and the acts and declarations of persons, being its organs, which are inconsistent with the very nature of the organization, are not acts and declarations of the State—are not its Law.

How can it be told whether a rule laid down by a court is to be deemed not the Law, either because such rule is inconsistent with the organization of the State as established by its rulers, or because it is beyond the limits of the power of the court as fixed by those rulers? The principal evidence that declarations of judges are inconsistent with the organization of the State, or beyond the limits fixed by it for their action, is the opinions of the members of the community to that effect. To determine whether such opinions are so strong and universal that they must be taken for the judgment of the rulers of the State, or whether the declarations, though much disregarded, are still to be deemed Law,[1] there seems to be no general definite rule, applicable to all cases.

It should be observed that the unexpressed, and, in formal shape, inexpressible, opinion of the rulers of society lies behind the Law none the less in those countries which possess written constitutions than in those which do not. The organization and powers of the ordinary legislative bodies may be indeed defined in a constitution, but whether there was power in any one to bring into effect the constitution, the constitution itself cannot determine, any more than a book can prove its own inspiration, or a man lift himself up by his boots. For instance: What are the geographical limits for which the constitution is to be in force? Who are to vote upon it, —men, women, or children? Can paupers, slaves, aliens, vote? By what collections of individuals, such as towns or boroughs, must representatives to frame a constitution be chosen? These are questions that the rulers of the State must determine; their decision is a prerequisite for the constitution coming into existence. The elephant may rest on the tortoise, but in the last result we have to go back to the wills of those who rule the society.

Indication of sources of the Law

The power of the rulers of the State or other community in reference to its judicial organs or courts is exercised in a twofold way,—first, by creating them, and secondly, in laying down limits for their action, or, in other words, indicating the sources from which they are to derive the rules which make up the Law. From what *sources* does the State or other community direct its judges to obtain the Law? These sources are defined for the most part in a very vague and general way, but one rule

[1] See pp. 105 *et seq. ante.*

is clear and precise. The State requires that the acts of its legislative organ shall bind the courts, and so far as they go, shall be paramount to all other sources. This may be said to be a necessary consequence from the very conception of an organized community of men.

The other sources from which courts may draw their general rules are fourfold,—judicial precedents, opinions of experts, customs, and principles of morality (using morality as including public policy). Whether there is any precedent, expert opinion, custom, or principle from which a rule can be drawn, and whether a rule shall be drawn accordingly, are questions which, in most communities, are left to the courts themselves; and yet there are probably in every community limits within or beyond which courts may, or, on the other hand, cannot, seek for rules from the sources mentioned, although the limits are not precisely defined. Take, for instance, a country where the English Common Law has prevailed. If a court in such a country should, in matters not governed by statute, absolutely refuse to follow any judicial precedents, it is not likely that the rulers of the country would recognize the doctrine of that court as Law; or, if a court should frame a rule based upon the principle that infanticide was not immoral, that rule would not be the Law.

Statutes as a source of Law

Though the commands by the rulers of a community as to the limits within which these last four classes of sources are to be sought by the courts are indefinite, while the command that legislative acts must be followed by the courts is precise and peremptory, the fact is that this latter rule, in its working, is almost as indefinite as those which are imposed on the courts with reference to the other sources; for, after all, it is only words that the legislature utters; it is for the courts to say what those words mean; that is, it is for them to interpret legislative acts; undoubtedly there are limits upon their power of interpretation, but these limits are almost as undefined as those which govern them in their dealing with the other sources.

And this is the reason why legislative acts, statutes, are to be dealt with as sources of Law, and not as part of the Law itself, why they are to be coördinated with the other sources which I have mentioned. It has been sometimes said that the Law is composed of two parts,—legislative law and judge-made law, but, in truth, all the Law is judge-made law. The shape in which a statute is imposed on the community as a guide for conduct is that statute as interpreted by the courts. The courts put life into the dead words of the statute. To quote again from Bishop Hoadly, a sentence which I have before given: "Nay, whoever hath an *absolute authority* to *interpret* any written or spoken laws, it is *he* who is truly the *Law-giver* to all intents and purposes, and not the person who first wrote or spoke them." [1] I will return to this later.

[1] Benjamin Hoadly, Bishop of Bangor. Sermon preached before the King, 1717, p. 12.

CHAPTER VI

LAW OF NATIONS

Relation between nations

IT is possible, perhaps probable, that men have lived together in certain modes and fashions, have, in other words, lived in society, and yet may not have formed an organized body. But the units of such unorganized bodies may be themselves organisms, and this has in all probability been generally the case. A horde of savages who are in the habit of wandering about together, without king or judge, may be composed of true organisms, families, each with its ruler (alike legislator and judge) and Law. The horde is made up of the family units, and not of the individual human beings who make up the family.

The consideration of the relations between the units of an unorganized collection of units seems to be a discussion remote from modern life, but, in truth, such relations not only exist to-day, but they are some of the most important factors in the life of the world. Such relations obtain between modern civilized nations. Each nation is an organized unit, but taken together, they do not form an organized body. The rules governing the relations of such nations between themselves constitute what is called the Law of Nations, or International Law. Is this really Law?

"International Law"

There are two matters which must be distinguished. *First.* On no subject of human interest, except theology, has there been so much loose writing and nebulous speculation as on International Law. In many parts of the vast field which it covers, no questions have been positively decided or, at any rate, judicially decided; one class, however, and a very important class, of questions has frequently come before courts for determination; that is, questions arising from the capture of neutral vessels by belligerents on the high seas. When a neutral ship is captured by a belligerent cruiser, on the alleged ground, for instance, that it is carrying goods belonging to a subject of the other belligerent nation, or is carrying contraband goods, or is attempting to break a blockade, it is carried into a port of the belligerent, and is there made the subject of a suit by the captors in the Admiralty. If the Court of Admiralty finds that there has been just cause of capture, the vessel is condemned; if there has been no just cause of capture, the vessel is released.

Now here the judge of the Admiralty Court is not acting as an organ of the nations generally, but as an organ of the particular belligerent State. The rules that he follows in determining the validity of a capture are the Law of that particular State, and he applies them because they are the Law of that particular State. The sources of that Law may be the customs which prevail among civilized nations, but he refers to these, not because such nations have commanded him so to do, but because he has been authorized so to do by the State of which he is the judge. If his State should pass a statute contrary to the general customs of civilized nations, the judge would be bound to follow it. The enactment of the statute may give rise to complaint on the part of neutral states, or may even be a *casus belli,* but the judge will follow the statute.

The relations between nations come in question before the courts of a State most frequently in cases of captures on the high seas, but other cases sometimes present themselves. For instance, the automobile of an ambassador runs over a man and kills him. The chauffeur is indicted for manslaughter. Can he be tried and convicted? This is a question which the courts of the country where the alleged crime has been committed must determine, but the rule which the judges follow is a part of the Law of that country, not of the country of the ambassador, nor of the nations generally.

"Private International Law"

Second. The rights of a man in any country, arising from a transaction which has occurred partly in one place and partly in another, or between citizens of different States, may depend, under the Law of that country, upon the difference of locality or citizenship. Suppose a contract is made for the carriage of goods. The offer is made by a letter written in Paris and is accepted in Madrid; the goods are to be carried from Lisbon, in a Liverpool ship, to Naples; one party is domiciled in Stockholm and the other in St. Petersburg; a suit is brought on the contract in Berlin; judgment is obtained there; and an action is brought on the judgment in New York. In what way and to what extent the Laws of France, Spain, Portugal, England, Italy, Sweden, Russia, Germany, and New York, respectively, are to be considered, must be determined by the New York court. The rules which that court follows in considering what effect shall be given to these several laws are a part of the

Law of New York, not of any or all of the other countries. The Laws of the other countries are simply facts which the court has to consider like other facts. They are no part of the Law of New York.

As it is obviously desirable that the effect to be given to differences of locality or citizenship should be alike in different countries, it is natural and proper that a court, in laying down rules, that is, in establishing the Law of its own country on the subject, should pay regard to the Law of other countries. And such has been the practice of the courts of most civilized nations. There is much similarity in the Law of different countries upon this subject, and, therefore, while some treatises on the subject confine themselves to the Law of a particular jurisdiction, there are others which approach the topic from the point of view of Comparative Jurisprudence, and deal with the doctrines which prevail among civilized nations generally.

Whichever treatment is adopted, the best title for the subject is that which Judge Story domesticated in English, the Conflict of Laws, the name he gave to the book which is his highest claim to reputation as a jurist. A nomenclature has, however, arisen from this branch of the Law, which, though favored by respectable writers, is unfortunate and pernicious,—Private International Law. I do not always agree with Mr. Holland, which makes me the more willing to borrow the excellent remarks in his treatise on Jurisprudence:[1] "'Private International Law' is wholly indefensible. Such a phrase would mean, in accordance with that use of the word 'international,' which, besides being well established in

[1] (11th ed.) 416.

ordinary language, is both scientifically convenient and etymologically correct, 'a private species of the body of rules which prevail between one nation and another.' Nothing of the sort is, however, intended; and the unfortunate employment of the phrase, as indicating the principles which govern the choice of the system of private law applicable to a given class of facts, has led to endless misconception of the true nature of this department of legal science. It has also made it necessary to lengthen the description of International Law, properly so called, by prefixing to it the otherwise superfluous epithet 'public.' It is most important, for the clear understanding of the real character of the topic which for the last forty years has been misdescribed as 'Private International Law,' that this barbarous compound should be no longer employed." It is cause for satisfaction that Mr. Dicey, in his work which is likely for long to continue a standard book, has returned to the title "Conflict of Laws."

Is International Law really Law?

Having cleared the ground, we come back to the question: Is International Law, so called, really Law from the point of view of independent nations? Austin denied that International Law had the qualities essential to Law, and, though this denial has been much carped at, it is hard to make out a case against it on any sound definition of Law. As we have seen, the rules of International Law, as they are laid down by the judges of a particular State, are the Law of that State; but the question here is: Are they the Law of the collection of civilized nations generally? They are not the rules laid down by international courts, for there are no international courts; they are not the commands of a common superior, for independent States have no common superior; they are not put in execution by joint force, for the civilized nations do not put forth their force jointly to carry them into effect. The sanction which makes them operative as between nations is not a physical sanction; it is the sanction arising from the opinion of civilized nations that the rules are right, and that civilized nations are morally bound to obey them. They are, as Austin says, precepts of positive morality.[1]

Law in becoming

On the term "International Law," Mr. Brown, in his valuable book on the Austinian Theory of Law[2] has some interesting, and perhaps prophetic, remarks: "As a matter of fact, the term International Law is at present too generally adopted to admit of questioning its propriety. But apart from this, the severest accusation that can be urged against the term is simply that it is a trifle previous. Just as in the history of particular societies there are periods when the differentiation between law and morality is in the process of becoming rather than actually realized—periods when a something which is to become positive law is being slowly differentiated from positive morality—so in relation to the society of nations to-day there is a body of rules in which a distinction is being established and developed between rules which must be obeyed, if certain penalties are not to be incurred, and rules which are merely the expression of international comity and good-will. Rules of the former class . . . are law in becoming—law struggling for existence, struggling to make itself good in contradistinction from international morality, and, like the customary law of undeveloped societies, entitled to be called law in virtue of their like-

[1] 1 Jur. (4th ed.) 187; 2 *id.* 593-594.
[2] § 157.

ness to law strictly so called—the Positive Law, which is the subject-matter of Jurisprudence."[1]

Since this was written, the International Conference has met; the establishment of an International Court of Arbitration has been discussed, and it seems not unlikely that it may be set up. When that is done, the nations which unite to establish it will become an organized body, which will have the court as an organ. The court will lay down and follow general rules. If the nations who have united to establish the court unite to declare that they will join in carrying out its decrees by force, if necessary, then the rules will become Law in the strictest sense, and each of the nations parties to the establishment of the court will have legal rights and legal duties.[2]

[1] See also article by Roland Gray, 32 Harvard Law Rev. 825.

[2] The author is speaking in 1908. The establishment of the League of Nations is a further step in the direction indicated.

CHAPTER VII

JURISPRUDENCE

JURISPRUDENCE is the science of Law, the statement and systematic arrangement of the rules followed by the courts and of the principles involved in those rules. There are three kinds of Jurisprudence: first, Particular Jurisprudence, or the science of the Law of a particular community; second, Comparative Jurisprudence, or the comparison of the Law of two or more communities; third, General Jurisprudence, or the comparison of all the legal systems of the world.

Particular Jurisprudence

Austin says that the appropriate subject of Jurisprudence is positive Law; that, as limited to any one system, it is particular or national; that many principles of Law are common to all systems; and that the principles common to maturer systems are the subject of General (or Comparative) Jurisprudence, or of the philosophy of positive Law.[1] Austin, it will be thus seen, speaks of Particular Jurisprudence as the science of the legal system of a particular country. Professor Holland objects to the term "Particular Jurisprudence"; he says it can only mean an acquaintance with the Law of a particular people.[2] It means that, but it means more; it means a scientific knowledge of the Law of a particular

[1] 2 Jur. (4th ed.) 1107.
[2] Jur. (11th ed.) 10.

people. It is desirable to have a special term to express this, and this is what "Particular Jurisprudence," as ordinarily, and I think rightly, used, does mean.

Indeed, there seems no objection to the usage which Professor Holland mentions as springing up in France, of referring to the "Jurisprudence" of a particular Court in the sense of *"La manière dont un tribunal juge habituellement telle ou telle question."* [1] Nor is it necessary that the courts, whose rules form the subject of Jurisprudence, should be those of a political community. It is right to speak of the Jurisprudence of the Roman Catholic Church; and if the Worshipful Company of Bellows Menders has courts with judicial functions, it may have a Jurisprudence.

Jurisprudence, it is true, is often used in a sense which it is impossible to defend. There are certain treatises, many of considerable merit, dealing with those facts, likely to arise in litigation, with which the members of certain professions or trades are or ought to be familiar; such books are often called treatises on Jurisprudence. Thus, works on Medical Jurisprudence are *vade mecums* for lawyers and doctors, containing a mass of useful information on poisons, parturition, etc., but without any scientific unity, or any pretension to be considered "Law" at all. So in France they speak of "Veterinary Jurisprudence," and there is no reason why, in like manner, we should not have "Builders' Jurisprudence," or "Jockeys' Jurisprudence."

Comparative Jurisprudence

Comparative Jurisprudence has for its object the systematic comparison of the Law of two or more countries or organizations, for the purpose of discovering the ele-

[1] Jur. (11th ed.) 4.

ments of agreement and difference. There are many bodies of Law of which, at present at any rate, we know little,—some in ancient times, as the Assyrian or Egyptian; others of to-day, as that of the Chinese or Zulus; but all of them were or are in a state of development so different from that of the systems under which we live, that the chief gain to be derived from considering them, in connection with the Common or Civil Law, would be rather from the light which might be thrown on the history of the past, than in expectation of improvement or change in the future.

But though there may be little practical advantage in the pursuit of Comparative Jurisprudence beyond the limits of the Common and Civil Law, there is plenty of material within those limits. The Law of England, of all of the United States except Louisiana, and of many of the English Colonies, including the whole continent of Australia, have one common root, yet the growths from that common root have been very varied, and the comparison of those growths is most instructive. So again, the Law of the different States of Continental Europe, of Scotland, of Louisiana, of South America, are based on the Roman Law, but so diversified by natural development and by codes that there is great opportunity for fruitful comparison of the systems of all these countries with each other and with those of communities where the English Common Law has formed the point of departure.

General Jurisprudence

The natural meaning of General Jurisprudence would seem to be a comparison of *all* (as distinguished from some) of the legal systems of the world. As we know nothing, or next to nothing, of the Law of many of the nations and tribes which exist, or have existed on the earth, and have only a very superficial acquaintance with the Law of many others, it is impossible, with our present materials, to construct such a science of General Jurisprudence, and it is likely long to continue impossible.

Another meaning sometimes given to General Jurisprudence is that it has, for its object, the rules of Law which are common to all legal systems. An objection exists also to the practicability of the science of General Jurisprudence in this sense. Under the first definition the product of the science would be extraordinarily bulky; on this second meaning, its product would be meagre in the extreme. The list of rules of Law received *semper, ubique et ab omnibus* from Kamschatka to Patagonia is likely to be a short one.

Supposed necessary principles of Law

General Jurisprudence has sometimes been declared to be the science of the *necessary* principles of the Law in all countries. Such a treatment of the subject is not likely to meet with much favor at the present day. There is no need of denying that the rules which courts have laid down have been compelled by a sequence of events as fixed as those which prevail in the material forces of nature. Such may have been the case. We know that language, which seems to be the sport of individual caprice, is in truth subject to rigorous rules which have operated controllingly without the conscious knowledge of those who have in fact obeyed them. But if this be so, we as yet know little of the general forces of human nature which have compelled the Law to develop as it has. Much has of late been done to show how particular institutes, like the jury, or particular doctrines, such as that of possession, have grown up in this or that country, but little, if anything, to show what universal forces of human nature have caused the Jurisprudence of the globe to be what it is; or, in other words, Jurisprudence, as a branch of anthropology, is yet in its infancy. *A priori* theories on the fundamental laws of human existence have been common enough, and far enough away from any known facts, but General Jurisprudence, as a science based on observation, does not yet exist.

But, further, we do know enough to render it extremely doubtful whether there are any principles of Law which are so ingrained in human nature as to be immutable and necessary. The possibility of General Jurisprudence as a science of *necessary* principles rests on a theory of the universe which has, in these last days, been badly shaken, a theory which supposes a permanence in social relations the existence of which is very uncertain. As Mr. Buckland well says:[1]

"The fact that principles of law change Professor Holland admits by calling Jurisprudence a progressive science. This admission is somewhat startling. A writer on the Jurisprudence of a single nation might make it readily enough. But what is likely to be the fate of a principle found in the law of, say, ten states which go on developing on different lines? The probabilities are against its continuance as a general principle. And the notion that some other general principle will arise to take its place appears to be rather an article of faith than a proposition on which a science can be based."

And, as Mr. Buckland goes on to point out, the generality to be looked for in such legal investigations is not a

[1] 6 Law Quart. Rev. 444.

generality of institutions and principles to be discovered fixed in the legal systems of all times and all countries, but the generality of laws by which institutions and principles themselves change.[1]

If we are to employ both terms, Comparative Jurisprudence and General Jurisprudence, with different meanings, it would seem as if the latter must apply to the world. Austin, however, uses it in a narrow sense. He says: "I mean by General Jurisprudence the science concerned with the exposition of the principles, notions, and distinctions which are common to systems of law; understanding by systems of law the ampler and maturer systems." [2] But all the "ampler and maturer systems" of which we have any knowledge, or are likely to have any knowledge, are derived either from the Roman Law or the English Common Law, and therefore come within the limits, as ordinarily defined, of Comparative Jurisprudence. It may be said that there is no great harm done by calling Comparative Jurisprudence "General," but it has the evil result of suggesting the universal, and even the necessary, character of certain legal propositions, when the fact merely is that they have been accepted as true or convenient by certain jurists in Rome and by certain judges in England.

[1] "Man *in abstracto,* as assumed by philosophies of Law, has never actually existed at any point in time or space." Wundt, Ethics, p. 566. Translation by Titchener and others, vol. 3, p. 160.

"I have seen in my life, Spaniards, Italians, Russians, etc.; I even know, thanks to Montesquieu, that there are Persians: but as to *man,* I declare that I have never come across one in my life; if he exists, I don't know it." J. de Maistre, Considerations sur la France, Œuvres, vol. 1 (ed. 1851), Chap. 6, p. 88. See also preface by Professor Kocourek to Science of Legal Method, p. *l* (Modern Legal Philosophy Series), and article by Professor Pound, 28 Harvard Law Rev. 343, 353, note.

[2] 2 Jur. (4th ed.) 1108.

Deontological or ethical element

In defining the limits of Jurisprudence, it is important to consider how far a deontological element should be introduced into the science.[1] Austin says that with the goodness or the badness of laws General Jurisprudence has no immediate concern, which distinguishes it from the Science of Legislation; that some of the principles which are the subjects of General Jurisprudence are necessary; and that others, though not necessary, yet "as they rest upon grounds of utility which extend through all communities, and which are palpable or obvious in all refined communities, occur very generally in matured systems of law." [2]

The Science of Legislation and Jurisprudence are, then, distinguished, according to Austin, by the circumstance that with goodness or badness of laws the latter has no concern; but Austin does not emphasize the distinction with the savage stress which he sometimes employs. "It is impossible," he says, "to consider Jurisprudence quite apart from Legislation." "If the causes of laws . . . be not assigned, the laws themselves are unintelligible." "In certain cases which do not try the passions [the teacher of Jurisprudence] may, with advantage, offer opinions upon merits and demerits." [3]

[1] One way of approaching the Law "starts from the needs of society, and considers how far the Law is adequate or inadequate to those needs. As it deals with what the law ought to be, we may designate it as the deontological or ethical." Nature and Sources of the Law, 1st ed., sec. 1. Sociological Jurisprudence appears to be neither more nor less than Deontological Jurisprudence as thus defined.

[2] Jur. (4th ed.) 1109.

[3] 2 Jur. (4th ed.) 1113, 1114. It must be borne in mind that the Science of Legislation, according to Austin, is concerned with the Law as it ought to be. He regards all changes and improve-

Austin, as we see, admits the impossibility of considering Jurisprudence, as he defines it, by itself, and any one who has tried to do so will agree with him. Writers have shrunk, on the one hand, from limiting Jurisprudence to a mere classified digest of established rules, and, on the other hand, from saying that Jurisprudence is the science of what ought to be the Law of Utopia. The existence of Law as a fact has always been recognized, though not always with precision, as a necessary element in the subject-matter of Jurisprudence.

There are, in truth, three ways of considering the Law; that is, the rules applied by the courts. First, we may consider only the rules which have been actually adopted. This excludes the discussion of those cases which do not fall within the established rules. We have only to determine what rules have actually been adopted. Or, secondly, we may consider the rules which have been actually adopted, and determine what those rules are, and may also consider what rules ought to be adopted in those cases which do not come within the established rules. Or, thirdly, we may consider what the Law ought to be in all cases.

This last method, it should be observed, does not involve going back to a *tabula rasa*. Rules based on statute and precedent may have become so bound up with institutions which are on the whole beneficial, that it may not be wise to interfere with them, although they would never be established at the present day in a new commu-

ments in the Law as made by legislation, direct or indirect. It is only the changes wrought by statutes which are commonly included in legislation, but Austin makes it cover changes and additions in the Law, however wrought.

nity. For instance, that a jury is to consist of twelve persons, that it must be unanimous, that its verdict of acquittal in a criminal case cannot be set aside,—all these might not be adopted in a brand new code for a brand new State, and yet it might not be wise to alter them in a country where they had long prevailed.

But though this be true in the third way of dealing with the Law, yet, under this method, the existence of present rules of Law is only one of the facts in the condition of a community, like their language or their usual occupations, which are to be taken into account in determining what is best for them. What the Law of that community *ought* to be, under all the circumstances, is the sole purpose of the inquirer. This third method of consideration must, therefore, be deemed appropriate to the Science of Legislation, but foreign to the Science of Jurisprudence.[1]

Ethical element necessary

The first mode is undoubtedly appropriate to Jurisprudence. Is the second? I conceive that it is. In older days, when the rules composing the Law were thought of, at any rate talked about, as deducible, with unerring certainty, from unquestioned principles, it was customary to speak of Jurisprudence as dealing only with rules already established, for those rules were feigned to hold within themselves all possible doctrines of the Law; but now that we know more of the mode of growth of the Law, it is not the immutability of legal principles which attracts the mind, it is the prospect of their future development.

[1] By many recent writers, especially those of the sociological school, the Science of Legislation is included in Jurisprudence, and the third method above stated is therefore adopted.

To illustrate: Whether a *donatio causa mortis*[1] *ought* to be good without delivery, is not a topic for English Jurisprudence, because it is settled that delivery is necessary. Neither is the question whether a devise to A. for life, remainder to his heirs, *ought* to give A. a fee, for the rule in *Shelley's Case*[2] settled that it does. On the other hand, whether the certification of a check by the bank on whom it is drawn, after delivery, *ought* to discharge the maker, was a topic for the Jurisprudence of Massachusetts before the decision of the Supreme Judicial Court of that State that it did.[3] Now the corresponding topic of Massachusetts Jurisprudence is that such certification *does* discharge the maker. To consider whether now in Massachusetts such certification *ought* to work a discharge, is a question for the Science of Legislation, not for the Jurisprudence of Massachusetts.

And yet, even in Jurisprudence, it may sometimes be necessary to consider the beneficial or injurious character of an established doctrine of Law, in order to determine whether it should be extended. For instance, in most of the United States it is the Law that a deed with covenant of warranty passes the legal title to land afterwards acquired. The wisdom of establishing such Law has been much doubted, but the Law itself is well settled. But on a question whether the doctrine should be extended to the case of a deed which in terms disclosed the want of title,—where, that is, the warranty was in effect only a promise of indemnity,—it would seem that the

[1] A gift to take effect on the death of the giver.
[2] 1 Co. 93.
[3] *Minot* v. *Russ*, 156 Mass. 458.

consideration of the beneficial or injurious character of the rule would be a matter for Jurisprudence.

Ethical element in Comparative Jurisprudence

In Comparative Jurisprudence there are first to be considered separately two or more systems of Law, and then the results are to be compared and their resemblances and differences noted; and further, when there is agreement on some points and difference on others, it seems within the scope of Comparative Jurisprudence to consider which system, taking into account the points agreed upon, holds the sounder view on those in which they differ. For instance, suppose that in two States the Law concerning bills and notes is on most points the same, but that in one of them a man who takes a promissory note in payment of a preëxisting debt is deemed a purchaser for value, and that in the other he is not; which State, on this particular point, has reached the better conclusion, is a question falling within the scope of their Comparative Jurisprudence. But to consider what *ought* to be the Law in a matter upon which, in both of the States, the Law is definitely settled the same way, falls outside of their Comparative Jurisprudence.

In General Jurisprudence, the only deontological question excluded from consideration is what *ought* to be the Law on those points where the Law is in fact uniform in all human communities. Except in this area, which is probably not large, the element of what ought to be the Law is properly a subject of General Jurisprudence, and General Jurisprudence swallows up, or, if one prefers to say so, is swallowed up by the Science of Legislation.

If I am right in thinking that Jurisprudence, within the limits indicated, comprises the consideration of Law as it ought to be, then, since the doctrines of morality are largely, as we shall see more clearly later, a most important source from which the judges draw and ought to draw the rules which make the Law, the true theory of morals comes properly within the purview of Jurisprudence; and I cannot, therefore, blame Austin, as some do, for dealing with the foundations of morality in his treatise. From his own point of view, indeed, it seems difficult to justify his procedure. He endeavors to confine Jurisprudence to the Law that has been actually settled, and to eliminate, as far as possible, the deontological element, and therefore the discussion of the foundations of morality seems out of place in this book. But on the definition of "Jurisprudence," which appears the sounder one, the true grounds of morality seem a proper subject of contemplation.

Jurisprudence as a purely formal science

There are three or four narrower definitions of Jurisprudence which should not be passed over. Professor Holland describes Jurisprudence as a formal analytical science as opposed to a material one: "That is to say, that it deals rather with the various relations which are regulated by legal rules than with the rules themselves which regulate those relations"; and he likens it to the science of Grammar; "Whether the possessive case of a noun substantive is expressed by a specific modification of its termination, or by prefixing to it a specific preposition, is a question of the matter of language; but that the possessive idea, however variously expressed, yet finds some expression or other in every family of human speech, is a proposition which relates to linguistic form." And he goes on to say that "Comparative Law collects and tabulates the legal institutions of various countries," and that Jurisprudence sets forth "an orderly view of the ideas and methods which have been variously realized in actual systems. It is, for instance, the office of Comparative Law to ascertain what have been at different times and places the periods of prescription. . . . It is for Jurisprudence to elucidate the meaning of prescription, in its relation to ownership and to actions. . . . A system of Jurisprudence might conceivably be constructed from the observation of one system of law only, at one epoch of its growth. . . . Jurisprudence is therefore not the material science of those portions of the law which various nations have in common, but the formal science of those relations of mankind which are generally recognized as having legal consequences."[1]

This sounds plausible, but a little reflection shows that it is true of Law, as it is of Logic, that "the notions of form and formal relations are by no means so simple and free from ambiguity that by their aid one can at once solve a complicated problem of philosophic arrangement."[2] Jurisprudence is, in truth, no more a formal science than Physiology. As bones and muscles and nerves are the subject-matter of Physiology, so the acts and forbearances of men and the events which happen to them are the subject-matter of Jurisprudence, and Physiology could as well dispense with the former as Jurisprudence with the latter. As Professor Platt has truly said: "Without resorting to acts and forbearances and to the states of fact under which they are commanded, Law cannot be differentiated at all; not so much as the bare framework of its chief departments can be erected.

[1] Holland, Jur. (11th ed.) 6-9.
[2] Prof. Adamson, on "Logic," Encyc. Brit. (9th ed.) p. 780.

An attempt to construct quite apart from all the matter of Law even the most general conception of ownership or contract would be like trying to make bricks not merely without straw but without clay as well." [1]

Let us take, for instance, the question of prescription,[2] which is one of the instances given by Professor Holland. Under the head of Prescription, the following matters have arisen and been determined differently in different countries. 1. Does prescription bar the remedy or actually pass title? And is the rule different with regard to ownership of land from what it is in the case of rights of way? 2. Must prescription begin with a possession taken in good faith? 3. Can successive independent adverse holders join their times to produce the period required for prescription? 4. Can constructive possession be given by color of title? 5. Can successive disabilities be joined? 6. After the period of prescription has begun to run, can it be suspended? 7. Does prescription run without the knowledge of the person against whom it runs? Are these and other like questions fit topics for Jurisprudence? If they are, then the whole subject of prescription, except the arbitrary determination of the periods of prescription, is within the domain of that science; if not, then Jurisprudence is confined to a jejune list of propositions, and indeed, it might be said that Jurisprudence teaches that property may be transferred from one person to another without a conveyance, and that Comparative Law furnishes us the cases of prescription in which this principle is applied.

[1] 24 Am. Law Rev. 605-606.

[2] *I.e.* the acquisition of property by lapse of time.

Essence of Juris-prudence is method

The real relation of Jurisprudence to Law depends not upon *what* Law is treated, but *how* Law is treated. A treatise on Jurisprudence may go into the minutest particulars, or be confined to the most general doctrines, and in either case deserve its name; what is essential to it is that it should be an orderly, scientific treatise in which the subjects are duly classified and subordinated. "Jurisprudence is the most general word we have to denote the scientific treatment of Law, and there is no reason to restrict its natural meaning." It is noticeable that, as Professor Platt remarks, Professor Holland is so far in practice from excluding the material of Law from his book on Jurisprudence that he has justly laid himself open to the charge of dealing with the special subject-matter of a particular system as if it were universal.

Mr. Lightwood, in his valuable treatise on Positive Law,[1] takes a somewhat different view of Jurisprudence. He says: "As long as we take our distinctions solely from English law and explain them merely by history, we do not enter upon science, for the distinctions and principles may be merely accidental, and the historical reasons may have no reference to utility. If, however, we were to show that these distinctions and principles have a real basis in the wants of the people, we should then treat the law scientifically, and we should work out the Particular Jurisprudence of the country. This at least is the only natural meaning I can give to this phrase."

But thus to reject from the domain of Jurisprudence all of the Law which a writer does not believe to "have a real basis in the wants of the people" is hardly ad-

[1] P. 10.

missible. It is true, as has been said, that Jurisprudence may extend to the consideration of the Law as it ought to be, so far as is consistent with the Law already established, but it also includes an orderly exposition of the Law that is established, and when we omit this latter element, we leave the domain of Particular Jurisprudence for that of the Science of Legislation.

Principles common to two systems

Mr. Lightwood then proceeds to General Jurisprudence. He says that the system of one country is to be compared with those of other countries; that certain common distinctions and principles are detected; that these "are assumed to have a more permanent value than others"; that, at last, it will be discovered that these "only differ from the rest in that they clearly follow the principle of utility"; and that "henceforth, then, we can provisionally guess that this principle is satisfied by comparing different systems; but when this method fails, we can apply the principle directly." [1]

But these assumptions and guesses seem unjustifiable. Are those elements which are common, say, to the English and Roman Law, of more permanent value than others? Compare the rule forbidding conditions restraining marriage with the rule of authorizing the disinheritance of children. In the Common and Roman Law alike, general conditions in restraint of marriage are void, but on the disinheritance of children the systems differ. Surely we cannot "assume" that the rules avoiding conditions in restraint of marriage "have a more permanent value" than the rules relating to the power of disinheritance. Nor do we "at last" discover that the former

[1] Lightwood, pp. 15, 16.

rules differ from the latter "in that they clearly follow the principle of utility."

And it is not only in reading Mr. Lightwood's book that one should bear in mind that rules of Law shown to be common to the Roman and English systems cannot necessarily be accepted as what the Law ought to be. It is undoubtedly in favor of a legal principle that it has been received by two able men so unlike as Ulpian and Lord Coke, but yet it is not only possible, but extremely likely, that on many points both Ulpian and Lord Coke were ignorant of what was best for a community. Is it so clear, for instance, that the *noxalis actio* [1] of the Roman Law, and the liability of a master for the acts of his servant in the English Common Law, are founded on a wise policy? Or take the question alluded to above on conditions in restraint of marriage. Many of the wisest and best men would be only too glad of the aid of the Law in restraining marriages. The question of population is looked at from a totally different point of view from what it was when the foundations of the Roman and the Common Law were laid.

The notions of personal righteousness may not have changed much, but certainly at the present day one would not wish to borrow one's ideas of the best mode in which society should interfere with its members, either from the "classical jurists" or the "sages of the Common Law," and would hardly feel safe in concluding that, because both those two highly respectable bodies thought alike on a question of social morality or political economy, they must be right; and yet this feeling that doctrines common to

[1] "Action for injury." This gave the same sort of right against the master as exists in English Law.

the Roman and English Law must be right and fundamental, has led writers to confound Comparative with General Jurisprudence, and to feel justified in laying down rules as universal and, indeed, necessary, because they found them both in the Digest and in the notes to Williams's Saunders.

Mr. Lightwood makes a further division between Pure and General Jurisprudence,[1]—the first dealing with distinctions, the second with principles. But it seems impossible practically to carry out this difference. What is a contract and what are the different kinds of contracts, would be, according to this division, matters of Pure Jurisprudence, while the question what contracts could be enforced would be for General Jurisprudence. But the kinds of contracts are innumerable; they may concern hats or cows, they may be between whites or negroes, they may be made at noon or at midnight, in town or in the country, in winter or summer, they may be written on white paper or on blue paper; there is a myriad of possible distinctions; but the only distinctions which are of consequence for Jurisprudence, for any kind of Jurisprudence, are those which affect the question of enforceability; and it is therefore practically impossible to consider distinctions and principles separately as the subject-matter of Pure and General Jurisprudence respectively.

Historical Jurisprudence

The history of institutions is no mean aid to the understanding of their nature. Especially is it useful with regard to the anomalies and lack of symmetry in an

[1] Pp. 13-17.

actual system which render its substance hard to classify and difficult to remember. It helps to distinguish those parts of the Law which correspond to modern ideas from those which are survivals of an earlier age. For instance: To the arrangement of the Law, according to our modern notions, with reference to the nature of rights and duties, the forms of action have been a hindrance, but that hindrance is greatly lessened when we understand how trespass, and trover, and assumpsit had their origin in a time when the Law was arranged with reference not to rights, but to remedies. Again, the difficulty of remembering legal doctrines which have no present rational excuse for being is alleviated if we can trace them to the times when they had their origin. A present reason is better than a past reason, but a past reason is better than no reason at all.

But the historical method has its disadvantages; it begets literary rather than practical study; it hinders the grasping of the Law of the present time as a whole. Mr. Frederic Harrison has some noteworthy remarks on this point.[1] Speaking of the historical study of the Roman Law, which was so stimulated by the discovery of Gaius, he says: "The result, to the overburdened memory of the student, is too often to lead to a spirit of legal anachronism thoroughly hostile to the really legal mind. . . . It is desirable to know how irregular, how arbitrary, and how archaic the Roman system once was; but the essential thing is to know how symmetrical, how wise, how scientifically right it ultimately became."

[1] 31 Fortn. Rev. 120-130; Jurisprudence and the Conflict of Laws, pp. 86-87.

PART II

SOURCES OF THE LAW

CHAPTER VIII

STATUTES

We have hitherto been considering the Nature of the Law. I have defined the Law as the rules laid down by the courts for the determination of rights and duties, and I have endeavored to point out the difference between the Law and the Sources from which the Law is drawn, and the confusion and errors which have arisen from not distinguishing between them.[1] We will now take up the consideration of these Sources.

Legis-
latures

The first Sources from which the courts of any human society draw the Law are the formal utterances of the legislative organs of the society. We can conceive of a society with judicial but no legislative organs. The courts of such a society would follow rules derived by them from other sources, say, from former decisions of their own, or from custom. But all modern civilized political societies have, in fact, legislatures.

In any organized society there may be, and, in political societies particularly, there often are, several bodies which,

[1] P. 84, *ante*.

within the limits marked out by the organization of the society, or by the orders or tolerance of the supreme legislative body, have legislative functions. In a country with a written constitution, the body of persons which enacts the constitution is the supreme legislature; all other bodies and persons having legislative powers, including the ordinary Legislature, Congress, Assembly, Cortes, are subordinate to it.

In most modern societies the chief legislative functions are given not to individuals, but to assemblies. In political societies these assemblies are now usually representative, but sometimes all the persons considered as having political power have met and voted, as, for instance, in the ancient Greek cities, in some of the Swiss cantons, and in the town meetings of New England. And in societies not political the legislatures are often composed of all the members of the society, as in the meetings of the stockholders of corporations and of the members of clubs.

Although at the present day the chief legislative functions are vested in bodies more or less numerous, whether representative or not, yet many legislative powers are given to individuals. Such is the power of the King or other head of the government to issue proclamations, of a Secretary of the Treasury or Postmaster-General to make regulations, of a Commander-in-chief to issue general orders; and so down, through all grades of officials, to a subaltern of infantry commanding a post.

Various designations of statutes

The variety of names given to the legislative acts of these bodies is great: constitutions, statutes, laws, acts, ordinances, proclamations, regulations, orders; among the Romans, *leges, plebiscita, senatus-consulta, edicta, consti-*

tutiones; among the Germans, *gesetze, verordnungen.* There is, unfortunately, no word recognized as the name of the *genus.* I know of no better way than to take the name which is given to the utterances of the highest ordinary legislature in a political society, apply it to the whole *genus,* and call them all *statutes.*

This variety of names has given rise to a notion that there is an essential difference between a statute and a proclamation, for example; and, of course, there may be the gravest distinction so far as politics are concerned, but from the point of view of Jurisprudence, the difference between statutes and proclamations is immaterial. They both set forth general rules which are equally binding, and binding in the same way, on the courts. The fact that in countries without a written constitution the power of the highest legislature is practically unlimited, while officials having legislative functions are generally closely limited in their use, tended to put the former into a separate class; but now that the existence of governments with written constitutions has familiarized us, at least in the United States, with frequent and strict limitations upon the powers of the highest ordinary legislative bodies, there seems small reason for distinguishing between statutes and proclamations. Every utterance of the most subordinate official, if it be within the legislative powers given to him, directly or indirectly, by the organization of the State, is as binding on the courts as any act of the supreme parliament or assembly, while every utterance of the highest legislative body which is beyond its constitutional competence is as invalid as an unauthorized order of the lowest official.[1]

[1] See pp. 110-112, *ante.*

The possession of legislative power is not confined to political bodies; every organized body of men may have a legislative organ, and most of such bodies do, in fact, have one, be they churches, business corporations, charitable societies, or social clubs.

The formal utterances of the legislatures of non-political organized bodies are not commonly called statutes; thus, we speak of the canons of a church, or the by-laws of a business corporation. But this is a matter of nomenclature only; for the purposes of Jurisprudence they are identical in character with the statutes of a State; that is, they are binding upon the courts of the organization of which they are the canons or by-laws.

A distinction should be noticed among organized bodies which are not States. Some of these bodies, although not States, are yet political; they are organs of the State, and are formed for carrying out its purposes; some of its powers are delegated to them for these purposes; and, if these bodies have legislatures, the general rules declared by such legislatures are really declared by the State; they are its statutes. Municipal bodies, like cities, are such political bodies, and the ordinances issued by them are, in truth, statutes of the State. So when legislative power is granted to an individual, as to a King, President, Secretary, or General, and he puts forth proclamations or regulations containing general rules, the rules are, in truth, put forth by the State; and for juristic purposes they are identical with the statutes of the ordinary supreme Legislature.

Rules of bodies other than the State

But a church, or a business corporation, or a charitable society, or a club, is not an organ of the State; it is not a political body created for political purposes; and its canons or by-laws or rules are not statutes of the State. It is true that such bodies often owe their existence to the State, and can legislate only on the subjects and within the limits prescribed by it, but the meeting of the stockholders of an automobile manufacturing company is not an organ of the State to carry out its purposes; it is the organ of the company to carry into effect the objects of the company. The State merely allows the company to carry out its objects; it does not make these objects its own.

If we should call the by-laws of a corporation the statutes of the State, because the State, if it saw fit, could prevent their being passed by the stockholders, and because it will open its courts to enforce the observance of them by the members of the corporation, we should have to call every general rule issued by a person whom the State permits to issue it, and which it will regard in its courts, a statute of the State. Thus, a general rule by the head of a household that the children shall go to bed at eight o'clock, or that the cook shall always boil eggs for two minutes and a half, would be a statute of the State.

Indeed, this would not be confined to general rules: every particular order given by any person who has a right to give such an order, although, from its lack of generality, it could not be called a statute or a law, would yet be a command of the State. A master has a right to tell a servant to bring him the mustard. Should she refuse, he has a right to dismiss her, and the State will protect him in this right; and, therefore, on the theory we are considering, the order to bring the mustard is a command of the State.[1] Even Austin, I think, would shrink from such a conclusion.

Though courts of the State often have occasion to enforce the legislation of non-political organizations, it is not a source of Law to them. Thus, suppose a member of a club is charged with improper conduct, and a committee is chosen, in accordance with the by-laws, to try him, the by-laws are the sources of Law to the committee as the judicial organ of the club; they are commands of the club to them and binding upon them; but suppose the peccant member is expelled and sues for reinstatement in a court of the State: in that case the by-laws do not come as commands to the judge from the State; they are simply facts, one of the elements of the contract which the member made with the club on joining it. The distinction would generally be brought out by the procedure. The club committee would take judicial cognizance of the club's by-laws; the court of the State would require them to be proved.

It should be observed that though the nature of that which is a source of Law for a non-political body but not for the State, is brought out with the most clearness in considering legislative enactments, it is also true that other sources of Law for a non-political body, precedents in a church court, for instance, cannot properly be considered sources of Law for the State.[2]

To put the whole matter in another way. A distinction is to be made between the general rules which the

[1] See p. 107, *ante*.

[2] Of course this has no application to courts which, while called church courts, are simply part of the State machinery, as is the case with the ecclesiastical courts in England. See p. 109, note, *ante*.

courts of a State lay down, that is, the Law, and the decisions which they make. In making the decisions they apply the Law to the facts. Among the facts may be the rules established by non-political bodies, and these rules are then elements or, if you please, sources of the *decisions,* but they are not sources of the Law.

It is convenient to distinguish those rules made by the State, either directly or through its agents, from those made by other bodies or persons by permission of the State, and to regard the former as sources of Law, and the latter as facts; but (except as to matters of proof, which are likely to be different in the two classes, but may be subject to a great number of artificial rules), there is little practical difference whether we say that the State has commanded children to obey their teacher's orders and that Mr. Barlow has ordered Tommy Merton to take his finger out of his mouth, or whether we say that the State has commanded Master Tommy to remove the misplaced member. In the suit of *Merton* v. *Barlow* for trespass *quia vi et armis,* the court would reach the same result on the one theory as it would on the other.

"Autonomy" in German law

The fact that the distinction is not of vital importance explains, perhaps, the persistence in Germany of what is called autonomy, and on which there has been much discussion. Autonomy is the legislative power of a body other than the State to make orders which are sources of Law to the courts of the State. On two things all late writers seem agreed. First, that the orders put forth by officials of the State are not autonomic; they are simply the commands of the State issued through these officials instead of through the ordinary legislature. Secondly, that the by-laws of ordinary private corporations are not autonomic; such by-laws are properly sources of Law to the corporation, but they are not sources of Law to the courts of the State; to them they are simply facts.

The truth seems to be that the whole conception of autonomy is an historical and not a logical one; that it springs from a lack of clearness of perception. In the loose political organization of the Middle Ages, many towns and other communities, though situated in a kingdom or duchy, were largely self-governed, and had written laws which were called *statuta*. Such communities were originally separate political bodies with independent organizations, but in a state of subjection, more or less well defined, to the feudal lord on whose territory they were situated. At present this condition of things has passed away, the towns have become simply municipal agents of the larger State, the kingdom or duchy, and any rules passed by them are to be considered as emanating from such larger State. During this process of degeneration, or at least of change, while these towns had ceased to be independent States, but were not yet recognized as simply organs of the larger State, these ideas of autonomy arose.[1]

Form of statutes

The form of a statute is, for the purposes of the Law, immaterial. Whether it is committed to writing or whether it is pronounced orally is indifferent, though, of course, for the sake of preservation, it is in fact always committed to writing.

[1] It is not impossible that a similar change is going on in the relation of the States of the American Union to the Federal Government; such changes are apt to be hidden from the eyes of contemporaries.

On autonomy see, further, Appendix IV.

The Romans made a distinction between *jus scriptum* and *jus non scriptum,* and took the phrases literally, including in the *jus scriptum* not only the statutes of the supreme legislative bodies, but also the *edicta magistratuum* and even the *responsa prudentium.*[1] As Savigny says,[2] it was the form of the Law at its origin that determined its name.

In France, during the Middle Ages, *jus scriptum* was used for the Roman Law as opposed to the customary Law, as in the Register of a Parliament of 1277, cited by Ducange (*sub voc. Jus scriptum*), "*Li Advocat ne soient si hardi de eux mesler d'aleguer Droit escrit, là û Coustumes ayent leu, més usent de Coustumes.*"

Sir Matthew Hale, in his History of the Common Law, confines the term *lex scripta* to Acts of Parliament, "which in their original formation are reduced into writing, and are so preserved in their original form, and in the same style and words, wherein they were first made." The rest of the English Law he calls *leges non scriptæ,* including the Civil and Canon Law, so far as they are in force in England.[3] Blackstone follows Hale.[4]

Thibaut says that *jus scriptum* is made up of the commands proceeding directly from the supreme power of a State, whether it be actually written or not;[5] and Austin gives this as the meaning of the word in the mouths of the modern Civilians, but justly remarks that "nothing can be less significant or more misleading than the language in which it is conveyed"; and that it is

[1] See p. 201, *post.*
[2] 1 Heut. röm. Recht. § 22.
[3] Hale, Hist. Com. Law (4th ed.) 23; (5th ed.) 27.
[4] 1 Bl. Com. 63.
[5] Thibaut, Pand. § 10.

unsuited to express any distinction of importance.[1] The terms *jus scriptum* and *jus non scriptum* seem to have been given up by the late German writers.

In view of the uncertainty of the meaning of the phrases "written law," and "unwritten law," of the inaptness of these phrases to any of the supposed meanings except that of the Romans, and of the unimportance of the distinction which they denoted among the latter, the best way is to follow the modern German practice, and discontinue the use of the terms altogether.

Generality of statutes

A statute is a general rule. A resolution by the legislature that a town shall pay one hundred dollars to Timothy Coggan is not a statute. This mark of generality which distinguishes a statute from other legislative acts does not seem to establish a very important distinction; both the statute and the resolution or other particular enactment emanate from the same authority, and both alike are binding on the courts. In a suit by Coggan against the town for not paying the one hundred dollars, or by the town against its treasurer's bondsmen for paying it without authority, the resolution would be as binding on the court as if it had been a statute which concerned every citizen. The difference between statutes and other legislative acts, though of little importance practically, is, however, of consequence in Jurisprudence, for Jurisprudence is a systematic and scientific arrangement of general rules; isolated particular commands are ordinarily no proper subjects for it.

The generality necessary in order that a legislative enactment be recognized as a statute, may come either from its applying to a whole community or class, or per-

[1] 2 Jur. (4th ed.) 530.

haps from its applying as a permanent (though not necessarily perpetual) rule to the conduct of an individual; for instance, an enactment that A. should never pay any taxes would perhaps be properly called a statute. There are some sensible remarks on the subject in Mr. Hammond's note to the first volume of Blackstone's Commentaries,[1] but it seems a trifling matter on which to spend much thought.

Foreign statutes

It is only the Acts of the legislative organs of a court's own State that come under the head of statutes as sources of Law for such courts. The Law of a State may direct that in certain contingencies the statutes of foreign States shall be taken account of by its courts, but such statutes are no more sources of the Law of the State than are the provisions of a contract or will which may be brought in question.[2]

Enactment of statutes

What is necessary for a statute to have power as a source of law? It must, of course, be passed by the legislative body, but, beyond this, is any publication required? The practice in the matter greatly varies.

Civil Law

In the republican period of Roman history the word *"promulgare"* meant to bring forward a project of a law; later it seems to have been used in the sense of issuing a law.[3] During the republic, no publication apart from

[1] P. 126, note 15.

[2] "Where foreign statutes are cited as authorities, as is done frequently, for instance, by Swiss courts with regard to German statutes, the foreign law is treated not as a statute but as 'written reason,' just as the opinions of an author might be cited." Eugen Ehrlich, Freie Rechtsfindung, Judicial Freedom of Decision, Ch. I, § 9. Transl. in Science of Legal Method, p. 59. (Modern Legal Philosophy Series.) The same sort of thing is occasionally done in the United States, when a court refers, for instance, to the terms of a Negotiable Instrument Law enacted in another State.

[3] Cicero, Phil. I, 10; V, 3; Livy, III, 9; Festus, De signific. verb. (ed. Müller), p. 224.

the passage of a statute appears to have been required as a condition precedent to its going into effect. Under the Empire, the Emperor had both the legislative and executive power; but in addition to the expression of his will as legislator, there does not seem to have been any further step necessary to be taken by him as an executive officer to make a statute a valid one. I am aware of no theory in the Roman Law that any "publication" in the sense of the modern Civilians was necessary to make a statute operative.[1]

According to the theory which now prevails generally on the Continent of Europe, four things are necessary in order for a statute to become a source of Law. It must be (1) passed by the legislature, (2) declared to be a law by a proper document, (3) ordered to be published, and (4) published. The first of these acts is performed by the legislative department of the Government, and the other three by the executive department. The name commonly used to indicate the performance of the second and third acts in France and in those countries which have taken their modern Jurisprudence from France is *promulgation;* in Germany it has usually been called *Ausfertigung.*

The distinction between promulgation and publication has been well put thus: *"On a quelquefois consideré ces deux termes comme synonymes; leur signification est cependant loin d'être identique. La promulgation est l'acte par lequel le roi en sa qualité de chef du pouvoir executif, atteste au corps social l'existence de la loi et en ordonne l'exécution; la publication, au contraire, est le mode de publicité à l'aide duquel la loi est portée a la*

[1] Krüger. Geschichte der Quellen, § 33, pp. 266, 267.

connaissance des citoyens." The distinction, however, seems often to be disregarded, and promulgation to be used as including publication.[1]

In some of the Continental countries, the chief executive officer has no part in legislation. This is the case with the Emperor of Germany and the President of the French Republic. In such countries he has no concern with the first of the acts mentioned; but generally in the monarchical countries of Europe he takes part in legislation and therefore shares in the performance of the first act. What he does as legislator is called "sanctioning," to distinguish it from the promulgation which is his act as administrator. Thus in the Constitutional Charter of the Bourbons on their return, in 1814, it was provided: *"Le Roi seul sanctionne et promulgue les lois,"* while in the Constitution of the French Republic for 1848 we read: *"Le Président de la République promulgue les lois au nom du peuple français."*

A corollary from the doctrine of the need of promulgation and publication arises from the promulgation being made known in different places and at different times. The Code Napoléon,[2] for instance, provides as follows: *"Les lois sont exécutoires dans tout le territoire français, en vertu de la promulgation qui en est faite par l'Empereur. Elles seront exécutées dans chaque partie de l'Empire du moment où la promulgation en pourra être connue. La promulgation faite par l'Empereur sera réputée connue dans le département où siégera le gouvernement, un jour après celui de la promulgation; et, dans chacun des autres*

[1] See 1 Aubry et Rau, Cours de droit, § 26; 1 Planiol, Traité élémentaire, § 173.

[2] Art. 1.

départements, après l'expiration du même délai, augmenté d'autant de jours qu'il y aura de fois dix myriamètres entre la ville où la promulgation en aura été faite et le chef-lieu de chaque département" ; and, save by the changes called for by successive revolutions or restorations, the Law has so remained, except so far as it is modified by an ordinance of the year 1816, which provides that the promulgation of laws shall result from their insertion in the *Bulletin des Lois,*[1] and that the promulgation shall be considered known in the Capital, in accordance with the Code, the day after the *Bulletin des Lois* is received from the government printer by the Ministry of Justice, the time in the departments being calculated from this according to the Code.

The fact of a statute going into effect in different parts of a country on different days would seem likely to produce difficult questions of the same kind as those which arise in the Conflict of Laws; in the case of the latter there being a conflict between the laws of different places, and in the case of the former a conflict between the laws of different times. Thus, suppose two Frenchmen, the *chefs-lieux* of whose departments are one ten, and the other thirty, myriametres from Paris should make a contract on September 20 by telegraph, and that on September 17 the *Bulletin des Lois,* containing a statute which affects the contract, has been received at the Ministry of Justice, —does the statute govern the contract?

The provision shows a striking difference between the French and the English mind. A Frenchman says a man cannot know the law until he has heard or seen it; it is

[1] The *Journal Officiel* was substituted for the *Bulletin des Lois* by decree of Nov. 5, 1870.

unjust to hold a man bound by a statute which he could not know; the further a man lives from the seat of Government the longer will it be before the news of the making of a statute reaches him; and not to have a provision like that of the Code Napoléon would be the greatest injustice. An Englishman would be likely to say: Who reads the *Bulletin des Lois?* If it contains a statute which is of great importance, the whole country will know that such a statute has been passed by the legislature long before it is promulgated. If the statute is not one that has excited public interest, the arrival of the *Bulletin des Lois* at the *chef-lieu* of a department is one of the most insignificant factors in the general knowledge. Is it immediately known by one in a thousand or one in twenty thousand of the inhabitants? It is foolish to worry about one or more grains of sand in such a heap of ignorance. Does any man know all the Law governing his actions? It is a serious evil to complicate the Law, and offer tempting opportunities for litigation by making a statute applicable to some citizens on one day and to other citizens on another.

The Scotch Statute of 1581, *c.* 128, recited "that oftentimes doubtes and questions arisis, touching the Proclamation of the Actes of Parliament, and publication thereof: It being sumtime alledged to be the lieges, that they are not bound to observe and keepe the samin as lawes, nor incur ony paines conteined therein, quhill the same be proclamed at the mercat croces of the head Burrowes of all Schires," and then proceeded to enact that all acts and statutes of Parliament "sall be published and proclamed at the mercat-croce of Edinburgh onely, Quhilk publication . . . to be als valiable and sufficient as the samin were published at the head burrowes of the haill Schires within this Realme. . . . The haill Lieges to be bounden and astricted to the obedience of the saidis Actes as Lawes, fourtie dayes, after the publication of the samin, at the said mercat-croce of Edinburgh, being by-past." [1] Since the Union there have, of course, been no Scottish Parliaments.

Enactment of statutes: English Law

In England the King assents to the passing of Acts of Parliament as one of the members of the legislature; to use the nomenclature common on the European continent, he "sanctions" them; but no "publication" is required for them. Those who are satisfied with the reason given by Blackstone can accept it; it is, he says, "because every man in England is, in judgment of law, party to the making of an act of parliament, being present thereat by his representatives." [2]

The reason indeed is much older than Blackstone. In early times the laws of each Parliament were transcribed on parchment and sent by the King's writ to the sheriff of every county, to be there proclaimed. Lord Coke [3] gives copies of a writ in the tenth year of Edward III., and another in the first year of Richard II., and says that the like writs continued until the beginning of the reign of Henry VII. But in the case of *Rex* v. *Bishop of Chichester*,[4] which was *præmunire* on a statute, upon Serjeant Cavendish, of counsel with the defendant, objecting that the statute had never been published in the county, Sir Robert Thorpe, C. J., said: "Although the proclama-

[1] See 1 Erskine, Inst. Bk. 1, tit. 1, § 37.
[2] 1 Bl. Com. 185. See Austin's sneer, 2 Jur. (4th ed.) 542, 543.
[3] 4th Inst. 26.
[4] Year Book, 39 Edw. III. 7 (1365).

tion be not made in the county, every one is bound to know it [the statute] as soon as it is made in Parliament; for as soon as the Parliament hath concluded anything, the Law intends that every person hath notice thereof, for the Parliament represents the body of the whole realm, and, therefore, it is not requisite that any proclamation be made, seeing the statute took effect before."

The distinction in England between public statutes and private statutes is well known. The courts take judicial cognizance of public statutes, and may consult any means of information they please;[1] and the reason which Dwarris gives may well be the true one, namely, the impossibility of proving important ancient public statutes by anything that would be legal evidence in cases of a private nature. In fact, there are several early English statutes which do not appear on the rolls of Parliament, and of which there is no official transcript or exemplification, and which yet have been constantly recognized as binding.[2]

The existence of private statutes must be proved in England by record evidence.

Enactment of statutes in the United States

In the United States the same doctrine as to public and private statutes would seem, at first sight, to have been laid down. Thus the Supreme Court of the United States in 1868[3] called attention to the impropriety of speaking of "extrinsic evidence" in reference to public statutes, and ruled "that whenever a question arises in a court of law of the existence of a statute, or of the time

[1] 2 Dwarris, Statutes (2nd ed.), 465-473.

[2] See Hale Hist. Com. Law, 12-15; Cooper, Public Records, 163-184; cf. *Rex* v. *Jefferies*, 1 Str. 446.

[3] *Gardner* v. *The Collector*, 6 Wall. 499.

when a statute took effect, or of the precise terms of a statute, the judges who are called upon to decide it have a right to resort to any source of information which in its nature is capable of conveying to the judicial mind a clear and satisfactory answer to such a question; always seeking first for that which in its nature is most appropriate, unless the positive law has enacted a different rule."

But the meaning of the words "always seeking for that which in its nature is most appropriate" is ambiguous. If they merely mean that the court is morally bound to weigh the information like reasonable men, and give credence to that which ought to convince such a man, the proposition, though somewhat unnecessary, is innocuous and suggests nothing new. But if they mean that the court, in reaching its conclusion, is bound by legal rules to consider certain facts to the exclusion of other facts, then a novel element is introduced in the mode of conveying knowledge of the existence of public statutes to the courts.

And this second meaning seems to be that which has generally, if not universally, prevailed in this country. It is true that the Supreme Court of California, in 1852,[1] recognized the power of the court to seek information from any sources as to the existence of a public statute, but this was disapproved and overruled by the same court fourteen years later,[2] and there appears to be no other like decision in this country. It seems to be generally conceded that with us the existence of both public and private statutes must be established, just as the existence of a private statute must be established in England, by

[1] *Fowler* v. *Peirce*, 2 Cal. 165.
[2] *Sherman* v. *Story*, 30 Cal. 253.

record evidence; and the only matter ordinarily discussed is what records are admissible and controlling. The principal question which has come up is how far the enrolled bill can be controlled by the journals of the Houses.[1]

Interpretation of statutes

It may be urged that if the Law of a society be the body of rules applied by its courts, then statutes should be considered as being part of the Law itself, and not merely as being a source of the Law; that they are rules to be applied by the courts directly, and should not be regarded merely as fountains from which the courts derive their own rules. Such a view is very common in the books. And if statutes interpreted themselves, this would be true; but statutes do not interpret themselves; their meaning is declared by the courts, and *it is with the meaning declared by the courts, and with no other meaning, that they are imposed upon the community as Law.* True though it be, that, of all the sources from which the courts draw the Law, statutes are the most stringent and precise, yet the power of the judges over the statutes is very great; and this not only in countries of the Common Law, but also on the Continent of Europe, where the office of judge is less highly esteemed.

A statute is the expressed will of the legislative organ of a society; but until the dealers in psychic forces succeed in making of thought transference a working controllable force (and the psychic transference of the thought of an artificial body must stagger the most advanced of the ghost hunters), the will of the legislature has to be expressed by words, spoken or written; that is, by causing sounds to be made, or by causing black marks to be im-

[1] On this question see *Field* v. *Clark*. 143 U. S. 649 (1891).

pressed on white paper. "Only in an improper sense can we speak of a communication or transfer of thought; the thought itself is not transferred, but the word gives only the impulse and the possibility of a *like process of thought*, the reproduction of a like spiritual movement in the mind of the hearer, as in that of the speaker. . . . The principle of communication by words is wholly the same as of that by signs; one means is complete, the other incomplete, but they *work* in the same way; neither gives the thought itself, however exact the expression of it may be; it gives only the invitation and the point of departure for it to *reconstruct* itself." [1]

A judge puts before himself the printed page of the statute book; it is mirrored on the retina of his eye and from this impression he has to reproduce the thought of the law-giving body. The process is far from being merely mechanical; it is obvious how the character of the judge and the cast of his mind must affect the operation, and what a different shape the thought when reproduced in the mind of the judge may have from that which it bore in the mind of the law-giver. This is true even if the function of the judge be deemed only that of attempting to reproduce in his own mind the thought of the law-giver; but as we shall see in a moment, a judge, starting from the words of a statute, is often led to results which he applies as if they had been the thought of the legislature, while yet he does not believe, and has no reason to believe, that his present thought is the same as any thought which the legislature really had.

The Judge has the last word

As between the legislative and judicial organs of a society, it is the judicial which has the last say as to

[1] 2 Ihering, Geist des röm. Rechts (4th ed.). § 44, pp. 445, 446.

what is and what is not Law in a community. To quote a third time the words of Bishop Hoadly: "Whoever hath an *absolute authority* to *interpret* any written or spoken laws, it is *he* who is truly the *Law-giver* to all intents and purposes, and not the person who first wrote or spoke them."[1] And this is now recognized even in Germany: "A judicial decree is as much as a statute the act of the law-making power of the State. Like the legislative determination of the Law, so the judicial determinations are filled with the power and compulsive force of the State. A judgment of a court has the force of Law; it carries the whole force of the Law with it. A judicial determination of Law has, in the region belonging to it, the power of a fixed, legally binding order, more fully, with stronger, more direct working, than the statutory, merely abstract statements of the Law. The power of Law is stronger than the power of Legislation, a legal judgment maintains itself if it contradicts a statute. Not by its legislative, but by its judicial determinations, the law-regulating power of the State speaks its last word."[2]

Legislative intent frequently non-existent

But the matter does not rest here. A fundamental misconception prevails, and pervades all the books as to the dealing of the courts with statutes. Interpretation is generally spoken of as if its chief function was to discover what the meaning of the Legislature really was. But when a Legislature has had a real intention, one way or another, on a point, it is not once in a hundred times that any doubt arises as to what its intention was. If that were all that a judge had to do with a statute, interpreta-

[1] See p. 125, *ante*.
[2] Bülow, Gesetz und Richteramt, 6, 7.

tion of statutes, instead of being one of the most difficult of a judge's duties, would be extremely easy. The fact is that the difficulties of so-called interpretation arise when the Legislature has had no meaning at all; when the question which is raised on the statute never occurred to it; when what the judges have to do is, not to determine what the Legislature did mean on a point which was present to its mind, but to guess what it would have intended on a point not present to its mind, if the point had been present. If there are any lawyers among those who honor me with their attention, let them consider any dozen cases of the interpretation of statutes, as they have occurred consecutively in their reading or practice, and they will, I venture to say, find that in almost all of them it is probable, and that in most of them it is perfectly evident, that the makers of the statutes had no real intention, one way or another, on the point in question; that if they had, they would have made their meaning clear; and that when the judges are professing to declare what the Legislature meant, they are in truth, themselves legislating to fill up *casus omissi.*[1]

Rules of construction for deeds and wills

In statutes any rules of interpretation ever suggested have been of the most general character, and the same

[1] "The intent of the Legislature is sometimes little more than a useful legal fiction, save as it describes in a general way certain outstanding purposes which no one disputes, but which are frequently of little aid in dealing with the precise points presented in litigation. Moreover, legislative ambiguity may at times not be wholly unintentional. It is not to be forgotten that important legislation sometimes shows the effect of compromises which have been induced by exigencies in its progress, and phrases with a convenient vagueness are referred to the courts for appropriate definition, each group interested in the measure claiming that the language adopted embodies its views." Mr. Justice Hughes, in 1 Mass. Law Quart. (No. 2), pp. 13, 15. On the point that the legislature sometimes deliberately leaves its intention doubtful, see Sir Courtenay Ilbert, Mechanics of Law Making, pp. 19-23.

is true of legal writings generally; but in two classes of instruments, deeds of real estate and wills, particularly the latter, the limited character of provisions, probable or possible, causes language of a similar nature to be often employed, and thus gives opportunity for the establishment of rules of construction.

The making of these rules was at one time carried too far in the Common Law; they were often pushed into such refinement that they lost their practical value, and, what is more, they sometimes attributed to a testator the very opposite of the intention which he was likely to have had, as with the rule that the words "dying without issue" meant an indefinite failure of issue.[1] Against this disposition there has of late years been a decided reaction on the part of the courts. Judges have spoken with contempt of the mass of authorities collected in Mr. Jarman's bulky treatise on Wills, have declared that the mode of dealing with one man's blunder is no guide as to the mode of dealing with another man's blunder, and especially have said that each will is to be determined according to the intention of the testator, and that the judicial mind should apply itself directly to that problem, and not trouble itself with rules of construction.

And yet it may be doubted whether the pendulum of judicial theory and practice has not swung too far in this direction. It undoubtedly sounds very prettily to say that the judge should carry out the intention of the testator. Doubtless he should; but some judges, I venture to think, have been unduly influenced by taking a fiction as if it were a fact. As is said above with reference to

[1] *I.e.* a failure of descendants at any time, even long after the death of the ancestor.

the legislature, when a testator has a real intention, it is not once in a hundred times that he fails to make his meaning clear. For instance, if a testator should have present to his mind the question whether a legacy to his wife was to be in lieu of dower, it is almost incredible that he should not make what he wished plain. When the judges say they are interpreting the intention of a testator, what they are doing, ninety-nine times out of a hundred, is deciding what shall be done with his property on contingencies which he did not have in contemplation. Now for cases in which a testator has not provided, it may be well that there should be fixed rules, as there are for descent in cases of intestacy.

It would seem that the first question a judge ought to ask with regard to a disputed point under a will should be: "Does the will show that the testator had considered this point and had any actual opinion upon it?" If this question be answered in the affirmative, then there is no doubt that the solution of the testator's intention must be sought in the will. But in the vast majority of cases this is not what has happened. What the judges have to do is, in truth, to say what shall be done where the testator has had no real intention; the practice of modern judges to which I have alluded is to guess from the language used in the particular will what the testator would have meant had he had any meaning, which he had not; the older practice was to look for an established rule of construction. In the modern practice the reasoning is often of the most inconclusive character, but the judges have got to decide the case somehow, and having turned their backs upon rules of construction, have to catch at the slightest straw with which to frame a guess.

Take, for instance, the word "heirs," so often, indeed almost always, put into a will to fill out the final limitations. There are jurisdictions where no counsel dares to advise on what is to be done with property that is bequeathed to "heirs." The judging of each will by itself leads necessarily to the bringing up of each will to be judged, and is responsible for a great deal of family dissension and litigation.

That the unsatisfactory character of many of the rules for the interpretation of wills is largely responsible for their present unpopularity with the courts cannot be denied; but I only wish to point out that what many judges are setting up against the rules of construction of wills is, not their opinion of what testators really intended, but their guess at what the testators would have intended if they had thought of the point in question, which they did not, a guess resting often upon the most trifling balance of considerations.

Methods of interpretation of statutes

The process by which a judge (or indeed any person, lawyer or layman, who has occasion to search for the meaning of a statute) constructs from the words of a statute-book a meaning which he either believes to be that of the Legislature, or which he proposes to attribute to it, is called by us "Interpretation," by the Germans "*Auslegung*."[1]

Interpretation is of two kinds, grammatical and logical. (Savigny's division into grammatical, logical, historical, and systematic [2] has not been generally followed.) Grammatical interpretation is the application to a statute of

[1] 1 Savigny, Heut. röm. Recht, § 32.
[2] *Id.* § 33.

the laws of speech; logical interpretation calls for the comparison of the statute with other statutes and with the whole system of Law, and for the consideration of the time and circumstances in which the statute was passed.[1]

It is sometimes said that the rules of interpretation applicable to statutes are in no way different from those applicable to other writings, and this, in a sense, is true, since statutes, like all writings, are intended to express in language the thoughts of human minds; but the statement needs some qualification, for a difference in the application of the rules for interpreting different writings must arise from the greater precision, definiteness, and accuracy with which a writer is speaking or purporting to speak; and so the rules of interpretation for an Act of Parliament may be very unsuitable to the Mécanique Céleste of La Place, or the Apocalypse of St. John, or the Frogs of Aristophanes.[2]

The dependence of the statutes upon the will of the

[1] The so-called "legal interpretation," as has been often remarked, is no interpretation at all. It contains two parts, authentic and usual interpretation. Authentic interpretation is defining the meaning of an earlier statute by a later. Usual interpretation is the attaching of a meaning to a statute by usage, or, with us, more commonly, by a judicial precedent. A judge, in adopting a meaning for a statute in accordance with its authentic or usual interpretation, is not ascertaining its meaning from the statute itself, but is adopting a meaning for it from some other authority.

[2] It may, by the way, be observed that the most remarkable results of attempting to apply to works of one class rules of interpretation adapted for those of a totally different class have been reached in the domain of theology. To interpret the poems and prophecies of Scripture as if they were the market ordinances of the City of New York, to deal with the fourth verse of the one hundred and tenth Psalm of David, as if it were the fourth section of the one hundred and tenth chapter of the 17 & 18 Victoria, has produced marvels of ingenuity, but of ingenuity wofully misplaced. On the other hand the statement often met with that "the Bible must be interpreted like any other book" is based upon the fallacy that all books are to be interpreted alike, and begs the question, "To what class of books does the Bible belong?"

judges for their effect is indicated by the expression often used, that interpretation is an art and not a science; that is, that the meaning is derived from the words according to the feeling of the judges, and not by any exact and foreknowable processes of reasoning. Undoubtedly rules for the interpretation of statutes have been sometimes laid down, but their generality shows plainly how much is left to the opinion and judgment of the court. Thus Savigny's three aids to interpretation are: *First*, the consideration of the law as a whole; *Second*, the consideration of the reasons of the statutes; *Third*, the excellence of the result reached by a particular interpretation.[1] But their lack of precision he himself notes, saying that the application of the second rule calls for much reserve, and that the third must be kept within the narrowest limits.[2]

Rules of the Common Law

The rules of the Common Law, as laid down in *Heydon's Case*,[3] are not more precise. "For the sure and true interpretation of all statutes in general (be they penal or beneficial, restrictive or enlarging of the Common Law) four things are to be discerned and considered: 1st. What was the Common Law before the making of the Act. 2nd. What was the mischief and defect for which the Common Law did not provide. 3rd. What remedy the Parliament hath resolved and appointed to cure the disease of the Commonwealth. And 4th. The true reason of the remedy; and then the office of all the judges is always to make such construction as shall suppress the mischief, and advance the remedy, and to suppress subtle inven-

[1] 1 Savigny, Heut. röm. Recht, §§ 33-37.
[2] See 1 Windscheid. Pand. § 21.
[3] 3 Co. 7 (1584).

tions and evasions for continuance of the mischief, and *pro privato commodo*, and to add force and life to the cure and remedy, according to the true intent of the makers of the Act, *pro bono publico*."

Of other rules of the Common Law, the principal seems to be that penal statutes are to be construed strictly, but this merely gives a turn to the judicial mind, and furnishes no clear rule where it shall go.

Yet some bounds on the power of interpretation there must be. How far can a judge go? Windscheid answers the question thus: "However clearly interpretation may recognize the real thought of the law-giver, it can recognize it as establishing Law only under the supposition that in the statement given by the legislator, an expression, if not a complete expression, of his real thought can be found. Therefore its principal, if not sole, activity will consist in quantitative extension and limitation of the Statute."[1] Suppose, for instance, in a country where the Common Law prevails, that a statute is passed providing that any person setting fire to a house shall be liable to a certain punishment, no court would so construe that statute as to include children under seven years of age, and yet the legislature has not excluded them, it never thought about them. The judge is clear that it would have excluded them had it thought about the matter, and so he attributes to it the actual intention to exclude them.

Plenty of instances where statutes have been so interpreted can be found at the Common Law; the instance which I have given was of a limiting interpretation; here is an instance of an extensive one. Originally the right

[1] 1 Windscheid, Pand. § 22.

to recover for a wrong did not generally survive the death of the person entitled to recover, but the St. 4 Edw. III. (1330), *c.* 7, reciting that "in times past executors have not had actions for a trespass done to their testators, as of the goods and chattels of the same testators carried away in their life," enacted "that the executors in such cases shall have an action against the trespassers." Under this statute the English courts have held that the survival is not confined to cases where executors sue trespassers who have carried away the goods of testators in the lifetime of the latter, but extends to suits by administrators; to actions for the misappropriation of goods; to an action against a sheriff for making a false return on legal process; to an action for wrongful disposition by an executor, or for removing goods taken on legal process before the testator, who was the debtor's landlord, had been paid a year's rent.[1] And the Court of King's Bench were equally divided on the question whether it did not extend to an action against a bailiff for allowing the escape of one arrested on preliminary legal process.[2]

But, on the other hand, it has been said over and over again, both in the Civil and in the Common Law, that the courts must not undertake to make the legislature say what it has not said. Is not the true rule that the judge should give to the words of a statute the meaning which they would have had, *if he had used them himself*, unless there be something in the circumstances which makes him believe that such was *not* the *actual* meaning of the legislature?

Interpretation of the Twelve Tables

The most remarkable instance of the grow[illegible] Law

[1] 1 Wms. Saund. 217.

[2] See *Le Mason* v. *Dixon*, W. Jones, 173.

by interpretation of statutes is to be found in the Roman Law. The Twelve Tables [1] formed in theory the foundation of the Law, but they were so extended, limited, and altered by *interpretatio*, that they retained but little of their original force. "A formal setting aside of the Law of the Twelve Tables (as statute) by an altering customary law must have appeared inconceivable to a Roman of that time. Down to the end of the Roman legal development, down to the Corpus Juris Civilis of Justinian, that is, for a whole thousand years, when finally, for already a long period, no stone of the Law of the Twelve Tables stood upon another, yet in theory the legal authority of the Twelve Tables was still the source of the collected Roman Law. This corresponded to the conservative, and in all legal matters, far-seeing judgment of the Romans. No letter of the Twelve Tables was to be altered, and yet it was possible to read a new spirit into the old letters. After the completion of the legislation of the Twelve Tables, the questions dealt with were of an '*interpretatio*' which developed, yes, changed the Law, while it left the letters of the Law undisturbed." [2]

Power of courts over statutes

Perhaps the best way to illustrate how much statutes are at the mercy of the courts is to take some one statute, and to see how different courts have attributed to the legislature entirely different meanings, so that the people of different communities are living under totally different Law, although there be the same enactments on their respective statute-books. Let us select the Statute of Frauds, an Act which requires certain transactions to be in writ-

[1] See p. 31, *ante*.

[2] Sohm, Inst. § 11. See 2 Ihering, Geist des röm. Rechts, 461 *et seq.*

ing, and of this only one section, the fourth, which has generally been reënacted in much the same terms in the several United States.

The section is as follows: "No action shall be brought (1) whereby to charge any executor or administrator upon any special promise to answer damages out of his own estate; or (2) whereby to charge the defendant upon any special promise to answer for the debt, default, or miscarriages of another person; or (3) to charge any person upon any agreement made upon consideration of marriage; or (4) upon any contract or sale of land, tenements, or hereditaments, or any interest in or concerning them; or (5) upon any agreement that is not to be performed within the space of one year from the making thereof; unless the agreement upon which such action shall be brought, or some memorandum or note thereof, shall be in writing and signed by the party to be charged therewith, or by some person thereunto by him lawfully authorized." [1]

In some jurisdictions the courts interpret "a special promise to answer for the debt, default, or miscarriage of another person" as including a promise by A. to B. to indemnify the latter for becoming surety to C. In other jurisdictions the courts put the contrary construction on the provision. Again, some courts interpret this clause as covering an indorsement of a note before delivery by one not a party thereto. Others hold the other way. Some courts again, interpret "land" as including a crop of growing grass; others do not. Some courts, further, interpret contracts "not to be performed within a year" as contracts either side of which cannot be performed in a year, while others construe the words as meaning contracts

[1] 29 Car. II, c. 3, sec. 4.

of which the part to be performed by the defendant cannot be performed within a year; and, so again, a memorandum in writing of an agreement is interpreted by some courts as meaning a memorandum containing not merely the promise but the consideration, while others interpret it as meaning a memorandum containing the promise only.[1]

One more case to illustrate the power of the courts. In Maine and Massachusetts there is a statute requiring three competent witnesses to a will, and providing that any legacy to a witness shall be void. In each State arose a case where a will containing a gift to a man had been witnessed by his wife. The Maine Supreme Judicial Court interpreted the statute extensively, and held the legacy bad and the will good, while the Supreme Judicial Court in Massachusetts, interpreting the statute strictly, held the whole will bad.[2]

When amendment is difficult, interpretation is free

One thing, however, is clear,—when legislation is rare, and can be procured with difficulty, the judges will allow themselves a freedom in interpreting statutes which they will not exercise when any ambiguous or defective statute can be easily remodelled by the Legislature. The history of the Law shows this to be so, and it is perhaps well that it should be so; but for this reason the practice of the courts, when legislation is difficult, will form an imperfect index of what is or ought to be their practice when legislation is readily attainable.

Perhaps the most striking instance in modern times

[1] Within a single jurisdiction, *e.g.* England, this section of the Statute of Frauds, and many other statutory enactments, "have been the subject of so much judicial interpretation as to derive nearly all their real significance from the sense put upon them by the Courts." Dicey, Law & Opinion, 2d ed., p. 362.

[2] *Winslow* v. *Kimball*, 25 Maine, 493; *Sullivan* v. *Sullivan*, 106 Mass. 474.

of the freedom of interpretation exercised by a court to modify legislation which could be altered only with great difficulty,—indeed the last modern instance of a fiction which, in its barefaced character, seems a late survival of the practice of the early Roman prætors [1]—is the doctrine of the Supreme Court of the United States on the right of corporations to sue in the Federal Courts. Had the question arisen under an Act of Congress, the Court would have left the difficulty which was felt to be dealt with by Congress, and not sought to mend an inconvenient state of affairs by a fiction; but the question arose under the Constitution, which could be altered only with great trouble and elaborate machinery. The action of the Supreme Court furnishes an excellent example of the extent to which courts will go when they despair of the amendment of defective legislation.

The history of the matter is this: The Constitution provides that the judicial power of the United States "shall extend . . . to controversies between citizens of different States," and under the statutes passed to give effect to this provision, it has been, from early times, uniformly held that if there are citizens of the same State on opposite sides of a controversy, the jurisdiction of the Federal courts on the ground of citizenship is ousted.[2] And it has also been held that a corporation is not a citizen of any State so as to be entitled to the privileges of citizenship.[3]

[1] See p. 31, *ante*.

[2] *Strawbridge* v. *Curtiss*, 3 Cr. 267 (1806); *Smyth* v. *Lyon*, 133 U. S. 315 (1890).

[3] *Bank of Augusta* v. *Earle*, 13 Pet. 519 (1839); *Paul* v. *Virginia*, 8 Wall. 168 (1868).

In *Hope Insurance Co.* v. *Boardman,*[1] it was held that a plaintiff described as a company incorporated by a State could not sue the citizens of another State under the clause in question, the plaintiff not being a citizen of any State. But this was followed in the same year by *Bank of the United States* v. *Deveaux,*[2] in which the Supreme Court decided that a petition by a corporation established by the United States which averred that the petitioners were citizens of Pennsylvania could be maintained in a Federal Court against citizens of Georgia. That is, the Court extended the meaning of citizen of a State in this clause to a corporation all of whose members were citizens of that State.

This was going a good way, but the court has gone much further, and now holds that the stockholders of a corporation will, for the purposes of jurisdiction, be conclusively presumed to be all citizens of that State by which the corporation was established, no evidence to the contrary being admissible.

This ruling leads to most extraordinary results. The Federal courts take cognizance of a suit by a stockholder who is a citizen, say, of Kentucky, against the corporation in which he owns stock, which has been incorporated, say, by Ohio. Since he is a stockholder of an Ohio corporation, the court conclusively presumes that he is a citizen of Ohio, but if he were a citizen of Ohio, he could not sue an Ohio corporation in the Federal courts. Therefore the court considers that he is and he is not at the same time a citizen of Ohio, and it would have no jurisdiction unless it considered that he both was and was not

[1] 5 Cr. 57 (1809).
[2] *Ib.* 61.

at the same time a citizen both of Ohio and Kentucky.[1]

Interpretation of compilations

The special character of a particular body of legislation will sometimes call for special rules of interpretation. The most marked instance is to be found in the legislation of Justinian: the main parts of this, the Digest and the Code, are composed almost entirely of what was originally not legislation; the Code is made up mainly of rescripts and decrees by the Emperors in particular cases, while the Digest contains some such rescripts and decrees, but is composed chiefly of extracts from the writings of jurists. In fact, therefore, to interpret rightly a passage in the *Corpus Juris*, it is necessary first to consider what it meant as used by its original author, and then how that meaning has been modified by reason of the passage being incorporated into the *Corpus*, where it has to be considered in connection with other passages which have also been appropriated by Justinian.[2]

It is obvious that in many ways a body of legislation thus made up must have its own rules of interpretation. For instance, when a statute declares that written instruments shall have a certain effect if made in a certain way, the *argumentum a contrario*, that instruments not so made will not have that effect, is much stronger than in the case of a judgment in which it has been declared that an instrument so made shall have the effect in question.

Whenever a code of laws is published and put forth as one new thing, it is to be interpreted very differently from a collection of statutes which is merely a revision and orderly arrangement of statutes already existing. Of this

[1] *Dodge* v. *Woolsey*, 18 How. 331 (1855).

[2] 1 Windscheid, Pand. § 25; 1 Savigny, Heut. röm. Recht, §§ 42-46.

latter sort are many, though not all, of the collections of statutes in the several States of the Union, and in them the original dates and context of the separate parts will influence the mode in which the courts construe their provisions. Any one familiar with the revisions of the statutes in any of the United States has had frequent proof of this.[1]

Legislative interpretation

The legislature can repeal a statute; it can pass a new statute saying what shall be the meaning of an old statute (although the new statute must be in turn interpreted by the courts), and it can, in the absence of any Constitutional prohibition, even make the new statute retroactive; this is simply an instance of its law-making power; but how far have legislatures undertaken to reserve to themselves the power, apart from new legislation, of interpreting statutes, a power which is ordinarily confided to the judicial organs of a community?

Justinian forbade any commentaries to be written upon the product of his legislation and added: "*Si quid vero ambiguum fuerit visum, hoc ad imperiale culmen per judices referatur et ex auctoritate Augusta manifestetur, cui soli concessum est leges et condere et interpretari.*"[2] If this provision was ever of any practical force, it forms no part of the Roman Law as received in the modern world.[3]

So far as Sovereigns during the Middle Ages inter-

[1] See an article by H. W. Chaplin on Statutory Revision, 3 Harvard Law Rev. 73.

[2] "But if anything shall seem doubtful, let it be referred by the judges to the Imperial Throne and it shall be made plain by Imperial authority, to which alone is given the right both to establish and to interpret laws." Cod. I, 17, 2, 21. See also Cod. I, 14, 12.

[3] 1 Windscheid, Pand. § 25; 1 Savigny, Heut. röm. Recht, § 49.

fered with the decisions of the courts it would seem to have been as supreme judges rather than as legislators interpreting their own statutes.[1]

In countries where the English Common Law prevails, no references have ever been made by judicial tribunals to legislatures to furnish them with interpretations of statutes.[2] In England and in some of the United States, legislative bodies can ask the opinion of the judges on the interpretation of statutes as on any other questions of Law, remaining free to follow or not to follow such opinion, as they see fit, but the reverse practice does not exist.[3]

The Prussian Code at one time directed the judges to submit their doubts on the interpretation of statutes to a legislative commission,[4] but this has now been done away with, and the judges have full and exclusive powers of interpretation.

It is in France that the idea of reserving to the legislature the power of interpretation has been most developed. Its history is interesting, but it will be sufficient to say

[1] See account of Henry II as judge, 1 Pollock & Maitland, Hist. of Eng. Law, 2d ed. 156-160.

[2] But see Y. B. 40 Edw. 3, p. 34. Thorpe, C. J., and Green, J., on a disputed question as to the construction of a recent statute about amending pleadings, went "to the Council, and there were 24 bishops and earls, and we asked of them who made the statute, if the record could be amended." In the middle ages, however, the functions of Parliament as a legislature and as a court were not clearly distinguished, so that such applications might be regarded as being made to a higher court. See also McIlwain, High Court of Parliament, 115, 326; Pike, Constitutional History of the House of Lords, pp. 50 *et seq.;* 2 State Trials, Case of the Postnati, p. 675.

[3] *Attorney-General* v. *Attorney-General,* [1912] A. C. 571; and see J. B. Thayer, Legal Essays, 42.

[4] 2 Austin, Jur. (4th ed.), 659, 681; Prussian Landrecht, 1794, §§ 47, 48.

here that, at present, the legislature is not charged with this judicial function.[1]

Desuetude of statutes

A statute once enacted continues to be a source of law until it comes to an end. Sometimes a statute itself provides that it shall be in force for only a limited time. But the usual way in which a statute ceases to be a source of Law is its repeal by the legislature which enacted it or by a legislature of higher powers. A legislature cannot bind subsequent legislatures, and therefore cannot pass an irrepealable statute. This is true of a supreme legislative body having an unlimited power of enacting statutes, but to an inferior legislative body may be delegated the power of making ordinances once for all, and when it has made them, it may be *functum officio;* and from the circumstance that the legislatures of the several States in the United States are limited by the Constitution of the United States has arisen another interesting class of statutes which the legislatures that passed them cannot repeal. That has come about in this way. The Constitution of the United States prohibits a State from passing any law impairing the obligation of contracts, and the prohibition was interpreted in the Dartmouth College Case[2] to cover not only executory contracts, but also grants, and therefore statutes of a State which are grants cannot be repealed by a subsequent legislature of that State. The statutes which have in this way become irrepealable are mainly those which have granted certain privileges, such as exemption from taxation, to corporations.

[1] 1 Laurent, Principes du droit civil, §§ 254-256; 1 Planiol, Traité élémentaire, §§ 208-214.

[2] 4 Wheat. 518.

Civil Law

The Civilians base their doctrine as to abrogation by desuetude upon a passage of the jurist Julianus, who flourished in the first half of the second century, which is taken up into the Digest.[1] "*Inveterata consuetudo pro lege non immerito custoditur, et hoc est ius quod dicitur moribus constitutum. Nam cum ipsæ leges nulla alia ex causa nos teneant quam quod judicio populi receptæ sunt, merito et ea, quæ sine ullo scripto populus probavit, tenuerunt omnes; nam quid interest suffragio populus voluntatem suam declaret an rebus ipsis et factis? Quare rectissime etiam illud receptum est, ut leges non solum suffragio legislatoris, sed etiam tacito consensu omnium per desuetudinem abrogentur*";[2] and there are other passages in the *Corpus Juris* which seem to be to the same effect.[3] On the other hand, a rescript of Constantine (A.D. 319), to be found in the Code, reads as follows: "*Consuetudinis ususque longævi non vilis auctoritas est, verum non usque adeo sui valitura momento, ut aut rationem vincat aut legem.*" [4]

On the attempted reconcilement of these passages, and on the existence and extent of the doctrine that statutes may be abrogated by disuse, there is a whole literature.

[1] D. I, 3, 32, 1.

[2] "Long continued custom is not improperly regarded as equivalent to a statute, and what is pronounced to be established by usage is law. For since the statutes themselves are binding on us for no other reason than that they are accepted by the people, it is proper also that what the people have approved without any writing shall bind everyone; for what difference is there whether the people declares its will by a vote or by its very acts and deeds? Wherefore very rightly this also is held, that statutes may be abrogated not only by a vote of the legislator, but also by desuetude with the tacit consent of all."

[3] Inst. IV, 4, 7; Cod. I, 17, 1, 10; Cod. VI, 51, 1, 1.

[4] "Custom and long usage have no slight weight, but not so great that they will prevail of themselves, or overcome either reason or a statute." Cod. VIII, 52 (53), 2.

Placentinus[1] taught that statutes could no longer be abrogated by disuse. But he has found few followers among the civilians. Of the divers theories held as to Constantine's rescript by those who allow that statutes may be abrogated by desuetude, Guyet[2] enumerates fourteen of the "weightiest," besides his own.

One of these theories is that the doctrine of abrogation by desuetude should be confined to those statutes which provide what is to be done in transactions where the parties have expressed no will of their own (*Dispositivgesetze*), and ought not to be extended to statutes which positively forbid or order certain acts. Thus, a statute directing that, in the absence of agreement, six per cent shall be the legal rate of interest can be abrogated by disuse, but a statute forbidding that more than six per cent shall be taken, cannot.[3] But this limitation of the power of abrogation by desuetude to the case of *Dispositivgesetze* has not met with general approval.[4]

Abrogation by desuetude is not merely a doctrine of the schools, but has been applied in practice in modern times. Thus, the following case was decided in the Court of Appeals at Darmstadt in 1827. The defendant had alleged that the provision of the statute Law (the Land Law of the Upper County of Katzenelnbogen) in relation to the formalities of a will had undergone modification through

[1] In his gloss to Cod. VIII, 52 (53), 2, just quoted. See 2 Puchta, Gewonheitsrecht, 204.

[2] In an article on *Das particuläre Gewonheitsrecht*, in 35 Arch. für civ. Pr. 12, 23-25.

[3] Seuffert, 11 Arch. für civ. Pr. 357.

[4] See 2 Puchta, Gewonheitsrecht, 208, 209; Busch, 27 Arch. für civ. Pr. 197. On the question of desuetude, see also Windscheid, Pand. § 18; 2 Puchta, Gewonheitsrecht, 203-215; 1 Savigny, Heut. röm. Recht, § 25; *Id.* Beylage 2, in 1 Heut. röm. R., p. 420; Gesterding, 3 Arch. für civ. Pr. 259.

customary Law. When the question came before the Court of Appeals, that tribunal held that the defendant should be allowed to prove the superiority of the customary Law which derogated from the provisions of the Land Law, for that through usage a positive statute could be abrogated or modified, and that this was good even in reference to the formalities for making wills.[1]

The practical use of a formal doctrine allowing the abrogation of statutes by desuetude is likely to be greatly limited by the freedom which the courts permit themselves to exercise in interpretation. It is not as speedy or as simple a process to interpret a statute out of existence as to repeal it, but with time and patient skill it can often be done. And the desire not to seem to disturb ancient landmarks has often occasioned a resort to "interpretation" rather than to a repeal to get rid of the weight of a statute which has become burdensome. Particularly was this the case in Rome. Referring again to the passage from Sohm,[2] a formal repeal of the Law of the Twelve Tables by customary Law would have appeared inconceivable to a Roman, and when for a long period no stone of the Law of the Twelve Tables had stood upon another, still, in theory, that legislation was regarded as the source of the collected Roman Law.[3]

Another circumstance which affects the practical employment of the doctrine of desuetude is the comparative ease of obtaining new legislation; when the legislative organ of a community is with difficulty called into action,

[1] 9 Seuffert, Arch. Nr. 3; see also 40 Seuffert, Arch. Nr. 269.

[2] Cited p. 181, *ante*.

[3] But see Inst. IV, 4, 7, which seems to recognize that a provision of the Law of the Twelve Tables could be abrogated by desuetude.

the courts are pretty certain, whatever legal texts may say, to exercise the power of either interpreting statutes out of existence, or else of holding that they may be abrogated by desuetude. But when new legislation can be easily obtained, there is little occasion to apply the doctrine of desuetude.[1]

Many of the German Codes provide that no customary law shall prevail against them. But some of the German jurists go so far as to declare that an express provision in a statute that it should not be abrogated by any customary law would be null and only empty words.[2] Windscheid, while condemning this view, adopts one which leads to the same result. He says that if a statute denies derogatory power to customary law, that provision of the statute is valid, and that, as long as the statute is in force, it must prevail against customary law, but that, notwithstanding, the statute itself may be derogated from by customary law.[3]

In France, the prevailing opinion is that statutes cannot be abrogated by desuetude.[4]

In Scotland statutes may fall into desuetude.[5]

Desuetude of statutes: Common Law

The doctrine of the English Common Law is that a statute can be abrogated only by an express or implied repeal, that it cannot be done away with by any custom or usage, that it cannot fall into desuetude.

[1] See p. 183, *ante*.
[2] See Zoll, 13 Jahrb. f. Dogm. 416 (1874); Maurer, 14 Krit. Vierteljahrsschr. 49 (1872); Eisele, 69 Archiv. f. civ. Pr. 275 (1886); Wendt, 22 Jahrb. f. Dogm. 324 (1884).
[3] 1 Windscheid, Pand. (9th ed.) § 18, note 3. See Rümelin, 27 Jahrb. f. Dogm. 225 (1889); 1 Stobbe, Handbuch, § 23.
[4] 1 Aubry and Rau Cours de Droit, § 29. See 18 Merlin, Rep. "Usage," 255 *et seq.;* 7 Merlin, Quest. de Droit, "Société," § 1.
[5] Erskine, Principles (21st ed.) p. 7.

To the rule that a statute cannot fall into desuetude, Lord Coke seems to allege an exception. His words [1] are, "If a statute in the negative be declarative of the ancient law, that is, in affirmance of the common law, there as well as a man may prescribe or allege a custom against the common law, so a man may do against such a statute"; and Mr. Hargrave [2] approves the rule that one may prescribe or allege a custom against a statute declaratory of the Common Law. But the truth seems to be that there are no statutes having force as such which are older than the time of legal memory,[3] and that, therefore, all rights acquired by prescription or custom are to be considered as existing before any statutes were enacted. So that the question is this: Is a custom or prescription contrary to the Common Law put an end to by a statute confirmatory of the Common Law passed subsequently to the establishment of the custom or prescription? In other words, the question is not of the effect of prescription or custom on a statute, but of the effect of a statute upon an existing prescriptive or customary right, which is merely a question of interpretation, and does not concern us here.

The theory that a statute cannot fall out of use is undoubtedly accepted law in England to-day, and the ease with which legislation can now be obtained renders the maintenance of such a theory easy. But it is not perfectly clear that the doctrine was always held with great rigidity. St. 15 Hen. VI. *c.* 4 is to the effect that "no

[1] Co. Lit. 115 *a*.
[2] In his note to this passage of Coke's.
[3] See Hale, Hist. Com. Law, *c.* 1. The time of legal memory begins with the commencement of the reign of Richard I, 1189. See 2 Bl. Com. 31.

writ of *subpœna* be granted from henceforth until surety be found to satisfy the party so grieved and vexed for his damages and expenses." This statute was, after a time, totally disregarded in the Chancery.[1] It may be observed that this statute was passed to diminish recourse to Chancery, and must have been disliked by the officers of that court, and that if the Chancellor disregarded the statute, he could not be proceeded against at Common Law either by *mandamus* or prohibition. It may also be noted that the statute is not in any of the exemplifications formerly preserved at the Tower of the lost statute roll of this year.[2]

The St. of 1 Hen. V. *c.* 1, requiring candidates for Parliament to be resident within the counties, cities, or boroughs from which they are chosen, and other statutes in the following reign *in pari materia*,[3] were not followed by the House of Commons; and in 1774, the St. of 14 Geo. III. *c.* 58, after reciting that "several provisions contained in the said Acts have been found, by long usage, to be unnecessary, and are become obsolete," enacted that, in order "to obviate all doubts that may arise upon the same," the said Acts are repealed. It should be observed that most of the acts forbidden by these statutes could be taken cognizance of only by the House of Commons, and therefore would escape the supervision of the regular courts.

Near the beginning of the seventeenth century (1617), Ferdinando Pulton published a calendar abridgment of the Statutes, in which he marked by the letters "OB"

[1] 1 Harrison, Prac. Ch. (8th ed.) 157.
[2] 2 Sts. of the Realm (ed. 1816) 296, note.
[3] Sts. 8 Hen. VI. *c.* 7; 10 Hen. VI. *c.* 2; 23 Hen. VI. *c.* 14.

every statute which was "*obsoletum*, that is, worn out of use."

The St. of 19 & 20 Vict. *c.* 64 (1856) is entitled "An act to repeal certain statutes which are not in use." It repeals one hundred and eighteen Acts, and it is to be observed that it is only in the preamble that it speaks of the statutes not being in use.[1]

The English statute book has undergone a pretty thorough purging from Acts applicable only to a state of things which has passed away. For instance, between the Restoration of 1660 and the Revolution of 1689 there were passed two hundred and seventeen statutes (omitting the private, personal, and local). Of these, one hundred and seventy-five have been expressly and totally repealed, and doubtless the judges would be astute in searching for, and successful in finding, implied repeals of other statutes that they did not like.

English statutes in America

The position among the English colonists in what is now the United States of the statutes passed by the English or British Parliament, whether before or after their departure from the mother country, presents an interesting question. Undoubtedly the principles embodied in those statutes were largely applied as rules by the American courts, but they were applied not as commands of the English or British Parliament, for no Act of Parliament extended to the colonies unless they were expressly mentioned,[2] but as part of a body of rules,

[1] See also St. 26 & 27 Vict. *c.* 125.

[2] Between the date of the first establishment of the American colonies in the beginning of the seventeenth century and the Revolution at the end of the eighteenth, the statutes passed by the Parliament of England or of Great Britain, which were made applicable to the colonies or any of them, were few in number.

known as the Common Law, which were, in fact, applied by the English courts, and which the courts in the colonies took over from them; and they dealt with these rules much more freely than they would have felt at liberty to do, had the statutes been made by the legislatures of their own communities. They said that they would consider as furnishing rules for decision only those English statutes which were "suited to our condition," a phrase giving them a wide discretion, of which they did not hesitate to avail themselves, and there was, therefore, no occasion to consider the effect of desuetude on true statutes.[1]

In South Carolina, indeed, an Act of the General Assembly of the Province, passed in 1712,[2] provided that certain Acts of Parliament, set forth at length, should be in "as full force, power and virtue as if the same had been specially enacted and made for this Province, or as if the same had been made and enacted therein by any General Assembly thereof." But in no other colony or province was there a local reënactment of English statutes.

Desuetude of statutes in the United States

There does not seem often to have come up any question of the desuetude of the statutes of the United States or of the several States. I suppose that the courts would generally follow the English doctrine that a statute cannot be abrogated by desuetude; but, doubtless, if they found a statute troublesome as a "survival of the unfittest," they could do much to get rid of it by "interpretation," or by declaring it the victim of an "implied repeal." The only States in which the question has been discussed seem to be South Carolina, Pennsylvania, Maryland, and Iowa.[3]

[1] See article by Professor Sioussat, in 1 Select Essays in Anglo-Amer. Leg. Hist. 416.

[2] 2 Cooper, Sts. of So. Car. p. 401.

[3] See Appendix V.

CHAPTER IX

JUDICIAL PRECEDENTS[1]

Precedents in general

THE second source of the Law, that is, of the rules by which the courts govern their action, is to be found in Precedents. Precedent has a very wide meaning. It covers everything said or done which furnishes a rule for subsequent practice, especially in matters of form or ceremony. Thus, at the Lord Mayor's Election Dinner, it is a precedent that "upon the Lady Mayoress retiring from the dinner table the senior alderman below the chair conducts Her Ladyship to the drawing-room"; and in the Law, "precedent" is often used to mean a paper employed as a model in drawing other papers; thus, we have precedents in conveyancing and pleading; but the precedents of which we have to speak here, Judicial Precedents, are former decisions which courts respect and follow because made by judicial tribunals.

As the weight attached to precedents in every department of life is closely connected with the force of habit, and has its roots deep in human nature, it is more than probable that Judicial Precedents have exercised great influence in all systems of Law; the feeling that a rule is morally right has often arisen from the fact that it has long been followed as a rule; but the degree in which

[1] This chapter is partly taken from the author's article in 9 Harvard Law Rev. 27, which contains a fuller citation of cases on some points.

judicial decisions have been openly recognized as authoritative, simply because they are judicial decisions, has varied very greatly in different systems. Judges are everywhere largely influenced by what has been done by themselves or their predecessors, but the theories to explain and control such influence have been diverse, and the development of the Law has not been unaffected by them.

Two things should be borne in mind. In the first place, the functions of courts are not in practice confined to the decision of particular causes. Either by authority expressly delegated, or of their own motion, courts have undertaken to legislate with regard to the conduct of litigation before themselves; they have published general rules, in the form of command or permission, setting forth the manner in which they will proceed. The most striking example is the Edict of the Roman prætor, which became a chief instrument in the development of the Roman Law. Doubtless special cases gave rise to many of its provisions, but, none the less, it was in form a legislative, not a judicial, act.[1] The Scotch Court of Sessions, in its Acts of Sederunt, assumed extensive powers of enacting laws,[2] and in our days, governments have frequently intrusted to courts a wide authority to make rules of procedure.[3] All this lies outside of our present limits. Such rules are not Judicial Precedents.

[1] The prætor, who was the principal judicial officer in the Roman republic, on assuming office made a proclamation, *edictum*, of the rules which he proposed to follow. These edicts affected not only the procedure but the substantive law. It was the custom for each prætor to adopt the edict of his predecessor with additions and amendments. This permanent body of rules was called the perpetual edict.

[2] Erskine, Inst. Bk. 1, tit. 1, § 40.

[3] As to the extent to which this has been done, and the advantages of it, see an article by Professor Pound, in 10 Illinois Law Rev. 163.

Judicial Precedents as sources of Law

Again, the peculiar quality and effect of a Judicial Precedent as a source of Law should be noted. It may be a source of Law as expressing the opinion of learned men, or as stating sound moral doctrine, but its peculiar force as a Judicial Precedent does not lie in its accordance with the opinion of the learned, or in the fact that it is right; it is a Judicial Precedent, not because it *ought* to have been made, but because it *has* been made. The decision of a court may unite the character of a Judicial Precedent with the character of an expression of wise thought or of sound morals, but often these characters are separated. To go no farther than our own Law, there is no difficulty in finding decisions standing as precedents, at which, like the Rule in *Dumpor's Case*,[1] "the profession have always wondered,"[2] or which, at any rate, are no expression of present opinion and would never be made for the first time to-day.

Roman Law

Of Judicial Precedents as a source of Law, we find nothing at Rome in the time of the Republic, except as far as the rulings of the Pontifical College had this character.[3] The manner in which the *pontifices* intervened in lawsuits between individuals is very obscure, but there is reason to believe that their position was an authoritative one, and it is likely enough that in the archives of the college were recorded decisions which they

[1] 4 Co. 119 b (1603). The decision was that where there was a condition in a lease that the lessee should not assign his interest without the lessor's consent, and the lessor consented to one assignment, the condition was gone, so that a second assignment could be made without his consent.

[2] Chief Justice Mansfield, in *Doe* v. *Bliss*, 4 Taunton, 735. Compare Lord Eldon, in *Brummell* v. *McPherson*, 14 Ves. Jr. 173.

[3] See Dig. I, 2, 2, 6.

followed as binding precedents;[1] but this remains largely a matter of conjecture.[2] At any rate, before the end of the Republic, their power of controlling litigation appears to have greatly diminished, and the practice of giving opinions had passed to the unofficial body of jurisconsults, *jurisprudentes*,[3] who seem to have enjoyed great public consideration; but the opinions of these jurisconsults, however worthy of respect, were not binding on the magistrates and judges. The jurisconsults did not form a judicial body.

But Augustus gave to certain persons *jus respondendi* by the authority of the Emperor.[4] All that we know of the *jus respondendi* is contained in three passages.[5] These three passages have called forth much comment, and given birth to many theories.[6]

From our present point of view the important question is, whether the *responsa* of those jurisconsults who had the *jus respondendi* were of effect only in the particular case in which they were given, or whether they were obligatory upon the courts as precedents in later cases. The probable opinion appears to be that they had the character of true Judicial Precedents.

By the time of Diocletian (A.D. 284-305) the *jus respondendi* seems to have ceased to be given, and, gradually, all the writings of the great jurists of the earlier years of the Empire came to be considered as authorities,

[1] Esmarch, Röm. Rechtsgeschichte, § 44.

[2] Ihering, 1 Geist des röm. Rechts, § 18 *a*.

[3] But see Cicero, Topica, 5, with commentaries of Boethius.

[4] The common opinion has been that the *responsa* of these persons were made binding upon the courts by Augustus, but some writers think that it was Hadrian who first gave them this binding character.

[5] Dig. I, 2, 2, 49; Gai. I, 7; Inst. I, 2, 8 *et* 9.

[6] See Glasson, Étude sur Gaius, 84-119.

without any distinction being made between their *responsa* and their treatises. It was as if Judge Story's judgments and treatises were to be considered of like weight. The power of adding to the Law or modifying it by judicial decisions had passed away. The Law, like the Empire, had reached a period of degradation and sterility. It had no vitality, and could only nourish itself indiscriminately on the past.[1]

Such was the state of things when Justinian began his legislation. But before speaking of this, we must consider another class of judicial utterances—those emanating from the Emperors themselves. The legal utterances of the Emperors were of two kinds, legislative and judicial. They were all classed together as *constitutiones*. Of the legislative sort were the *edicta* and *mandata;* it is unnecessary here to consider their special character; they were in their nature statutes.

The judicial acts of the Emperor were *decreta* and *rescripta*. The *decreta* were decrees, final or interlocutory, in a cause. The *rescripta* were letters sent to the judge or to a party in a suit, giving the decision which

[1] "The writings of jurists who had not possessed the *jus respondendi* were cited as entitled to an authority in no way inferior to that of the writings of privileged jurists, provided only they were supported by the same *literary* prestige which distinguished the writings of the illustrious privileged jurists. . . . Considering that, in the case of the privileged jurists, their other writings which, of course, had nothing to do with their *jus respondendi*, were ranked on a par with the writings on the *responsa*, it was altogether absurd to insist on the *jus respondendi* as a condition of judicial authority. The practice of not discriminating between the different kinds of writings necessarily led to the practice of not discriminating between the authors themselves—which is only another way of saying that the transfer of the authority of the *responsa* to juristic literature in general had become an accomplished fact." Sohm, Institutes, § 17, Ledlie's trans. p. 83; see also the Law of Citations (A.D. 426), Cod. Theod. I, 4, 3; p. 264, *post*.

ought to be rendered. There seems to have been no substantial difference in their effect upon a suit; unquestionably they were alike obligatory upon the judges in the cases in which they were given. But the question arises, as with the *responsa prudentium*, were they binding as precedents?

First, as to *Decreta*. That in the classical period of the Roman Law *decreta* had sometimes at least the force of precedents, seems the more probable opinion; Justinian says that the binding force as precedents of the Imperial decrees had been doubted by some, adding, "*Eorum quidem vanam scrupulositatem tam risimus quam corrigendam esse censuimus*";[1] and he declared that a decree made by the Emperor in a cause should be a rule (*lex*) not only in that cause, *sed omnibus similibus.*

Secondly, as to *Rescripta*, with their sub-varieties of *adnotationes, subscriptiones, epistulæ, pragmaticæ sanctiones.* These, as I have said (though the word may have been sometimes used more loosely), were answers to requests of a party or of the judge in a suit for instructions how the case should be decided. These rescripts were obligatory on the court in that suit. Originally they seem, in some cases at least, to have been binding as precedents.[2]

The danger which there was that a case would not be fully or fairly presented to the Emperor brought rescripts into disfavor. Trajan (A.D. 98-117) is said to have refused to issue rescripts in answer to requests, "*ne ad alias causas facta præferrentur, quæ ad gratiam composita*

[1] "Their foolish over-nicety we laugh at, as well as order to be amended." Cod. I, 14, 12.

[2] Krüger, Quellen, § 14, pp. 97, 98.

viderentur," and Macrinus (A.D. 217, 218), referring to this, gave orders, *"omnia rescripta veterum Principum tollere, ut jure, non rescriptis, ageretur,"* saying, *"nefas esse leges videri Commodi et Caracalli et hominum imperitorum voluntates."* [1] Still later, it was ordered by Arcadius and Honorius (A.D. 398) that rescripts should not be regarded as precedents;[2] and they were forbidden by Justinian (541).[3]

The idea of Judicial Precedents was therefore familiar to the Roman Law, at least at some periods of its development.

The form of Justinian's Digest was peculiar: a mass composed of the decisions of judges and the opinions of jurisconsults in particular cases was taken up bodily into it and enacted as a statute; but in spite of this, it was impossible, in interpreting them, to treat them as if they had been enunciated in the usual statutory form; they had to be dealt with as if they were precedents, and the mode of reasoning adopted in their exposition had, to a considerable extent, to be that applicable to precedents;[4] and it would have been well if this had been carried to a greater extent.

A similar state of things is to be found in the Codes passed by the Legislative Council of India for that country. Macaulay set the example, which has been followed

[1] "Lest decrees which were evidently made as a favor should be brought forward in other cases." "To eliminate all the rescripts of former Emperors, in order that suits might be conducted according to law, not rescripts." "It is not right that the whims of Commodus and Caracalla and unskilled men should be regarded as laws." Capitolinus, Life of Macrinus, c. 13.

[2] Cod. Theod. I, 2, 11.

[3] Nov. 113, 1; see 1 Savigny, Heut. röm. Recht, § 24.

[4] P. 186, *ante*.

by his successors, of inserting illustrative cases in the body of the statutes. The character of such parts of the Law, their resemblance to and their difference from cases decided in the courts, are well given in the introduction of Macaulay to his Criminal Code.[1]

German Law

In Germany during the Middle Ages the Courts were composed of a judge (Richter) and Schöffen.[2] The Richter presided, kept order, and gave judgment, but on a doubtful point of law he took the opinion of the Schöffen, who were the Urtheiler,[3] and often the Schöffen sought the opinion of the Schöffen of another city or town, either because of their reputation as depositaries of the Law, or because such city or town stood in the relation of mother city to that from which the request came.[4]

The opinions of the Schöffen were generally called Weisthümer. There is a great collection of them by Grimm, the publication of which covered the interval between 1840 and 1878.[5] They took a variety of forms; sometimes they were put as general rules, sometimes as answers to hypothetical cases, and sometimes as opinions in particular real cases. These last availed, it would

[1] Cited 1 Stokes, Anglo-Indian Codes, xxiv *et seq.*

[2] Sheriffs, or Assessors.

[3] Doomsmen, Deciders.

[4] The court to whose Schöffen the request was sent was called the Oberhof, but the relation was not at all the same as that which prevails between a court of first instance and the appellate court, for the Schöffen of the Oberhof were not bound to answer. See 1 Stobbe, Geschichte d. deutsch. Rechtsquellen, § 27; 1 Planck, Deutsche Gerichtsverfahren im Mittelalter, §§ 15-19, 43; Gaupp, Das alte Magdeburgische und Hallische Recht; Schultze, Privatrecht und Process, §§ 6-14.

[5] Others will be found in Gaupp's little book, cited in the preceding note, in Wasserschleben, Deutsche Rechtsquellen, and in Tomaschek, Der Oberhof Iglau und seine Schöffengesprüche. A list of books containing Weisthümer will be found at the beginning of Planck's book, above cited, and in 1 Stobbe, Geschichte d. deutsch. Rechtsquellen, § 56, note (2).

seem, not only in the cases in which they were delivered, but also as binding in future cases in the same court, and as having a weight beyond their intrinsic merits in other courts.[1]

The introduction of the Roman Law into Germany and the driving out of the ancient Law were due mainly to the doctors of the Civil Law acquiring judicial position. This seems to be the conclusion reached by all late writers.[2] But the modern German civilians have rather ungratefully kicked down the ladder by which they themselves climbed, and exhibit a great repugnance to recognize judicial decisions, or *Gerichtsgebrauch*, in any form, as a source of Law. Perhaps the dislike felt toward the old Schöffen courts may have something to do with this attitude.[3]

At the beginning of the last century, Thibaut indeed stated the doctrine of Judicial Precedent in a form nearly as strong as prevails in the Common Law. "If in a court a rule has been frequently and constantly followed as Law, *that* court must follow these hitherto adopted rules as Law, whether they relate to simple forms or to the substances of controversies, if they do not contradict

[1] 1 Stobbe, Handbuch d. deutsch. Privatrechts, § 24; Gaupp, 90-94. So in the Imperial Court, in 1235, the Emperor Frederick II. established a standing judge and decided: "*Idem scribet omnes sententias coram nobis in majoribus causis inventas maxime contradictorio juditio obtentas, quæ vulgo dicuntur* gesamint urteil, *ut in posterum in casibus similibus ambiguitas rescindatur, expressa terra secundum consuetudinem cujus sentenciatum est.*" "He shall write down all the opinions delivered in our court in the more important cases, especially where there was dissent, which in the vulgar tongue are called 'The body of dooms', in order that for the future in similar cases doubt may be resolved,—express statement being made of the district according to whose custom the sentence was pronounced." 1 Stobbe, Geschichte, § 48.

[2] See article by W. S. Holdsworth in 28 Law Quart. Rev. 39, 49.

[3] See A. Duck, De Auth. Jur. Civ. II. *c.* 2, §§ 10-19.

the statutes, but yet only on the points on which the former judgments agreed. Coördinate courts do not bind each other with their judgments, but upper courts do bind the lower, so far as an earlier practice has not formed itself in the latter; and one ought not to treat the opinions of jurists as equal to the practice of the courts, although the former may, under certain circumstances, be of importance as authorities." [1]

But Thibaut's opinion does not seem to be followed, and Jordan, in a long and much-cited article,[2] summed up his own theory thus:—

A. Judicial usage (*Gerichtsgebrauch*) as such, that is, by reason of its being judicial usage, has formally no binding force, and materially, only so much value as on the principles of a sound jurisprudence belongs to it by reason of its inner nature; that hence—

B. A court cannot be bound to follow its own usage or the usage of another court as a rule of decision, but rather has the duty to test every question with its own jurisprudence, and ought to apply usage only when it can find no better rule of decision; that again—

C. Judicial usage makes binding law for the parties as soon as a judgment based on it has taken effect; that hence—

D. Many judicial usages have in this way come gradually to be accepted and practised, notwithstanding they have met with theoretical disapproval; that again—

E. On the other hand, on account simply of their real excellence, in so far as they by means of this have acquired not only a hold in approved courts, but also the

[1] Thibaut, Pand. § 16.
[2] 8 Arch. f. civ. Pr. 191, 245 *et seq.* (1825).

approval of theorists, and, on the theory that for cases not provided for in the statutes, they give the rules of decision which best correspond to the presumptive will of the legislature, many of these judicial usages become pretty generally recognized legal principles which cannot be left out of account. The fact that the legislature prescribes no other rules for future cases may be considered an approval of them by the legislature; that finally—

F. The lower courts act in accordance with the will of the legislature, if they follow the clear usage of the higher courts, although they are not bound to do so absolutely, but are only held to such following so far as they find it grounded in the will of the legislature according to their own examination, from which they are never excused.

Later writers seem generally to deny that *Gerichtsgebrauch* is a source of Law at all, and consider judicial decisions to be merely evidence (just as many other things might be evidence) of Customary Law. This seems to have been Savigny's opinion.[1] Such are the views of Wächter;[2] and of Keller.[3] So Stobbe,[4] "Practice is in itself not a source of Law; a court can depart from its former practice, and no court is bound to the practice of another." "Departure from the practice hitherto observed is not only permitted, but required, if there are better reasons for another treatment of the question of Law."

Dernburg is the only recent author whom I have observed fairly to admit that *Gerichtsgebrauch* is a source of law; and even he says, "Single decisions of a court,

[1] See 1 Heut. röm. Recht, § 29.
[2] 23 Arch. f. civ. Pr. 432.
[3] In his Pandekten, § 4.
[4] 1 Handb. d. deutsch. Privatrechts, § 24, pp. 144, 146.

even of the highest, do not make *Gerichtsgebrauch*," which he defines as "the general, uniform, and long-continued exercise of a legal tenet by the courts of the country." [1]

Nor are these views as to *Gerichtsgebrauch* confined to the text-writers. They are shared by the courts themselves. As is shown, for instance, by an interesting decision of the Imperial Court.[2] In New Hither Pomerania there had for a long time prevailed a doctrine of the courts (*Gerichtsgebrauch*), supported by decisions of the earlier Tribunal in Wismar and of the later Oberappellationsgericht in Greifswald, and recognized as binding by the Prussian Obertribunal, that discontinuous servitudes (*e.g.*, rights of way) are not acquired by a ten or twenty years' user, but only by immemorial prescription. The Imperial Court reversed a judgment founded on this view, on the ground that the doctrine was not based upon rules peculiar to the law of the special locality, but upon an erroneous interpretation of the Roman Law.[3]

One point especially in the views of the German writers seems very strange to those brought up in a different school. To a Common Law lawyer, the duty of a lower court to follow the precedents set by the court of appeal seems one of the clearest of judicial obligations. To delay a party of what will be declared his right in the end and to put him to the expense and trouble of an appeal seems wrong; but the German writers are all express in denying the duty of following the precedents set by

[1] 1 Dernburg, Pand. § 29.

[2] 3 Entscheidungen des Reichsgerichts, Civilsachen, Nr. 59, p. 210; S. C. 36 Seuffert, Arch. Nr. 254, p. 385 (1880).

[3] See another case, 7 Entscheid. d. Reichsg. Civ. Nr. 50, p. 154; S. C. 40 Seuf. Arch. Nr. 86, p. 130.

the court of appeal, even Thibaut[1] conceding that the upper courts bind the lower only so far as an earlier practice has not established itself in the latter. And Maurenbrecher, who at one time held the contrary,[2] appears to have weakened on his first statement. Gengler is the only writer cited by Stobbe as maintaining unconditionally the duty of following the precedents set by an upper court.[3]

At various times and places in Germany statutes have been passed on this subject; some of the statutes direct that courts shall follow their own precedents, and others that decisions of the highest court shall be followed by the lower courts. An account of several of these statutes will be found in Stobbe;[4] and that practically *Gerichtsgebrauch* is having an increased influence on the development of German Law is shown by the increasing publication of decisions of the courts, which in England has gone on for hundreds of years, but in Germany began only in the latter part of the nineteenth century.

French Law

In France, as in Germany, it would seem that decisions of courts are not binding precedents, even on inferior courts. Collections of decisions have, however, been for a long time published in France and are cited by counsel and judges.[5]

Scotch Law

In Scotland the position assigned to Judicial Precedents appears to be intermediate between that occupied by them on the Continent and that to which they are raised

[1] *Loc. cit.* p. 207, *ante.*
[2] See 1 Stobbe, Handb. § 24, p. 144.
[3] See pp. 119-120, *ante.*
[4] 1 Handb. §24, pp. 144-146.
[5] Aubry et Rau, Cours de droit, §§ 39 *bis.*, 51, E; 1 Planiol, Traité élémentaire, §§ 205-206.

in England. The example of the courts, and indeed the whole tone of the Law, in England, may have had an influence in elevating the reliance on precedents, as it is now found in Scotland, beyond the condition in which we find it on the Continent; and the power given to the Court of Session to formally legislate by means of Acts of Sederunt, may have aided in giving weight to their expressed judgment in litigated cases.[1] On the other hand, the fact that the court of ultimate appeal, the House of Lords, was a tribunal composed entirely of English judges, for I believe no one was ever called from the Scotch bench or bar to the House of Lords until the Appellate Jurisdiction Act of 1876 (except Lord Colonsay in 1867) and the irritation which prevailed in Scotland over this state of affairs, has had probably considerable effect in maintaining the view that precedents do not make Law which seems to have prevailed in the earlier times.[2]

English Law

In England, and in the countries where the English Common Law prevails, a very different theory as to Judicial Precedents exists.

While on the Continent of Europe jurists have insisted and still insist that a decision by a court has, apart from its intrinsic merit, no binding force on a judicial tribunal, even on a tribunal from which an appeal lies to the court rendering the decision, it is Law in England and in the United States that, apart from its intrinsic merits, the decision of a court is of great weight in that court and all coördinate courts in the same jurisdiction, and that it is absolutely binding on all inferior courts.[3]

[1] P. 199, *ante*.
[2] See Erskine, Inst. Bk. I, tit. 1, § 47.
[3] Cf. p. 124, *ante*.

The cause of this distinction between the English and the Continental Law is one of the unsolved problems of Comparative Jurisprudence. Is it due to a difference in race, or in political organization, or to the presence on the Continent of the systematic body of the Roman Law? Apparently, there was originally in the English Law no special regard for Judicial Precedents. If there had been, there would be more traces to be found of it in the earlier treatises and reports.

Glanville, who was probably the real author of the *Tractatus de Legibus*, commonly attributed to him, died in 1190. There appears to be but one reference in his treatise to decisions of the courts.[1]

Bracton's treatise, *De Legibus et Consuetudinibus Angliæ,* was written in the middle of the thirteenth century. Bracton is an exception to what had gone before, and what came after, his time. He abounds in references to cases. But Mr. Maitland, in his remarkable book, has shown that, with trifling exceptions, the cases cited by Bracton were all decided at courts in which Martin Pateshull and William Raleigh were judges.[2] "His is a treatise on English law as administered by Pateshull and Raleigh."[3]

The exceptional character of Bracton is shown by the later history of the Law. Fleta, which was written towards the end of the thirteenth century, was largely drawn from Bracton, but in only one chapter does it, so far as I have observed, refer to particular decisions; in this chapter, which is the third of the second book, there are

[1] It will be found in Book VII, c. 1.

[2] 1 Maitland, Bracton's Notebook, 40, 45, 48, *et seq.*

[3] *Id.* § 60; and see Introduction to the Twelfth Volume of the Year Book Series of the Selden Society, p. xviii.

three cases as to the jurisdiction of the Steward of the King's Court when the King was out of England, two of them being in Gascony and one in Paris; the last being a decision of the French King's Council, that the King of England had jurisdiction over Ingelramus, caught in the English King's hotel with stolen goods; Ingelramus was tried before the Steward and *"suspensus in patibulo Sancti Germani de Pratis."* [1]

Britton also wrote about the close of the thirteenth century, and his treatise was in like manner taken to a great extent from Bracton, but there appears to be no reference whatever in it to any decision of the courts.

As to the two legal treatises of the fifteenth century: in Fortescue, *De Laudibus Legum Angliæ,* there is no reference to any decided case; and in the original text of Littleton's Treatise on Tenures, of seven hundred and forty-nine sections, some ten cases only are referred to.

The Year Books

The first of the long series of reports which have been printed begins in 1292.[2] Professor Maitland, the greatest historian whom the English Law has ever had, has shown, almost to demonstration, that the Year Books were not authoritative collections of cases to serve as precedents, but were the notebooks of students under the bar, apprentices, as they were called. What Professor Maitland says is so interesting that I will quote at length from his Introduction to the Third Volume of the Year Book Series of the Selden Society.[3]

"The term 'Law Reports' inevitably suggests to us books that are to be cited in court. It is true that our

[1] "Hanged on the gallows of St. Germain des Prés."
[2] Year Book 20 & 21 Edw. I. Rolls Series.
[3] P. ix *ad fin.*

modern reports serve more purposes than one. They have an educational value. Young men will read them in order to learn the law, and older men will read them in order to amplify their knowledge. Still on the whole we might say that to serve as 'authority,' to be the base of judgments and of 'opinions' that should forestall judgments, is in our own time the final cause of the report. Now when we turn to these earliest Year Books this final cause seems to fall far into the background and almost to vanish. If these books themselves prove anything, they prove that they are rarely, if ever, cited by counsel or justices. The voucher of a precedent is, to all appearance, an uncommon event. We shall hardly find more than a couple of instances in any one term; and when the voucher comes, it looks much more like a personal reminiscence than a reference to a book. It will begin with 'I saw,' or 'I remember,' or 'Don't you remember?' and when Chief Justice Beresford recalls a case in this way, the reporters do their best to write down the tale that he tells, for it is unknown to them but memorable. No contrast could be stronger than that which we find between these vague vouchers, if vouchers they may be called, and Bracton's precise citations of cases that stand upon the plea rolls. Having regard to what Bracton did, we may indeed say that already in his time the English common law showed a strong natural inclination to become the 'case law' that it ultimately became; but, free access to the records of the Court being impossible, a long period seems to elapse before this tendency can prevail." [1]

[1] See further Introductions to Sixth Volume of Year Book Series of the Selden Society, pp. ix-xxviii, xxxviii; to Seventh Volume, p. xxxi; and to Twelfth Volume, p. xviii.

And in a later place in the same Introduction, Professor Maitland adds.[1]

"And let us not explain this by saying that the men of the time could do no better. On the contrary, we must remember that the educated men of the time were great citators of 'authorities.' The medieval scholar, were he divine, philosopher, canonist, or civilian, could give you a text for everything, and a text that you could find without much labor if you had a copy of the book to which he referred."

I have gone down through the time covered by the Year Books,[2] taking the cases of a whole year at intervals of fifty years, and the result quite bears out the accuracy of Professor Maitland's statement as to the scarcity of the references of judicial decisions. In the later years they are slightly increased, but only slightly.[3]

Early reporters

Coming down a generation after the close of the Year Books, we find one of the most famous and accurate of reporters, and one of those who reports what passes in court at the greatest length, Plowden. Taking the first ten cases in his second part, we find they occupy seventy-four quarto folios, or, leaving out the pleadings, which Plowden gives at length, over fifty folios, or one hundred pages. An examination of the use of precedents shows that about thirty cases are cited and stated as authority by court or counsel.

It must be remarked that in other reporters of about the same period a somewhat larger number of references will be found, but, with every allowance, the contrast

[1] P. lx.

[2] See 9 Harvard Law Rev. 27, 36-38.

[3] See Introduction to Sixth Volume of the Year Book Series of the Selden Society, p. xxix.

between all or any of the earlier reporters and Lord Coke is enormous, for with Lord Coke the citation of cases reached a height which it has never equalled since. Opening in the middle of his reports, we find in the first twenty-five folios of the seventh volume two hundred and forty citations of cases, or sixteen times as many as in Plowden. And although English judges and lawyers of modern times are not so prolific in their citations as Lord Coke, the weight attached to precedents has not diminished since his time.

There are four questions under the English Law as to Precedents to consider:—

1. How great is the authority of a decision in the court which made it, or in a court of coördinate jurisdiction?
2. Is there any court which is absolutely bound by its own decisions?
3. Does a lower court ever decide in opposition to a higher court of appeal?
4. Can decisions of the courts be properly considered as sources of Law?

Decisions in same or coördinate court

First. It is impossible to answer the first question with precision; precedents, in the English Law, have *great* weight but they have not irresistible weight; decisions can, I mean can according to the theory of the English Law, be overruled or not followed. Any attempt at a more exact determination would simply be a theory of the particular writer as to what would be desirable rules, and not as to what rules do in fact actually govern. The best statement of the circumstances which add to or diminish the weight of precedents is to be found in Ram on Judgments. The fact that precedents in the English Law are to be *generally* but not *always* followed, and that no rules have been, or apparently ever can be, laid down to determine the matter precisely, shows how largely the Law in England is the creation of the judges, for they not only make precedents, but determine when the precedents shall be departed from.

House of Lords bound by its own decision

Second. The only English court which is absolutely bound by its own prior decision is the highest, the House of Lords.[1] No such doctrine governs, however, the Judicial Committee of the Privy Council, which is also for Colonial and certain other matters a court of ultimate appeal. Thus the decision that a colonial legislature had a Common Law power to punish contempts, which was made in *Beaumont* v. *Barrett*,[2] was overruled in *Kielley* v. *Carson*,[3] the same judge, Baron Parke, delivering the opinion in both cases.

The theory that the House of Lords is bound to follow its own precedents is not an ancient one. As late as 1760, in *Pelham* v. *Gregory*,[4] the House of Lords decided contrary to a previous decision of its own. But the prevailing view now seems to be that the House of Lords cannot depart from its own precedents in judicial matters.[5]

Decision in higher court

Third. Does a lower court in England ever decide in opposition to a precedent furnished by a court of appeal? Never, unless there has been an obvious blunder made by the upper court. I can recall but two instances in the

[1] See the author's article in 9 Harv. Law Rev. 27, 39. But see also Pollock, First Book of Jur. (3d ed.) 328-334.

[2] 1 Moore, P. C. 59 (1836).

[3] 4 Moore, P. C. 63 (1842); and see *Read* v. *Bishop of Lincoln*, [1892] A. C. 644, 654.

[4] 3 Bro. P. C. (Toml. ed.) 204.

[5] *London Street Tramways Co.* v. *County Council*, [1898] A. C. 375. In Peerage Cases, the House of Lords is not bound by its previous decisions. *St. John Peerage Claim*, [1915] A. C. 282, 308.

English books. The first is *Hensman* v. *Fryer,*[1] where the court of appeal held that legatees of sums of money and legatees of specific articles or pieces of land must contribute *pro rata* to the payment of a testator's debts, contrary to the well-settled rule that the legatees of money must bear the burden. The lower courts have repeatedly refused to follow this decision, saying that it was clearly a mistake. The other instance is a ruling of Lord Westbury, when Chancellor, in *Cookney* v. *Anderson,*[2] made in ignorance of a statute.

Are decisions sources of Law?

Fourth. Can decisions of the courts be properly considered as sources of Law? If the object of asking this question is to ascertain the fact, there can be but little doubt of the answer. Certainly the judges, in deciding cases, draw rules from precedents. They decide cases otherwise than they would have decided them had the precedents not existed, and they follow the precedents, although they may think that they ought not to have been made. Why has any question, therefore, been raised on this? It is because the judges have been unwilling to seem to be law-givers, because they have liked to say that they applied Law, but did not make it, while, if the decisions of courts were sources of Law, it could not be denied that the judges, to that extent, did make Law.[3]

Sir Matthew Hale, in his History of the Common Law, which was first published in 1713, after his death, says:—

"The decisions of courts of justice . . . do not make a law properly so called (for that only the King and Parlia-

[1] L. R. 2 Eq. 627; 3 Ch. 420 (1867).

[2] De G. J. & S. 365 (1863). See *Tompkins* v. *Colthurst,* 1 Ch. D. 626, and *Dugdale* v. *Dugdale,* L. R. 14 Eq. 234.

[3] See p. 99, *ante.*

ment can do); yet they have a great weight and authority in expounding, declaring and publishing what the law of this kingdom is. . . . And though such decisions are less than a law, yet they are a greater evidence thereof, than the opinion of any private persons, *as such,* whatsoever. . . . Because they [the judges] do *sedere pro tribunali,* and their judgments are strengthened and upheld by the laws of this kingdom, till they are by the same law reversed or avoided."[1]

But the classical passage is in Blackstone's Commentaries:—

Blackstone's theory

"As to general customs, or the common law, properly so called; this is that law, by which proceedings and determinations in the king's ordinary courts of justice are guided and directed. . . . How are these customs or maxims to be known, and by whom is their validity to be determined? The answer is, by the judges in the several courts of justice. They are the depositaries of the laws; the living oracles, who must decide in all cases of doubt, and who are bound by an oath to decide according to the law of the land. . . . These judicial decisions are the principal and the most authoritative evidence that can be given of the existence of such a custom as shall form a part of the common law. . . . For it is an established rule to abide by former precedents, where the same points come again in litigation; as well to keep the scale of justice even and steady, and not liable to waver with every new judge's opinion; as also because the law in that case being solemnly declared and determined, what before was uncertain, and perhaps indifferent, is now become a per-

[1] Hale, Hist. Com. Law (4th ed.) 67; (5th ed.) 141.

manent rule, which it is not in the breast of any subsequent judge to alter or vary from, according to his private sentiments, he being sworn to determine, not according to his own private judgment, but according to the known laws and customs of the land; not delegated to pronounce a new law, but to maintain and expound the old one. Yet this rule admits of exceptions where the former determination is most evidently contrary to reason; much more if it be clearly contrary to the divine law. But even in such cases the subsequent judges do not pretend to make a new law, but to vindicate the old one from misrepresentation. For if it be found that the former decision is manifestly absurd or unjust, it is declared, not that such a sentence was *bad law,* but that it was *not* law; that is, that it is not the established custom of the realm, as has been erroneously determined. . . . The doctrine of the law then is this: that precedents and rules must be followed, unless flatly absurd or unjust: for though their reason be not obvious at first view, yet we owe such a deference to former times as not to suppose they acted wholly without consideration. To illustrate this doctrine by examples. It has been determined, time out of mind, that a brother of the half blood shall never succeed as heir to the estate of his half brother, but it shall rather escheat to the king, or other superior lord. Now this is a positive law, fixed and established by custom, which custom is evidenced by judicial decisions; and therefore can never be departed from by any modern judge without a breach of his oath, and the law. For herein there is nothing repugnant to natural justice; though the artificial reason of it, drawn from the feodal law, may not be quite obvious to everybody. And therefore, though a modern judge, on account of a supposed hardship upon a half brother, might wish it had been otherwise settled, yet it is not in his power to alter it. But if any court were now to determine, that an elder brother of the half blood might enter upon and seize any land that were purchased by his younger brother, no subsequent judges would scruple to declare that such prior determination was unjust, was unreasonable, and therefore was *not law*. So that *the law* and the *opinion of the judge* are not always convertible terms, or one and the same thing; since it sometimes may happen that the judge may *mistake* the law. Upon the whole, however, we may take it as a general rule 'that the decisions of courts of justice are the evidence of what is common law': in the same manner as, in the civil law, what the emperor had once determined was to serve as a guide for the future." [1]

Blackstone's statement, in short, is this: The Common Law consists of general customs, but what these customs are must be known from the decisions of the courts; former precedents must be followed, a decision of a court makes what was before uncertain and indifferent a permanent rule, which subsequent judges must follow; but precedents are not absolutely binding, they can be disregarded when flatly absurd or unjust.

There seems little occasion to find fault with this statement, so far as it concerns the force and effect of precedents as a source of Law, but Blackstone's attempt to carry back further the source of Law into general cus-

[1] 1 Bl. Com. 68-71.

tom, and make the decisions only evidence of that custom, is unfortunate.

The notion that judicial decisions are only evidence of a preëxisting law was fallen foul of by Bentham;[1] but in Austin it found its most influential opponent. It may be questioned whether he has not devoted himself too exclusively to this part of Blackstone's remarks, and neglected the substantially accurate view of the force and effect of precedents which the commentator gives. Austin speaks of "the childish fiction employed by our judges, that judiciary or common law is not made by them, but is a miraculous something made by nobody, existing, I suppose, from eternity, and merely *declared* from time to time by the judges." [2]

Austin's views have met general acceptance.[3] But Blackstone has not wanted defenders. One of the latest attempts to rehabilitate him is by his editor, Professor Hammond. As perhaps the most serious attempt, it is worth while to examine it in detail. It is contained in a note to the passage of Blackstone quoted above.[4]

Professor Hammond begins by saying that "no passage of Blackstone has been the object of more criticism and even ridicule than this," and he refers to Austin, to Digby's History of the Law of Real Property, to Pomeroy's Municipal Law, and "to the swarms of minor writers who have held Blackstone up to ridicule in small books and legal periodicals." "Such writers," he goes on to say, "may not think themselves answered by the

[1] *E.g.* Benth. Works (1843), vol. 5, p. 546; vol. 6, p. 552.
[2] 2 Jur. (4th ed.) 655.
[3] See Holland, Jur. (11th ed.) 65.
[4] Hammond's ed. of Blackstone, pp. 213-226.

unbroken testimony of the judges themselves, who from the earliest Year-books to the latest reports of the highest courts have unanimously agreed that they neither made nor could make new law in deciding cases which come before them for adjudication." Though it is doubtless true that judges have often disclaimed the authority to make law, Professor Hammond's two citations are not felicitous. In *Abbot of Everwike* v. *Abbot of Selby,* 8 Edw. III. 69, pl. 35 (not 8 Edw. III. 6, pl. 35, fol. 327 as cited) Herle, J., speaking of a point as "law before we were born," says, "we *will* not change that law," which is certainly no proof that on a point not settled he could not make law. The other passage is a remark in 1304 by the same man (but not by the same judge, as stated by Professor Hammond, for he was not a judge till sixteen years later) in argument to the court: "The judgment to be by you now given will be hereafter an authority in every *quare non admisit* in England,"[1] which, so far as it goes, asserts that a decision of the judges does make Law.

The learned editor then goes on to say that the effect of the contradiction of Blackstone's doctrine "in making the rule of law identical with the mere point decided in the given case, and relieving the student or practitioner from any attempt to seek for underlying principles, will always make it popular with busy attorneys and students incapable of abstract thought." That is one way of putting the matter. Another way of putting it would be to say that the effect of Blackstone's doctrine in denying

[1] *Prior of Lewes* v. *Bishop of Ely,* Y. B. 32 Edw. I. (Horwood's ed.) p. 32. "*Quare non admisit*" is the title of a writ concerning church patronage.

to judicial decisions the effect of making law, and relieving the student or practitioner from any attempt to find out from them the law which they have made, will always make it popular with lazy attorneys and students too weak in intellect to grasp the real significance of facts. But perhaps remarks of this sort, on the one side or the other, do not tend to aid in the search for truth.

Historically Judges make Law

"The position of Austin and his followers rests upon a confusion between the historical and scientific aspect of that doctrine. Historically considered, it is true that our judges make law." Here Professor Hammond gives away his whole case. "Historically true," means really true, that a thing is a fact. To say that a thing is historically true but scientifically false means that it is a fact, but that it cannot be logically fitted into a certain system; and that is undoubtedly the case here. That judges make the Law is a fact, and it is true that this fact cannot be logically deduced from Blackstone's doctrine. Austin and his followers have said, "so much the worse for Blackstone's doctrine." Professor Hammond says, "so much the worse for the facts."

The learned editor then proceeds, in the strongest and most emphatic manner, to declare the law-making work of the judges. He says: "In the historical aspect of the system they have actually made new law." And then he spoils it all. "So it is in every science. We can trace historically the growth of creeds, the development of theological, philosophical, or scientific truths in the utterances of successive thinkers and students. No one infers from this that these men have made theological or scientific truth." But it is not true that we can trace historically the development of theological, philosophical, or scientific truths in the utterances of successive thinkers; what we can trace is the development of human knowledge and belief of those truths; but the truths themselves are entirely independent of human knowledge and belief, and therefore "no one infers from this that these men have made theological or scientific truth." Take the doctrine of Transubstantiation: the origin or growth or decline of belief in it has been doubtless dependent on the declarations of eminent men, but whether the doctrine is true, whether the mysterious change in the consecrated elements occurs, is independent of the opinion of Loyola or Luther or Zwingli. So the laws of light do not depend upon the ideas of Sir Isaac Newton or any other physicist with regard to them.

"We do not infer that philosophers make the laws of nature; how then can we infer that judges make the law of the land?" is what Professor Hammond says. Because philosophers do not make the laws of nature, but, as Professor Hammond has just said, judges do make "historically" the laws of the land. Because the laws of nature are independent of human opinion, while the Law of the land *is* human opinion. The heavenly bodies have been governed by the same laws after the birth of Ptolemy and Copernicus and Newton that they were before, but the English people have not been governed by the same Law since Lord Mansfield's time that they were before. His decisions have made that to be Law which was not Law before, and the Law of England since his time is different from what it would have been, had he been a man of a different cast of mind.[1]

[1] Compare the part of Lord Stowell in the creation of prize law. Roscoe's Life of Stowell, pp. 49-52.

Or, to take an instance from the Constitutional Law of the United States, suppose Chief Justice Marshall had been as ardent a Democrat (or Republican, as it was then called) as he was a Federalist. Suppose, instead of hating Thomas Jefferson and loving the United States Bank, he had hated the United States Bank and loved Thomas Jefferson,—how different would be the Law under which we are living to-day.

It is quite true, as Professor Hammond goes on to say, that the courts will sometimes refrain from making new law. No one has ever dreamed of denying that in their law-making power they are confined by statutes and by the decisions of their predecessors, and no one has ever thought the existence of such confining limits to be "a childish fiction," as the editor complains.

Consequences of Blackstone's theory

The examples which Professor Hammond employs to show the scientific soundness of Blackstone's theory, and the advantages of carrying it into practice, will hardly seem to most persons to have been happily selected. Suppose that A., in New York, makes a note payable in New York to the order of B.; that B., in New York, in fraud of A., transfers the note to C., as collateral security for a preëxisting debt; and that C. sues A. in New York. If C. is a citizen of New York, he will fail; if he is a citizen of New Hampshire, he can go into the Federal Court and succeed.

Again, suppose that A., living in Newport in the State of Rhode Island, gives property to B., to pay the income to C., A.'s son, for life, without any power of anticipation on C.'s part or any liability for his debts; and that C. makes a contract with D., a Newport butcher, to furnish him with meat, and then refuses to pay him. D.

gets a judgment in the Rhode Island courts against C. and tries to enforce it against the trust fund. If B. or C. are citizens of Rhode Island, D. can get paid for his meat, but if they are both citizens of New York, they can remove the case into the Federal Court, and C. can then, according to the *dictum* in *Nichols* v. *Eaton,*[1] cheat his creditor with impunity.

Now I am not here considering any practical advantages resulting from this state of things, nor how far it is the natural or necessary consequence of our complex form of government. But certainly, from a "scientific" point of view, nothing could be more shocking. It seems a recurrence to barbarism, to the time when Burgundians, Visigoths, and Romans, living beside each other, had their own separate and tribal laws.

And how did this state of things have its origin? Professor Hammond truly says that it was by *Story,* J., in *Swift* v. *Tyson,*[2] adopting the Blackstonian theory: "In the ordinary use of language it will hardly be contended that the decisions of Courts constitute laws." These particular consequences of Blackstone's theory are hardly such as to recommend the theory itself.

Municipal bond cases

But the Supreme Court of the United States has, since this state of things was established, been compelled, by what Professor Hammond would call the aspect of historical as against that of scientific truth—that is, by the stress of the real facts of life—to abandon the theory of Blackstone in a most important class of cases, those concerning municipal bonds. I do not undertake to establish the court's consistency, but it is interesting as an

[1] 91 U. S. 716.
[2] 16 Pet. 1, 18. See p. 251, *post*.

example of how an elaborate theory, sustained by great names, will break down when it is in irreconcilable conflict with facts.

In several of the United States, bonds were issued by towns and cities, generally in aid of railroads; the Supreme Courts of the States declared that the bonds were validly issued; on the faith of these decisions the bonds were sold: and then new judges were elected and the bonds were declared invalid. Blackstone's theory was urged with great force, that the decisions of the courts did not make Law; and that the Law must be taken to have been always what the latest decisions declared it to be. But the Supreme Court ruled otherwise, and has always held firmly to the doctrine that if a contract, when made, was valid by the Law as then laid down by the courts, its obligation could not be impaired by any subsequent decision. I will consider these cases more fully later.[1]

Professor Hammond then points out a supposed inconsistency in Austin, and his tacit adoption of Blackstone's views while criticizing Blackstone himself. Blackstone,[2] speaking of the rescripts of the Roman Emperors, and describing their character, says: "In like manner the canon laws, or decretal epistles of the popes, are all of them rescripts in the strictest sense. Contrary to all true forms of reasoning, they argue from particulars to generals." [3]

Austin, in his unmannerly fashion, adverts to this as

[1] P. 256, *post.*
[2] 1 Com. 59.
[3] Austin takes Blackstone as if speaking of the Emperor's *decreta* or judgments on appeals, and not of their rescripts or interlocutory advice (p. 203, *ante*), but for the argument this seems immaterial.

a foolish remark (and indeed it is not a very wise one, nor does Professor Hammond seek to defend it) and he goes on: "The truth is, that an imperial decrete of the kind to which Blackstone alludes is a judicial decision establishing a new principle. Consequently, the application of the new principle to the case wherein it is established is not the decision of a general by a particular, but the decision of a particular by a general. If he had said that the principle applied is a new principle, and, therefore, an *ex post facto* law with reference to that case, he would say truly. But the same objection (it is quite manifest) applies to our own precedents." [1]

Here, says Professor Hammond, is a logical fallacy, for in assuming that the principle established by the decision or decrete is a new one, Austin contradicts his own statement that the process is "the decision of a particular by a general," for, "if these latter words mean anything, it is that the principle must have existed before the decision, so that the decision may have been made by it."

But is this the meaning? Had it not been for the difficulty which so careful a reader and accurate a thinker as Professor Hammond appears to find, Austin's meaning I should have thought quite clear. What Austin says is this: These prayers for instructions were brought to the Emperors in cases where there was no existing Law which could guide the magistrate. It was necessary, therefore, to make a new Law, or the case would have been undecided, but instead of issuing a general *ex post facto* statute, the Emperor established a new prin-

[1] 2 Jur. (4th ed.) 654.

ciple in accordance with which the case ought to be decided, and directed a decision accordingly. Whether the Emperors always, in fact, acted in so logical and philosophical a manner may be reasonably doubted, but there appears to be no fallacy in Austin's reasoning.

Sense in which rule must exist before decision

In fact, Professor Hammond has, it would seem, confounded two things,—the order of the intellectual processes that go on in a judge's mind when a case is brought before him, and the succession of events outside of his mind. Suppose a matter is brought before the judge, for which, "as an historical fact," there is no Law, no rule for decision in existence; and disguise the matter as we will, such cases are not infrequent. If the judge is a sensible and conscientious man, he will not decide the case by rule of thumb, but will endeavor to establish a principle on which such cases ought to be decided, and then, having determined that principle, he will apply it to the case. But all this has no tendency to prove that, before the case was brought into court, there was a rule of law in existence governing the case; in fact, it distinctly negatives that view, and reduces it to a pure fiction, which it is.

"Plainly, his [Austin's] mistake is the common one of confounding the *principium essendi* and *principium cognoscendi.*"[1] May we not rather say that, plainly, his learned editor's mistake is to assume that, because a judge has decided a case in accordance with a general rule, the rule must have existed before the case came into court; and this mistake is strengthened, if not caused, by the misleading comparison with physical science, to which reference has been made.

[1] The existence of a thing and the fact of its being known.

Professor Hammond then sets up an adversary who says if the Law in question existed before the decision of the court, it must have existed from eternity. Over this foolish person Professor Hammond wins an easy victory. But if it be true, as it undoubtedly is, that the rule of Law on which a case is decided *may* have existed before the case comes before the court, and yet may not have existed for all time, that carries us very little way towards the proposition that the rule of Law on which a case is decided *must* have existed before the case itself.

Decisions often change the Law

"The doctrine of precedent, correctly stated, forbids the assumption that a new law was created by the prior decision—or that, in Austin's words, 'the imperial decrete established a *new* principle,' in the sense of creating a new law. If it did, and the present case arose under the law so created by the precedent, we should be deciding the later case by a different law from that under which the precedent arose." And so we are. Suppose it has been generally believed that an action will lie for verbal slander, but upon the case coming before the court of final appeal, they decide, perhaps by a majority of one, that it will not. Does not any later case come before a judge under a different state of the Law? Is a judge in the same position as he was before that decision? Is there not a new element introduced? How must the Law be the same, when there is now an element, all but necessarily conclusive, which there was not before? Professor Hammond declares we must not say that the Law is changed, because such change cannot be reconciled with the simplest rule of justice; but, say what we will, the fact is that there is a new controlling element introduced into the Law. One can understand a German jurist considering such a state of things as unjust, and therefore refusing to give any weight to Judicial Precedents, but how a Common Law lawyer, who regards the system of precedent with complacency, can suppose that he can turn injustice into justice by inventing a fiction is a remarkable instance of the power of conventional expressions.

"The falsity of Mr. Austin's theory results also from a correct statement of the true nature of judicial power"; and Professor Hammond goes on to show that courts are charged with executive duties; but this does not in the least tend to show that they may not also be charged with legislative duties, as indeed, in the case of their power to make rules for practice, is notoriously true.[1]

I do not understand that Professor Hammond thinks that any change ought to be made in the mode of administering justice; if the judges have cases come before them which present questions for whose decisions there are no rules, I do not understand that he would have the judges leave the cases undecided, or that he would have the decisions based on whim or instinct; but he deems it important that the judges should say, and that the people should believe, that the rules according to which the judges decide these cases had a previous existence. Whether it is desirable that such remarks should be made, or whether, if made, it is desirable that they should be believed, or whether it is desirable that the judges' power and practice of making Law should be concealed from themselves and the public by a form of words, is a matter into which I do not care to enter. The only thing I am concerned with is the fact. Do the judges make Law?

[1] P. 199, *ante*.

I conceive it to be clear that, under the Common Law system, they do make Law.[1]

Mr. Carter's theory

The opinions of another writer on the question of the law-making power of the judges, a writer whose opinions deserve to be treated with the highest respect, remain to be considered. Mr. James C. Carter published an article[2] on "The Ideal and the Actual in the Law," in which he maintained that the judges were the discoverers and not the makers of the Law. That excellent man has since gone to his rest, but there has lately been published a book entitled "Law, Its Origin, Growth and Function," which he had completed before his death,[3] and which contains his matured opinion on the subject.

Mr. Carter, at an earlier period of his life, was a strenuous opponent of the adoption by the State of New York of Mr. David Dudley Field's Civil Code. In his opposition he was successful. I suppose it was largely by his endeavors that the State was saved from the threatened danger. The remembrance of this great struggle was always in his mind, and was, I feel sure, the *raison d'être* of his essay and of his book, and has affected his whole point of view.

Judge-made Law and the Sovereign

The main thesis of Mr. Carter's essay is the erroneousness of the theory that all Law proceeds from the commands of the sovereign. He admits fully "that all the knowledge which we really have of the law comes from the judge,"[4] but he shrinks from saying that the judge makes Law, because he fears that this would recognize

[1] See Maine, Anc. Law (Pollock's ed.) 34-37, 46; Dicey, Law & Opinion (2d ed.) 491; and pp. 93-99, *ante*.
[2] 24 Am. Law Rev. 752.
[3] In 1905.
[4] 24 Am. Law Rev. 758.

the theory that all Law comes from the command of the sovereign.[1] If I shared the fear, I should be equally unwilling to use the expression that judges make Law. But is this objectionable result a consequence of holding that judges make Law?

What is meant by judges making Law? It is meant that a decision *suo vigore,* without regard to its agreement or disagreement with some ideal, is a source of Law; not the only, not necessarily the controlling, source of Law, but something which has an independent and not merely evidential value. To decide cases is the necessary function of a judge; it is of the essence of judgeship; but whether a judge can establish precedents or not is not of the essence of judgeship. In England judges have the power; in Germany, generally, they have not. The sovereign might interfere to give them the power, or to deny them the power, but generally he has not interfered, and therefore, if they have the power, it does not arise from the command of the sovereign (unless we adopt the theory of Austin that whatever the sovereign permits he commands, a theory which I am at one with Mr. Carter in disapproving), but whether decisions shall establish precedents is left to the free action of the judicial mind, affected by ideas of public policy, by popular custom, and by professional opinion. These motives, operating on the minds of English and American judges, have led them to recognize decisions of the courts as sources of the Law. Judges, then, may make Law, *i.e.* establish precedents, and yet such Law may not be the product of the sover-

[1] See pp. 85 *et seq. ante.*

eign's command, and therefore the dilemma which Mr. Carter feels does not, it seems to me, in truth exist.

In his essay Mr. Carter does not seem to regard the effect of a judicial decision as evidential. "Inquiry," he says, "is made by the judge concerning what his predecessors have done, and if he finds that a similar state of facts has been considered by them and the law pronounced in reference to it, he declares the same rule." But he says a judge rather *discovers* than makes the Law. The expression "discovered" throws light on the processes of the judicial mind. To speak of "making" the Law suggests an arbitrary will, while to speak of "discovering" it suggests the process of reason and reflection. Indeed Mr. Carter adopts the same view substantially as to the legislature, properly so-called. "Its liberty of action so far exceeds that of the judicial tribunals as to justify, for ordinary purposes, such a designation of its functions [*i.e.* making Law]; but the deeper and more philosophical view would assimilate its office more nearly to that performed by the judicial tribunals, namely, of affixing the public mark and authentication upon customs and rules already existing, or struggling into existence, in the habits of the people." [1] But while I recognize the reason which led Mr. Carter to use the word "discover," and also the fact that the word "make" may, although improperly, carry with it a suggestion of arbitrariness, I must yet regret Mr. Carter's substitution of the term "discovery" as misleading.

Law as created by custom

But, in his posthumous treatise, Mr. Carter has pressed the idea of the evidential character of precedents farther than in his essay. The theory of his book seems to be

[1] 24 Am. Law Rev. 766.

that the Law is created by custom; that when the judges declare the Law, they are declaring that to be Law which already existed; and that the declaration is only evidence, though a high kind of evidence, of the Law. If this be his matured opinion, and I think it is, I must say, with all diffidence, I cannot agree with him. *Amicus Plato, sed magis amica veritas.*

I have already several times tried to point out the difference between a discoverer in the fields of physical science and a judge. A discoverer in chemistry does not make the natural law which he discovers. Water was composed of oxygen and hydrogen before its composition was discovered,—the discovery in no way affected the natural law; the existence of the natural law was entirely independent of human opinion,—but the Law of the land is made up of human opinion. Expressions of human opinion are its sources, and an important class of those expressions of opinions are the declarations of the judges.

It is very easy to weave plausible general theories, but there is only one test of their correctness. Do they agree with the facts? I have constantly endeavored, in these lectures, to apply that test, the only conclusive test, and to determine whether a theory is true by seeing how it fits the facts of a concrete case. Let us apply that test here.

Often no custom before decisions

In the year 1620, the court of King's Bench decided the famous case of *Pells* v. *Brown.*[1] It was this: Land was devised to Thomas Brown and his heirs, but if he died without issue in the lifetime of his brother William, the land was to go to William and his heirs; that is, Thomas

[1] Cro. Jac. 590.

took an estate in fee simple, with an executory devise, as it is called, over to William, in case Thomas should die in the lifetime of William without issue. Thomas parted with the land by a conveyance known as a common recovery,[1] and the question was whether Edward Pells, who claimed the land under this conveyance, held it subject to the executory devise to William or free from it, or, in other words, whether an executory devise after a fee simple is destructible by the holder of the fee.

The court, by three judges to one, decided that the executory devise continued, that Pells took the land subject to it, that Thomas could not destroy it; and so the Law has been held ever since. Therefore, in England and America, future contingent interests can be validly created by will. This is by no means a necessary state of things. In Germany, in France, in Louisiana, and generally, I believe, where the Civil Law prevails, future contingent interests are allowed, if at all, only to a very limited extent.[2]

Mr. Carter, I understand, would say that this doctrine as to the validity of future interests was created by custom, and was Law before the case of *Pells* v. *Brown*. Now, what is custom? Custom is what is generally practiced in a community and believed by the community generally to be a proper practice.

Now is it conceivable that in England, at the beginning of the seventeenth century, a belief was prevalent in the community that an executory devise could not be destroyed by a common recovery with a single voucher?

[1] A "common recovery" was a collusive suit at law, highly technical in its procedure, which was used as a means of conveying land. 2 Bl. Com. 357-364, 533.

[2] Gray, Rule against Perpetuities, §§ 753-772.

Why, there was not one man in England out of ten thousand, not one out of fifty thousand, who had any belief upon the question, or who would even have understood what it meant. To say that there was a custom that future contingent interests were indestructible is a baseless dream, invented only to avoid the necessity of saying that judges make Law.

But, further, before the decision in *Pells* v. *Brown,* so far was there from being a general opinion in the community that executory devises were indestructible, there was no such opinion among the judges. One judge of the four, as I have said, dissented, and the decision was far from meeting a favorable reception among the judicial brethren. In *Scattergood* v. *Edge,*[1] *Powell,* J., said that the notion that an executory devise was not barred by a recovery "went down with the judges like chopped hay"; and *Treby,* C. J., said, "These executory devises had not been long countenanced when the judges repented them; and if it were to be done again, it would never prevail"; and stronger statements were made by Latch, as counsel in *Gay* v. *Gay.*[2] But the point having been decided by the court in favor of executory devises, the Law has stood so ever since.

How, in the face of all this, is it possible to say that the judges in *Pells* v. *Brown* only declared Law which custom had previously created, or, to use an expression of which Mr. Carter is very fond, that the fair expectation of the community was that a doctrine should have in its favor three judges out of four, instead of one out of four? It is possible to make such a statement, but

[1] 12 Modern, 278.
[2] Styles, 258. See Gray, Rule against Perpetuities, § 159.

what support has it in the real facts? If Law was ever made by any one, Montagu, C. J., and Chamberlayne and Houghton, JJ., made Law.

It is hard to overestimate the importance of the Law which these three men made. It lies at the root of the Law of future interests. Millions upon millions, probably billions upon billions, of property have gone to persons to whom they would not have gone, if two of the judges of the majority had agreed with their brother Doderidge.

And this is only one case out of thousands where the Law stands as it does to-day upon the opinions of individuals in judicial position on matters as to which there was no general practice, no custom, no belief, no expectation in the community.

Part played by individual Judges

It has been a matter greatly disputed, how much or how little part is played in the development of human affairs by individuals. It is contended that the *Zeitgeist*, or the great underlying forces and instincts of human nature, will have their way without regard to, and in spite of, the acts of individuals; that such acts are but ripples upon the mighty stream of time. I do not deny that there is truth in this. It may be that the ultimate goal of human experience will be the same as if Cæsar or Napoleon or Mahomet had never existed. That may be true of the ultimate goal; but the road by which humanity, through long periods of its history, will travel towards its goal is largely determined by the beliefs, the opinions, the acts, of great men.

And not of great men alone; very small men may produce great results; it was a very small man who murdered Henry IV, a very small man who murdered President Lincoln. Especially is this true if a small man happens to be put in a great place. I know no reason to suppose that Montagu, C. J. and Chamberlayne and Houghton, JJ. were in any way great men, but the fact that they said one thing rather than another has seriously affected the course of human affairs in an important department of the Law.

CHAPTER X

JUDICIAL PRECEDENTS IN THE UNITED STATES

Turning now from the doctrine as to Judicial Precedents in the Common Law in general, let us see what modifications, if any, that doctrine has received in the United States. Besides the four points as to the English Common Law discussed in the last chapter, a question arises in the United States with reference to the weight in one of the States of decisions made by the Federal courts or the courts of another State or of England; so that we have now to consider five matters in the Law of the United States:—

1. How great is the authority of a decision in the court which made it, or in a court of coördinate jurisdiction?
2. Is there any court which is absolutely bound by its own decisions?
3. Does a lower court ever decide in opposition to a higher court of appeal?
4. What is the weight in the courts of one jurisdiction of decisions made in the courts of another jurisdiction?
5. Can decisions of the courts be considered as sources of Law?

Decision in same or coördinate court

First. The general rule and practice as to the authority of a decision in the court which made it, or in a court of coördinate jurisdiction, is substantially the same in the United States as in England. Naturally, owing to the character of the people and of the institutions, the weight attached to Judicial Precedents is somewhat greater in England than in America, but the difference hardly admits of any precise statement, and it does not seem worth while to attempt it. The peculiar position of the State and Federal courts towards each other will be discussed farther on.

No court bound absolutely by its own decision

Second. Is there any court in the United States which is absolutely bound by its own decisions? We have seen that the House of Lords will not overrule its own prior decision, but will leave the matter with the legislature.[1] No such doctrine prevails in America; the highest courts in the respective States and the Supreme Court of the United States all consider that they have the power, however inexpedient it may be to exercise it, to depart from their former rulings.

Thus, the Supreme Court of the United States has overruled its previous decisions in matters of the greatest importance. In 1825, the court decided that the Admiralty Jurisdiction did not extend to the great rivers above the ebb and flow of the time,[2] and reaffirmed the doctrine in 1837.[3] But in 1851 it overruled these cases and held that the Admiralty Jurisdiction extends over navigable rivers.[4] Again, in 1870, that court held the Legal Tender Act to be unconstitutional.[5] The judges stood five to three. One of the majority resigned, and two new judges were appointed; the question was again brought up in another case, and the court, in 1871, over-

[1] P. 217, *ante*.
[2] *The Thomas Jefferson*, 10 Wheat. 428.
[3] *The Orleans*, 11 Pet. 175.
[4] *The Genesee Chief*, 12 How. 443.
[5] *Hepburn* v. *Griswold*, 8 Wall. 603.

ruled its former decision, the two new judges uniting with the previous minority of three, and turning it into a majority of five.[1] Great feeling prevailed in some quarters as to the supposed mode in which this change had been brought about; but the power of the court was not questioned.

Decision in higher court

Third. The same rule as to the duty of a lower court to follow a precedent established by a higher court prevails in America as in England. It has been said in the United States that a judgment made by an equally divided court, though conclusive in the particular case, should have no weight attached to it as a precedent.[2]

Decision in another State

Fourth. In any one of the United States, the decisions of the courts of another State are recognized as determining the Law of such other State, according to the general doctrine of the Common Law. As to their authority in the former State on its own Law, it does not seem that they can properly have a greater weight than the opinions of equally learned non-judicial persons who have had the same advantages and same motives for arriving at a just conclusion.

In one way, indirectly, they do carry a greater weight; they have authority as settling the Law for the States in which they are made, and it is a reason, and a strong reason, why Law should be established in a State in a certain way that it is settled in the other States in the same way.

Another interesting point arises from the fact that, in several States, for instance, Maine and West Virginia,

[1] *Legal Tender Cases,* 12 Wall. 457.

[2] See *Bridge* v. *Johnson,* 5 Wend. 342, 372; *People* v. *Mayor of New York,* 25 Wend. 252, 256; *Etting* v. *Bank of United States,* 11 Wheat. 59, 78.

the systems of Law are derived from another State, of which each formed originally a part. In such a case, the decisions of the courts of the parent State, made before the separation, continue to have the same force in the new State that they had in the old.

English decisions

The question as to the authority of English decisions in the United States is more difficult. There are three periods to be considered: the period before the planting of the American Colonies; the period between the planting of the Colonies and the Revolution; the period subsequent to the Revolution.

As to the decisions made before the establishment of the English Colonies in America, there seems to be little doubt that, in the absence of legislation to the contrary, they must be considered as Judicial Precedents. It is true that only so much of the English Law as was applicable to the altered conditions of life was adopted here. This doctrine, which is generally approved, leaves a wide door for judicial discretion to abrogate or alter the Common Law, but does not affect this part of the Law more than any other, the Statute Law, for instance.[1]

It is clear that the decisions of the English courts since the Revolution cannot strictly have any weight in the United States as precedents, although they still have a value, as showing the opinion of learned men as to what the Law was, or ought to be.

In the intervening period between the settlement of the country and the Revolution, there lay, in general, no appeal to the English courts, nor to any tribunal having a control at the same time over the English and the

[1] P. 196, *ante*.

Colonial courts, and it seems, therefore, that the decisions of the English courts during this period were strictly not precedents, but were admissible only upon the grounds just stated for considering decisions of the English courts subsequent to the Revolution.

The practical difference, however, between the state of things which existed from the early part of the seventeenth century to the Revolution, and that which would have existed had the American Colonies been subject to the jurisdiction of the English courts, is, so far as concerns the matter in question, but slight. The deference felt for the learning and abilities of the English judges was so great, and the value attached to their opinions on matters of Law so high, even after the Revolution, that they would have carried but little more weight had they been true precedents.

Since the beginning of the last century, however, this has gradually ceased; the judgments of the English courts are regarded with less awe, and the courts in America do not hesitate to depart from their rulings.[1] In some opin-

[1] However excessive may have been the deference paid to English authority by courts and lawyers in some parts of the country, there was an exhibition of the contrary feeling in other places, at times when political feeling against England was high. The Kentucky Legislature, in 1808, enacted "That all reports and books containing adjudged cases in the Kingdom of Great Britain, which decisions have taken place since the 4th day of July 1776, shall not be read nor considered as authority in any of the courts of this Commonwealth, any usage or custom to the contrary notwithstanding." Morehead & Brown's Stats. 613. The attempt was made in the legislature to prohibit reference to English decisions of any date. Schurz, Life of Henry Clay, vol. 1, p. 49. There were similar statutes in Pennsylvania and New Jersey. Loyd, Early Courts of Penna. 150; Professor Pound, 48 Am. Law Rev. 676, 680. See Sullivan, Land Titles in Massachusetts, 337. In the same year in which this Kentucky statute was passed, the case of *Hickman* v. *Boffman* (Hard. 348, 364) came before the Court of Appeals. Counsel offered to read from 3 East part of an opinion which recapitu-

ions in the United States the judges strive to show that a doctrine which they disapprove has come into the English Law since the Revolution, but the true question would seem to be: Has it come in since the founding of the Colonies?

lated the adjudged cases. The Chief Justice stopped him. Counsel urged that they did not reply upon the opinion, that they only used the book to show what other books contained, and that the legislature had no more power to pass the statute than they would have to prohibit a judge the use of his spectacles. But the court said: "The book must not be used at all in court;" and a like decision was made later in the same year. *Gallatin* v. *Bradford*, Hard. 365 *n*. In 1821 the Kentucky court began to show a disposition to evade, if not to disregard the statute. In *Noble* v. *Bank of Kentucky* (3 A. K. Marsh. 262, 264), Boyle, C. J., said: "The use of English post-revolutionary cases in the courts of this country having been proscribed by the legislature, we can avail ourselves of the light those cases have shed upon the point now in controversy only through the medium of the elementary treatises upon the subject." He then referred to a late edition of Chitty on Bills as containing decisions in point, and added: "We do not suppose that this rule ought to be received here, merely because it is the established rule in England; but we apprehend the rule is intrinsically proper; and it is certainly no slight confirmation of its intrinsic propriety that it has been sanctioned by the enlightened tribunals of the most commercial country in the world." In the same year the court appear openly to neglect the Statute by quoting "an able opinion" of Lord Redesdale, salving their conscience, perhaps, by omitting to give the place where the opinion can be found. *Reed* v. *Bullock*, Lit. Sel. Cas. 510, 512. But in 1823, Mr. Littell, the reporter, in the preface to the first volume of his reports, although he speaks of the statute with contempt, says that it has been "very generally acquiesced in." Gradually, however, it came to be generally disregarded: thus, for instance, in the 12th volume of B. Monroe's reports, containing cases decided in 1851, the year before the Revised Statutes, there are a dozen or more references by name and place made by the court itself to post-revolutionary decisions in England, although reference to cases of all kinds are rather sparse. Indeed this Kentucky statute seems the nearest approach in a Common Law country to a Statute abrogated by desuetude. See Dembitz, Kentucky Jurisprudence, 7, 8. In the Revised Statutes of Kentucky adopted in 1852 we find the provision in an emasculated form: "The decisions of the courts of Great Britain, rendered since the fourth day of July, one thousand seven hundred and seventy six, shall not be of binding authority in the courts of Kentucky, but may be read in court and have such weight as the judges may think proper to give them." C. 61, § 1.

A highly respectable writer has asserted that the decisions of the English courts were binding precedents down to the Revolution: "While colonization continued—that is to say, until the war of the Revolution actually commenced,—these decisions were authority in the Colonies, and the changes made in the common law up to the same period were operative in America also if suited to the condition of things here." [1] But the only support to the doctrine appears to be a *dictum* of Chief Justice Marshall. In the case of *Cathcart* v. *Robinson,*[2] Cathcart, having made a voluntary conveyance to his wife, made a subsequent conveyance to Robinson. The Supreme Court found the conveyance to the wife to be actually fraudulent. It was, therefore, unnecessary for it to consider whether the English doctrine, that a later conveyance absolutely avoids a former voluntary conveyance, without actual fraud, was Law. The Chief Justice says that at the time of the Revolution this doctrine seems to have been settled, and that later decisions go too far and ought not to be followed. "The received construction in England at the time they [British Statutes] are admitted to operate in this country, indeed to the time of our separation from the British Empire, may very properly be considered as accompanying the statutes themselves, and forming an integral part of them. But, however we may respect subsequent decisions, and certainly they are entitled to great respect, we do not admit their absolute authority." I am aware of no case where a court has felt itself bound to decide against its own opinion by

[1] Cooley, Const. Lim. (7th ed.) 53.
[2] 5 Pet. 263, 279 *et seq.*

reason of an English judgment given between the colonization and the Revolution.[1]

Decisions as sources of Law: Federal and State courts

Fifth. Are decisions of the courts to be properly considered in the United States as sources of Law? Whether decisions are to be considered as true sources of Law, or whether they are only evidence of what the Law is, is a question which the relations of the Federal to the State courts have brought to the front as a practical matter, by the discussions upon the weight to be attributed by the Federal tribunals to the decisions of the State courts. The discussion has taken place principally in controversies between citizens of different States in which the Federal courts have jurisdiction concurrent with that of the State courts.

The Federal and State courts are the judicial organs of different political communities, and they are subject to the statutes passed by the legislatures of the communities of which they are respectively the organs; and if Congress should pass statutes for the conduct of the Federal courts which were in conflict with those of any or of all the States,—for instance, that writing should not be a necessary requisite to the validity or enforcement of any contract,—it may be that a State Statute of Frauds would not be a defence to an oral contract, say, for the sale of land, in any Federal tribunal. There seems to be nothing in the express language of the Constitution to forbid such a statute. And in all matters of procedure and evidence the Laws of the States have been dealt with by Congress at their pleasure. For instance, procedure in

[1] On the whole subject of adoption of the English Common Law, and the authority of English decisions in the U. S., see articles by Professor Pope, in 24 Harvard Law Rev. 6; and Professor Reinsch, in Select Essays in Anglo-American Legal History, 367.

equity is the same in all the Federal courts, whatever be the practice of the courts of those States in which the Federal tribunals sit.[1]

But in the absence of Congressional legislation to the contrary, the position of the Federal courts would seem to be this: Those courts are not (with the exception of the Supreme Court in a few cases) courts of appeal from the State courts. They are courts substituted in certain cases for the ordinary State courts. They are coördinate with the State courts. The Federal and State courts are independent, with no common superior; they derive their authority from different political bodies.

The Federal courts were constituted, not to avoid the danger of the State courts laying down improper rules, but to avoid the danger of the State courts applying their rules unfairly to the advantage of their own citizens. As both classes of courts are exercising their functions in the same territory, it is desirable that they should apply the same rules, that is, the same Law; and since the Federal jurisdiction is of an exceptional character, it would also seem desirable that the Federal courts should draw their rules from the same sources from which the State courts draw theirs, namely, from the statutes of the State legislatures and the decisions of the State courts. Such would seem to have been the right position of the Federal courts, even in the absence of special legislation by Congress on the subject.

Congress has legislated, but its legislation has been

[1] Whether the doctrine that the limits of equity jurisdiction have been fixed by Congress and that no State legislature can change them, was really called for by any Act of Congress, and, if it was, whether the doctrine has been applied consistently by the Supreme Court, is not a matter of inquiry here.

confirmatory of this position. In the formation of the Constitution and its ratification by the States, the powers of the Judiciary attracted comparatively little attention, and that little was mostly directed to supposed dangers which have since shown themselves chimerical; but by the Judiciary Act, U.S. St. 1789, *c.* 20, § 34, it was enacted that "the laws of the several states, except where the Constitution, treaties or statutes of the United States shall otherwise require or provide, shall be regarded as rules of decision in trials at common law in the courts of the United States in cases where they apply." Procedure in cases, civil and criminal, has been dealt with, as I have said, by later Acts of Congress, but the section cited has remained, without addition or alteration, the only statute touching the substantive Law on this point.

The question obviously presented by Sec. 34 of the Judiciary Act was the meaning of "the laws" of a State. Did it mean the body of rules which the State courts applied in deciding cases, or was its meaning limited to the statutes of the State? To use the German expression, did it mean *Recht* or *Gesetze?* The difference between "*the* Law," which generally means the body of rules, and "*a* law," which generally means a statute, has been noted.[1] The term here, "the laws," is ambiguous, and lends itself to either construction.

That the Congress which passed the Judiciary Act intended to limit "the laws" to statutes, seems very improbable; if for no other reason, because in many of the States the statute Law was so meagre; and for the first fifty years of the Government no such limitation was

[1] See p. 87, *ante.*

put on the expression "the laws" by the Supreme Court of the United States. In no case did that court sanction a refusal by a Federal court to follow a rule laid down by the State courts. It is to be observed, however, that the only cases during this period which came before the Supreme Court where any question as to following the decisions of a State court was presented, were cases concerning land or involving the interpretation of a State constitution or statute.

Swift v. Tyson

In the year 1842, the case of *Swift* v. *Tyson*[1] came before the Supreme Court. It was a suit against the acceptor of a bill of exchange, which had been accepted in New York. The plaintiff had taken the bill in payment of a preëxisting debt, and the question was whether he was to be considered a purchaser for value. Judge Story, who delivered the opinion of the court, after speaking of the decisions of the New York State courts as not being clear in favor of the defendant, went on to say that, "admitting the doctrine to be fully settled in New York," it would not bind the Supreme Court of the United States; and that Sec. 34 of the Judiciary Act was strictly limited to local statutes and local usages, and did not extend to contracts and other instruments of a commercial character.

The doctrine of *Swift* v. *Tyson* has not only been maintained by the Supreme Court, but it has been extended, though with many vacillations, from "general commercial Law," through "rules of Common Law," and "general Law," to "general Jurisprudence"; and that there is a distinction in the treatment of the decisions of State courts

[1] 16 Pet. 1.

in Federal tribunals, that some will be followed and some not, is now too firmly settled to be shaken; but it is not easy to draw the line, and I believe that, except on one occasion, the Supreme Court has not, since *Swift* v. *Tyson,* given any reason for the distinction, or undertaken to justify it. It has said *sic volo, sic jubeo,* and that is the end of it.

The sole exception is in *Baltimore & Ohio Railroad Co.* v. *Baugh.*[1] It was there held that liability for injury, in Ohio, to the fireman of a locomotive engine by the carelessness of the engine-driver, was to be determined by the "general Law," contrary to the Law laid down by the Ohio courts. The Supreme Court here, for the first and only time, gives reasons for following and extending the doctrine of *Swift* v. *Tyson.* Those reasons are two: *First.* That, notwithstanding *Swift* v. *Tyson,* Congress has never altered Sec. 34 of the Judiciary Act. *Second.* The second reason is stated in the form of a question: "If to a train running from Baltimore to Chicago it [the Railroad Company] should, within the limits of the State of Ohio, attach a car for a distance only within that State, ought the law controlling the relation of a brakeman on that car to the company to be different from that subsisting between the brakemen on the through cars and the company?"[2] The answer to this last question would seem to be another question. "Ought the Law controlling the relation of a brakeman on a car to the Company to be different from the Law controlling the relation of another brakeman on the same car to the

[1] 149 U.S. 368 (1892).
[2] P. 378.

Company, because one has his domicil in Pennsylvania and the other in Ohio?"

Mr. Justice Field was unwilling to carry the burden of *Swift* v. *Tyson* any longer, and confessed openly, "*mea culpa, mea maxima culpa.*" In his dissenting opinion, he declared that *Swift* v. *Tyson* was indefensible from the beginning. He says: "I am aware that what had been termed the general law of the country—which is often little less than what the judge advancing the doctrine thinks at the time should be the general law on a particular subject—has been often advanced in judicial opinions of this court to control a conflicting law of a State. I admit that learned judges have fallen into the habit of repeating this doctrine as a convenient mode of brushing aside the law of a State in conflict with their views. And I confess that, moved and governed by the authority of the great names of those judges, I have, myself, in many instances, unhesitatingly and confidently, but I think now erroneously, repeated the same doctrine."[1]

Among the causes which led to the decision in *Swift* v. *Tyson,* the chief seems to have been the character and position of Judge Story. He was then by far the oldest judge in commission on the bench; he was a man of great learning, and of reputation for learning greater even than the learning itself; he was occupied at the time in writing a book on bills of exchange, which would, of itself, lead him to dogmatize on the subject; he had had great success in extending the jurisdiction of the Admiralty; he was fond of glittering generalities; and he was possessed by a restless vanity. All these things conspired to produce the result.

[1] P. 401.

Swift v. *Tyson* inconsistent with any theory

The judgment in *Swift* v. *Tyson* seems at first view to have its root in the Blackstonian theory, which I have previously discussed, that judicial decisions are not sources of the Law,[1] and, indeed, Judge Story says: "In the ordinary use of language it will hardly be contended that the decisions of Courts constitute laws. They are, at most, only evidence of what the laws are; and are not of themselves laws." But, in truth, *Swift* v. *Tyson* seems impossible to reconcile with this theory.

Suppose the English High Court should adopt an interpretation of an Act of Parliament; that interpretation would be adopted by all the lower courts, and would be enforced by the executive authority; it would be the Law in England. Suppose the High Court should announce a rule of non-statutory commercial Law; that rule would be followed by all the lower courts; it would be enforced by the executive authority; it would be the Law in England. If the Supreme Court of the United States had to pass upon a case involving that statute, or upon a case on a contract made in England involving that general rule of non-statutory commercial Law, they would look in precisely the same manner, in the one case as in the other, to the decisions of the High Court to determine the Law of England.

Suppose, however, that the Court of Appeals in New York should adopt an interpretation of a New York statute or a rule regarding the creation of easements; such a decision would be followed by all the lower courts of the State, and would be enforced by its executive authority; it would be the Law in New York. And sup-

[1] P. 219, *ante*.

pose, again, that it should announce distinctly a rule of non-statutory commercial Law; such a decision would be followed by all the lower courts of the State, and would be enforced by its executive authority; it would be the Law in New York. But if the Supreme Court of the United States had to pass upon a case involving a New York statute or the creation of easements in New York, it would follow the decisions of the Court of Appeals of New York, while if called upon to pass upon a case arising in New York under the non-statutory commercial Law, it would not follow the State decisions.

If "the laws of a State" in the 34th section of the Judiciary Act mean its statutes only, then the decisions of the State courts should stand alike, and none of them should have the binding weight that is now given to some of them. If, on the other hand, "the laws" are to include "decisions," the Judiciary Act would allow no difference between them and statutes. On the general question, therefore, whether decisions are sources of the Law, the doctrine of the Supreme Court of the United States in *Swift* v. *Tyson* throws no light. If they are sources of Law, they should be followed even when dealing with non-statutory commercial matters. If they are not, then they are not binding when dealing with real estate or the construction of statutes. The doctrine of *Swift* v. *Tyson* is an anomaly, and does not lend a support to either theory.

The language of the Supreme Court varies. When the court wishes to depart from the State decisions, it says, with Judge Story, that the decisions of courts "are, at most, only evidence of what the laws are, and are not of themselves laws." On the other hand, when the court is about to follow the decision of the State court, it says: "Inasmuch as the States have committed to their respective judiciaries the power to construe and fix the meaning of the statutes passed by their legislatures, this court has taken such constructions as part of the law of the State."[1] Decisions of the State courts have "a binding force almost equivalent to positive Law."[2] The interpretation of the land Laws of a State "becomes a part of the law of that State, as much so as if incorporated into the body of it by the legislature."[3]

Municipal bond cases

But while the practice of the Supreme Court of the United States on questions like that raised in the case of *Swift* v. *Tyson* is anomalous, and is inconsistent alike with the theory that decisions of courts make the Law, and with the theory that they are only evidence of the Law, there is a series of cases in that court of the greatest importance, which must find their support in the former theory. These cases are of the following character: The courts of a State have declared that a certain class of contracts is valid, a contract of the class is subsequently entered into, but, after the making of the contract, the State courts reverse their decisions and hold that such contracts are invalid. Here, if the decisions are simply evidence of the Law, the Law, as declared by the courts in the later cases, must be considered to have been the Law from the beginning, and the contract to have been void at its inception; if, on the other hand, decisions make the Law, then the contract was good when made. The

[1] *Carroll* v. *Carroll*, 16 How. 275, 286.
[2] *League* v. *Egery*, 24 How. 264, 267.
[3] *Christy* v. *Pridgeon*, 4 Wall. 196, 203.

Supreme Court, in these cases, has thrown over fiction, has insisted upon looking at the truth of the case, and has held such a contract valid.[1]

In 1853, Chief Justice Taney said,[2] "The sound and true rule is, that if the contract when made was valid by the laws of the State, as then expounded by all departments of its government, and administered in its courts of justice, its validity and obligation cannot be impaired by any subsequent act of the legislature of the State, or decision of its courts, altering the construction of the law."

In the great case of *Gelpcke* v. *Dubuque* [3] it appeared that the Supreme Court of Iowa had repeatedly decided that municipal corporations had the constitutional power to issue bonds; that subsequently the City of Dubuque had issued bonds; but that afterwards the Supreme Court of Iowa had, in a very elaborate opinion, overruled its former decisions. The Supreme Court of the United States held the bonds good. The opinion of the majority, delivered by Swayne, J., is singularly feeble both in form and substance, while the dissenting opinion of Miller, J., is masterly. But it is not an uncommon phenomenon for minority opinions to be far superior in force to those of the majority, and yet for the doctrine of the majority to be right, and in the end to prevail.

Mr. Justice Miller said: "I understand the doctrine to be in such cases, not that the law is changed, but that it was always the same as expounded by the later deci-

[1] See Holmes, J., in *Kuhn* v. *Fairmount Coal Co.*, 215 U.S. 349, 371.
[2] *Ohio Ins. Co.* v. *Debolt*, 16 How. 416, 432.
[3] 1 Wall. 175 (1864).

sion, and that the former decision was not, and never had been, the law, and is overruled for that very reason. The decision of this court contravenes this principle, and holds that the decision of the court makes the law, and in fact, that the same Statute or Constitution means one thing in 1853, and another thing in 1859."[1] That is exactly so. The majority opinion did necessarily mean that the courts make and change the Law, and because the majority recognized this, though dimly, it was right and has prevailed.[2]

In *Douglass* v. *County of Pike,*[3] in 1880, the language of the Supreme Court became firmer.

"The true rule is to give a change of judicial construction in respect to a statute the same effect in its operation on contracts and existing contract rights that would be given to a legislative amendment; that is to say, make it prospective, but not retroactive. After a statute has been settled by judicial construction, the construction becomes, so far as contract rights acquired under it are concerned, as much a part of the statute as the text itself, and a change of decisions is to all intents and purposes the same in its effect on contracts as an amendment of the law by means of a legislative enactment. . . . The new decisions would be binding in respect to all issues of bonds after they were made; but we cannot give them a retroactive effect without impairing the obligation of contracts long

[1] P. 211.

[2] See *Havemeyer* v. *Iowa County,* 3 Wall. 294 (1886); *Thompson* v. *Lee, Id.* 327; *Mitchell* v. *Burlington,* 4 Wall. 270 (1867); *Lee County* v. *Rogers.* 7 Wall. 181 (1869); *City* v. *Lamson,* 9 Wall. 477 (1870).

[3] 101 U.S. 677.

before entered into. This we feel ourselves prohibited by the Constitution of the United States from doing."[1]

If, after a State court has decided that certain contracts are valid, a contract of the kind is made, suit is brought on it, and the court reverses its former ruling and holds the contract invalid, no appeal lies to the Supreme Court of the United States. This seems, at first sight, inconsistent with *Gelpcke* v. *Dubuque,* but such is not, in fact, the case. In the provision of the Constitution that no State shall pass any law impairing the obligation of contracts, "law" is construed to mean "statute," a law formally passed by a legislative body, while the impairment in the case supposed arises from a change in the judge-made law, and therefore is not within the protection of the Constitution.[2]

[1] P. 687. See *Thompson* v. *Perrine,* 103 U.S. 806; 106 U.S. 589; *Taylor* v. *Ypsilanti,* 105 U.S. 60; *County of Ralls* v. *Douglass,* 105 U.S. 728; *Green County* v. *Conness,* 109 U.S. 104; *Anderson* v. *Santa Anna,* 116 U.S. 356. And now in *Muhlker* v. *N. Y. & Harlem R. R. Co.,* 197 U.S. 544, the court has carried this doctrine to a further extreme. See *Sauer* v. *New York,* 206 U.S. 536, and articles by Mr. Larremore in 22 Harvard Law Rev. 182, and Professor Pope in 24 Harvard Law Rev. 6, 8-10, 23.

[2] The best statement of the situation created by *Swift* v. *Tyson* and *Gelpcke* v. *Dubuque* will be found in an article by William H. Rand, Jr., of the New York Bar, 8 Harvard Law Rev. 328. See also preceding note.

CHAPTER XI

OPINIONS OF EXPERTS

Opinions of experts as sources of Law

A THIRD source of Law, and one of great importance, is found in the opinions of experts. Sometimes these opinions have been taken up by the legislative organ of a community and published as part of the Statute Law. The most familiar and striking instance of this was when Justinian compiled the Digest from the treatises of the Jurists.[1] Again, the opinion of a new and unknown writer is sometimes adopted and applied by a court, not because the author possesses any authority, but because his arguments and conclusions appear to the court to be sound, just as the arguments and conclusions of an advocate in a particular case might appear to be sound.

It is not the effect of opinions on the Law in either of these two modes that is to be considered here; but, intermediate between them, stand the opinions of persons which carry a weight, because those persons are recognized experts. To use the common phrase, they are authorities. It is with the opinions of experts as authorities that we have here to deal.

In the physical sciences, authority had once great weight, but at the present day, as an ultimate principle, it is frankly and energetically repudiated. In theology, the extent to which authority should be admitted as a

[1] See p. 186, *ante*.

ground of belief has been a matter of the liveliest controversy. But whatever may be its value in theology and kindred sciences, in Jurisprudence, at any rate, where our primary objects of contemplation are the rules laid down by the judges, and where the existence of those rules, and not their conformity to our notions of a divine ideal, is the chief topic of inquiry, authority is unquestionably a matter with which we have much to do, for authority is an important source of the rules followed by the courts,—that is, of the Law.

One of the forms of authority, that which it bears when it takes the shape of Judicial Precedent, we have already considered. In the present chapter, we are to deal only with authority which does not take that shape. In a system where great respect is paid to Judicial Precedent, comparatively slight regard is likely to be rendered to opinions not coming in that form; this we see in the manner in which the Common Law subordinates treatises to decisions. In Germany, on the other hand, where the decisions of courts do not have a binding force,[1] the authority of jurists not occupying judicial position is often very great.

Obiter dicta of Judges

It must be observed that at the Common Law not every opinion expressed by a judge forms a Judicial Precedent. In order that an opinion may have the weight of a precedent, two things must concur: it must be, in the first place, an opinion given by a judge, and, in the second place, it must be an opinion the formation of which is necessary for the decision of a particular case; in other words, it must not be *obiter dictum*. That is, over against

[1] Pp. 205 *et seq. ante.*

Judicial Precedents stand not only the opinions of non-judicial persons, but the *obiter dicta* of judges.

I have spoken in an earlier place[1] of Savigny's theory that the opinion of jurists is the expression of the popular consciousness, and have shown that this is a fiction or, at best, an empty form of speech. I will not recur to it here. I shall deal simply with the undoubted fact that, besides Judicial Precedents, the opinions of persons learned in the Law are influential on its formation.

Text writers

How are the opinions of experts made known to the courts? The treatises of text writers have been spoken of as the mode of communication. But it must be borne in mind that the greater part of most text-books at the Common Law, and the whole of many of them, are not devoted to the statement of such opinions; they do not contain, nor profess to contain, any original or independent thinking or conclusions; they are simply collections of statutes and precedents; their merit or demerit lying solely in their good or bad arrangement.

But a more important matter is that the opinions of experts are often communicated to the courts in other ways than through treatises. Of course, in primitive times, such communication was exclusively oral, and though, in the course of years, it has taken more and more a written, or rather a printed, form, yet a very important source of Law—and perhaps at the present day it is quite as influential as it ever has been—is the opinion of experts, not printed, and indeed not formulated in any express statement, but known or believed by the courts to be their general opinion; such knowledge or belief being gained through some of the means by which knowledge

[1] See pp. 89 *et seq. ante.*

or belief of general opinion is acquired. That the bar who practise before a judge would be universally or generally of opinion that a certain decision ought not to be made, although not conclusive on his judgment, ought to have, and, what is more to our present purpose, does have, an influence on him, and an influence of a distinctly more stringent character than the knowledge or belief that the unlearned laity would disapprove of the decision.[1]

To say what makes one writer an authority in the Law and another not, is as hard as to say what makes one man an authority in medicine or in "practical politics," while the opinion of another man has no weight in either. Authority is the result of reputation, and the causes why one writer has a reputation are, if not infinite, at least indefinite. Attempts to weigh the authority of jurists by any exact balance, or to bring them to any test, conventional or otherwise, are rare; something of the kind was attempted in the later Roman Law.

Comparative weight of different jurists: in the Civil Law

I have spoken in a preceding chapter[2] of the important place that the jurisconsults occupied in the later times of the Roman Republic; how there was given to certain of them by the Emperors the *jus respondendi;* and how the *responsa* of these favored jurists had probably the weight of Judicial Precedents. But there were other jurists, some of great reputation, who never possessed the *jus respondendi;* the most famous of these was Gaius.

In the later Empire, the *jus respondendi* ceased to be given, and a natural consequence was that the writings of all jurists came to be considered as belonging to the same class, and to be distinguished only by the relative

[1] See *e.g. Hall* v. *Corcoran,* 107 Mass. 251, 253.
[2] Pp. 201 *et seq.*

reputation of their authors. And the writings of the jurists were now practically the source from which the Law was drawn; the Twelve Tables, even the Edict of the prætors,[1] had retired into the background, and it was only through the commentaries and treatises of the jurists that they were brought to the notice of the tribunals. Authority was given by reputation. But how was reputation to be determined? The situation was very confused. The Emperors intervened.

In A.D. 321, the Imperial Government of Rome decreed that the notes of Ulpian and Paullus on Papinian should not be cited,[2] but six years later it was decreed, "*Universa, quæ scriptura Paulli continentur, recepta auctoritate firmanda sunt et omni veneratione celebranda.*"[3] A hundred years later, we have the celebrated Law of Citations: "*Papiniani, Paulli, Gaii, Ulpiani atque Modestini scripta universa firmamus ita, ut Gaium quæ Paullum, Ulpianum et cunctos comitetur auctoritas, lectionesque ex omni ejus opere recitentur. Eorum quoque scientiam, quorum tractatus atque sententias prædicti omnes suis operibus miscuerunt ratam esse censemus ut Scævolæ, Sabini, Juliani atque Marcelli, omniumque, quos illi celebrarunt, si tamen eorum libri, propter antiquitatis incertum, codicum collatione firmentur.*[4] *Ubi autem diversæ sententiæ proferuntur, potior numerus vincat auctorum vel, si numerus æqualis sit, ejus partis præcedat auctoritas, in qua excellentis ingenii vir Papinianus emineat,*

[1] See pp. 31, 199, *ante*.

[2] Theod. Cod. I, 4, 1.

[3] "All the contents of the writings of Paullus are approved by authority, and are to be affirmed and treated with all respect." Theod. Cod. I, 4, 2.

[4] See Sohm, Inst. § 17.

qui, ut singulos vincit, ita cedit duobus. Notas etiam Paulli atque Ulpiani in Papiniani corpus factas (sicut dudum statutum est) præcipimus infirmari. Ubi autem pares eorum sententiæ recitantur, quorum par censetur auctoritas, quod sequi debeat eligat moderatio judicantis. Paulli quoque Sententias nuper valere præcipimus." [1]

Justinian, when ordering the Digest to be compiled, did away with the provisions of the Law of Citations, as it was called, and directed the commissioners, *"ea quæ antea in notis Æmilii Papiniani ex Ulpiano et Paulo nec non Marciano adscripta sunt, quæ antea nullam vim optinebant propter honorem splendidissimi Papiniani, non statim respuere."* [2]

After the revival of learning, special authority was attributed to favorite doctors in some countries. Thus, in Spain, at one time, *"tribuitur vis legis, non solum, jure*

[1] "All the writings of Papinian, Paullus, Gaius, Ulpian and Modestinus we confirm, so that the same authority shall belong to Gaius as to Paullus, Ulpian and all the rest, and passages from all his works may be cited. Also we approve the doctrine of those whose treatises and opinions any of the aforesaid writers have inserted in their own works, such as Scaevola, Sabinus, Julian and Marcellus, and all those whom the first-named writers have quoted, provided however that the books containing their writings, on account of the uncertainty resulting from their antiquity, are verified by a comparison of manuscripts. But when different opinions are expressed, the greater number of writers is to prevail, or, if the numbers are equal, the authority of that side is to take precedence, on which stands Papinian, that man of surpassing abilities, who outweighs any single opponent, but yields to two. And further we direct that the notes of Paullus and Ulpian on the works of Papinian (as has been formerly decreed) are to be of no force. But where an equal number of opinions are cited on each side, of those whose weight as authorities is considered equal, he who gives judgment may choose at his discretion which should be followed. We have recently decreed that the Opinions of Paullus are of weight." Theod. Cod. I, 4, 3.

[2] "The notes to Æmilius Papinian derived from Ulpian, Paullus and Marcian, which formerly had no force, on account of the reputation of the illustrious Papinian, you are not invariably to reject." Preface I (De conceptione digestorum), 1. 6.

Cæsareo et canonico, sed et doctorum interpretationibus; in Cæsareo, Bartolo et post eum Baldo; in canonico, Johanni Andreæ et post eum Panormitano." [1] So in Portugal, *"Lege enim Lusitana judicibus mandatum est, ut deficientibus legibus regni et jure civili Romanorum, ad Accursii glossas et Bartolum recurratur."* [2]

In some of the earlier civilians there are rules for marshalling authorities, but they are so general and vague as to have trifling practical value.[3] Duck's fifth rule is this: *"Cum doctorum sententiæ inter se pugnantes reperiuntur, eos potissimum sequendos esse existimavit clarissimus Galliæ Jurisconsultus, Guido Coquillus, qui dignitates et fortunas contemserunt, quales fuerunt Bartolus, Castrensis, Speculator,*[4] *Masnerius, Petrus Jacobi, Carolus Molinæus, aliique, qui in jure investigando affectibus suis et sordibus non indulserunt."* [5]

Comparative weight of different jurists: In the Common Law

In the Common Law no rule has been laid down as to marshalling authorities according to their weight. Lord Eldon, in *Johnes* v. *Johnes,*[6] is reported to have said that

[1] "The force of law is accorded, not only to the Imperial and canon law, but to the interpretations of the learned; on the Imperial law, to Bartolus and after him to Baldus; on the canon law, to Johannes Andreas and after him to Panormitanus." A. Duck, De Auth. Jur. Civ. II, *c.* 6, § 29.

[2] "For by Portuguese law the judges are directed, in case the laws of the kingdom and the Roman civil law are insufficient, to have recourse to the commentaries of Accursius and to Bartolus." *Id.* I, *c.* 8, § 6.

[3] See 1 Menoch. De Præsumpt. II, 71; A. Duck, I, *c.* 8, § 14.

[4] *I.e.* Durandus.

[5] "When the opinions of the learned are found to be in conflict with each other, the famous French jurisconsult, Guido Coquillus, considers that those should preferably be followed who have disregarded honor and wealth, such as were Bartolus, Castrensis, the Speculator, Masnerius, Petrus Jacobi, Carolus Molinæus, and others, who in the study of the law did not allow themselves to be influenced by their personal feelings or desire for filthy lucre."

[6] 3 Dow, 1, 15.

"One who had held no judicial situation could not regularly be mentioned as an authority"; but there is probably no marked distinction between a treatise written by one who is or has been a judge and one written by a man who has never held judicial office.

There is a short colloquy reported in *Ion's Case.*[1] "*Metcalfe* [referring to Welsby's edition of Archibold's Criminal Pleading]. Mr. Welsby, who may be cited as authority, comments on the words 'utter or publish.'

"*Pollock*, C. B. Not yet an *authority*.

"*Metcalfe*. It is no doubt a rule that a writer on law is not to be considered an authority in his lifetime. The only exception to the rule, perhaps, is the case of Justice Story.

"*Coleridge,* J. Story is dead."

The reporter appends the following note: "This rule seems 'more honored in the breach than in the observance.' The annotations of Mr. Greaves, Russell on Crimes, and the learned work of Mr. Pitt Taylor on Evidence, are constantly cited in Crown cases; and the writings of Chitty, Starkie, and also of Story, were referred to in the same way in their lifetime."[2]

Necessity of some authority besides statutes

It is almost a matter of necessity that authority in some form, either in the shape of Judicial Precedents or in the shape of the writings of jurists, should be one of the sources of the Law. Legislation covers but a small part of the field, and, as we have seen, legislation has

[1] 2 Den. C. C. 475, 488.

[2] It has been said that some of the old text-books constitute a distinct class of "books of authority." Pollock, Jurisprudence, 3d ed., 246. If a technical distinction of this sort was ever recognized by the courts, it is probably of very little practical importance at the present day.

to be interpreted by the courts before it becomes a part of the Law. If judges were always going back to establish fundamental propositions by independent processes of reasoning, the work of the world would never get itself done. Take a simple case of a sale of goods—how many questions may arise. What is a contract? How far can an intention contrary to the words of the parties be shown? Is a delivery necessary to pass title? Was there in the eye of the Law a delivery? When is one dispensed from keeping his contract? What authority has an agent? If courts had to examine all these questions *de novo* in each case, and not take them as established by authority, an army of judges would not suffice to keep society moving.

Even when a judge is not following a judicial precedent or the opinion of any jurist, he is constantly acting on authority, on his own authority, so to speak. He remembers having arrived at certain results; he does not recall the reasoning by which he reached them, but nevertheless he acts upon them with confidence. "We refer to a foregone process of inquiry, as a ground of present belief, in the faith that it was adequately performed, but without feeling the force of the reasons by which our mind was originally satisfied."[1]

Comparison of the Civil and the Common Law

The most striking difference between the Civil and the Common Law lies in the greater relative importance which, in the former system, is attributed to the opinions of the jurists as compared with prior decisions of the courts. In this, as in other matters, it is much to be regretted that the discussion of the comparative merits of the two systems has been carried on so largely upon *a priori* grounds.

[1] Sir G. C. Lewis, Influence of Authority in Matters of Opinion, c. 2, § 4.

It is said that in such a matter the Common Law *must* have the advantage, and on such another the rules of the Civil Law *must* be better; but whether they actually work better, is a matter of which little has been said, and in the ignorance which the lawyers of either system have of the practical working of the other, little can be said. One of the greatest services that could be rendered to the advancement of the Law would be for some intelligent and well-educated man to carry on real professional work, first under the Civil and then under the Common Law, or *vice versa*, and to tell the legal world the results of his experience.

There are three classes in a community who take part in the development and application of the Law,—the judges, the practising lawyers and the jurists. The accidental division of the second class in England into barristers and attorneys is, for our present purpose, unimportant. In most of the countries where the Civil Law prevails, the three classes are distinct, and distinct from the beginning. In Germany or France, a man intending to devote himself to the Law begins his career either in the lower orders of the magistracy, or in the ranks of the advocates and notaries, or as a teacher and writer on the Law; from one of these occupations he seldom passes to either of the others; and it is the latter class, that of the teachers and writers, who are the jurists and exercise the greatest influence on the development of the Law.

This must not be pushed too far. Among the Romans, the chief factor in the early development of the Law is commonly, and probably justly, considered to have been that of a succession of judges, the prætors, publishing the

Edict and fashioning Prætorian Law;[1] and the great work of introducing the Roman Law into Germany was, as I have said, performed by the doctors who were placed in judicial positions.[2]

And at the present day, notwithstanding the tenacity with which most of the German writers still continue to deny authority to Judicial Precedents, it is plain, from the increasing number of reports of decisions published upon the Continent, and the frequency with which they are cited, that the difference between the Common and Civil Law, though still existing, is less accentuated than it was some years ago.[3] With every allowance, however, a chief element in the development of the modern Civil Law has been the writings of jurists who have had no experience either on the Bench or at the Bar.

Under the Common Law in England and America, we have a very different state of things. There is not that line of demarcation, if not impassable, at least rarely passed, which in France and Germany separates the judge's career from the advocate's. The English and American judges have not been all their lives simply public officials to decide legal questions which are presented to them; they have had to deal with affairs in practice at the bar. Since the great seal was taken from Archbishop Williams in 1625, no one other than a practising barrister has been called to high judicial position in England in the Courts of Common Law or Equity, except Lord Shaftesbury, who was Chancellor in 1672-1673 for less than a year. Since that time, no one in England, and since the inde-

[1] P. 199, *ante*.
[2] P. 206, *ante*.
[3] P. 210, *ante*.

pendence of the United States, no one with us, has held a seat in any superior court of Common Law or Equity, the judgments of which would have any weight as precedents, without having practised at the bar the profession of the Law.

There was one exception in England and one in the United States. The peculiar constitution of the House of Lords, by which persons not learned in the Law can vote on judicial questions, has continued in existence to the present day, but the last occasion on which such persons have attempted to vote was in 1883.[1] The like power in the Senate of the State of New York came to an end in 1846.[2] In a few of the States high judicial powers survived in the Governor for some years, even after independence. Thus, the Governor of New Jersey, besides being Captain General, was also Chancellor and Ordinary, or principal Judge of Probate.[3]

But, further, in England and America, not only is there no line between the careers of judges and advocates, but there is no line between the judges and advocates and the jurists. Indeed, a large proportion of those text writers who could properly be cited as authority have either filled high judicial position, or have been actively engaged in some branch of practice. Omitting the names of living writers, we have, in England, Bracton, Littleton, Coke, Hale, Doderidge, Gilbert, Foster, Blackstone, Fearne, Hargrave, Butler, Preston, Wigram, Abbott, Sug-

[1] 17 Law Quart. Rev. 357, 369-370.

[2] See 14 Columbia Law Rev. 1, 2. As to the exercise of judicial powers by the Legislature of Rhode Island, see 14 Yale Law Jour. 148.

[3] Clevenger and Keasbey, Courts of New Jersey, 118 *et seq.;* appendix, 4 C. E. Green Ch. 580; *Coursen's Will,* 3 Green Ch. 408, 413.

den, Stephen, Byles, Williams, Blackburn, Benjamin; and in the United States, Kent, Story, Redfield, Washburn, Rawle.

The Law of a country at any time is made up of the rules that its courts are then applying in the decision of cases. In countries where the Common Law prevails the courts draw those rules mainly, so far as they are not derived from statutes, from the former decisions of judges. In countries which have adopted the Civil Law they draw those rules mainly from the treatises of writers, without regard to prior decisions. What difference in results is likely to arise from this difference in the sources?

Practical differences of method

One thing strikes at first sight. The method of the Civil Law tribunal is more deductive than that of the Common Law court. The jurist works undoubtedly to a great extent by induction. His general doctrines are not perceived by him intuitively. He considers cases of conduct, real or imaginary, and from them he extracts general rules, expressed, if he have the genius of the great Roman lawyers, in elegant propositions and definitions, and illustrated by apposite examples. But the result of his work, as it presents itself to the judge, who turns to him for instruction, is not a collection of concrete cases, but a series of general rules, and it is the natural tendency of the judge's mind to bring the case before him under one of those general rules, or, in other words, to fit it somehow into the system with which the writer has furnished him.

But the judge who is working with precedents in the form of earlier concrete cases is slow to accept any general doctrine or to lay down any rule as final. Each new state of facts brings a new element into the Law, and the old results are to be reconsidered in view of this new element. The principles extracted from the old cases are always being reëxamined in the light of new facts.

Each system has its merits and its defects. The method of the Common Law is the more scientific, and it would be entirely so, were it not that it gives an artificial weight to prior decisions by assuming them to be correct. The Common Law judge is like an experimenter in chemistry, who is always testing his theory by new and varied experiments, but who is not ready enough to admit that the record of former experiments may be wrong; while the Civil Law judge, on the other hand, is like a chemist who, having arrived at a theory, insists upon applying it as the true rule of nature. And the civilian has not the opportunity of discovering his mistakes which is given the chemist. If the latter's theory requires that the union of two bodies should produce a blue solid, and, instead of that, it yields a yellow gas, the most obstinate of doctrinaires is driven to revise his theory; but if in the Law a theory requires the decision that a certain transaction is right, it will be often difficult to demonstrate that the theory is wrong. The correctness or incorrectness of legal theories cannot easily be brought to the test of tangible proof. If one asserts a legal doctrine to be sound, he cannot be refuted by the assertion of some one else that it is not.

Of course, if the judge, be he of the Common or of the Civil Law, is a sensible man, he will not push his way of looking at things to an extreme. The Common Law court will admit that a former decision may have been wrong; and the Civil Law court will admit that a legal writer, though one of the admired masters, may have laid down a general principle too broadly or too narrowly; but notwithstanding this, there will be a tendency the one way and the other, and this tendency will make itself felt.

The Common Law system has one incidental advantage. It establishes a test which is easily applied to determine the comparative weight to be attached to opinions. It avoids that endless clash of opinions which prevails in those countries where there is no fixed precedency in the weight of authority, and where one doctor's opinion is as good as another doctor's opinion.

On the other hand, in a country like Germany, where each writer can emit his opinion, not only of what the Law ought to be, but of what the Law is, notwithstanding the judgment of Ober or Oberst tribunal to the contrary, and free from any conventional discredit, there is, possibly, a better chance in the end for a result to be reached which will be wisest as a final conclusion.

And yet, to a Common Law lawyer, considering that the end of the Law is to work out the happiness of the community, and not to establish a system however elegant and logical, it is hard not to prefer the method of his own jurisprudence. In both systems the legislature sits supreme, to knock to pieces, at its will or whim, with equal hand, the precedents and theories of judges and jurists alike. It can correct any errors of judgment into which the courts may fall, and in that large class of cases where there is no difficulty worthy of such a *deus ex machina,* the measure of good order and certainty which is brought about by the Common Law system of precedent seems preferable to the wild waste of contending doctors.[1]

[1] But see Maine, Village Communities (3d ed.), 48.

The inductive method of the Common Law makes the system more "elastic"; the readiness to adopt a new decision as soon as made into the family of precedents, the fact that there is no rule in formal shape to which the decision of a court must conform, makes it more easy to adapt the Law to the changing circumstances of real life; at the same time, from its being always ready to change the form of its general principles, it is inexact in its terminology.[1]

The Civil Law, on the other hand, is simpler, easier to acquire, easier to apply in ordinary cases, and it has a more exact nomenclature. The uniformity in style and expression of the great Antonine jurists is very remarkable and could exist only where there was a perfectly defined and universally recognized vocabulary. The fixity of statement and definition in the Roman Law has not, however, been an unmixed good. It established a strong, harmonious system, which was a wonderfully good one, because of the ability of the men who framed it; but, after all, they were men of the second century, not of the twentieth, and their system, while in many respects an admirable framework for modern law, has yet served to cramp it.

Sir Henry Maine attributes the "wealth of principles" in the Roman Law to the uncontrolled multiplication of imaginary cases, because all combinations of fact were on the same footing, without regard to their truth.[2] If this be correct, yet I doubt much whether it has operated to the advantage of the civilians. In the Common Law

[1] For a comparison of the practical advantages of the two systems, see address of Professor Pound, 37 Rep. Amer. Bar. Assn., 975.
[2] Ancient Law (Pollock's ed.), p. 41.

courts the arguments of counsel have always abounded in imaginary instances, and the judges, in their opinions, constantly suggest them. The argument from analogy which fosters the use of imaginary cases flourishes nowhere more than in the Common Law.

Dangers of imaginary cases

The true distinction is not, I suspect, that the Common Law judge neglects imaginary cases, but that the Civil Law jurist is in danger of neglecting real cases. It is comparatively easy to frame a rule when you can state your own examples. Putting simple extreme cases, it is not difficult to draw a line between them, but when you come to the cases which real life presents, with their complications and limitations, the theorist is apt to divert his eyes. I venture to quote some words that I wrote many years ago: "There is something which gives a judge a great advantage over a text writer, an advantage of which it may be said that the more a man watches the processes of his own mind, or those of others, the more weight he is disposed to lay on it, I mean the circumstances under which questions are presented to a judge for decision. . . . While the faculty of large generalization is perhaps the noblest of human reason, the power of sound generalization is perhaps the rarest. To keep close to facts in laying down principles, to resist the constant (often unconscious) temptation to overlook the limitations and qualifications of a doctrine, which would render its exact statement a most difficult and laborious task, but the absence of which makes the statement often false, or at best a useless platitude, is a quality given to few who deal with moral and legal subjects. I do not mean that judges are free from this common weakness of humanity,—far from it,—but the facts in the case are a constant aid and warning. The judge has his facts given to him. The text writer makes his own typical cases, and the temptation to make them such as to render easy the deduction of general doctrines is well-nigh irresistible."[1]

And here the admission of Bentham, the ablest, as he was the bitterest, of the opponents of judge-made law, is very noteworthy: "Traverse the whole Continent of Europe,—ransack all the libraries belonging to the jurisprudential systems of the several political states,—add the contents all together,—you would not be able to compose a collection of cases equal in variety, in amplitude, in clearness of statement—in a word, all points taken together, in instructiveness—to that which may be seen to be afforded by the collection of English Reports of adjudged cases."[2]

And there is unquestionably one evil caused by the habit of considering imaginary cases rather than real ones, —a tendency to develop distinctions purely theoretical and to complicate the Law with principles and deductions which have no place in the conduct of life,—and this tendency certainly shows itself in the Civil as compared with the Common Law. Think, for instance, of the discussions and doctrines on necessary and impossible conditions,—on legacies if Titius goes to the moon, if Titius does not go to the moon, if Titius never dies, etc.[3] So

[1] 22 Am. Law Rev. 756, 758.

[2] 4 Benth. Works, 461.

[3] See Inst. III, 19, 11; D. XXVIII, 3, 16; Swinburne on Wills, pt. 4, § 6, pl. 3, 12. Compare the question whether the will of Lazarus was valid after his resurrection, quoted in 27 Law Quart. Rev. 392. Another defect of the civilian method of relying on treatises is the small amount of information given in them as to the legal transactions which actually take place. "It is possible to dig through a

again, the subject of gratuitous loans has, as Judge Story says, "furnished very little occasion for the interposition of judicial tribunals," but the civilians have debated on it at great length, discussing whether, if Caius's house be on fire, it is lawful for him to save an urn of his own in preference to a vase which he has borrowed from Balbus, etc., etc.[1]

Multitude of theories in the Civil Law

I have spoken of the advantage which the form of the Civil Law gives it over the Common Law, and the precision and exactness of its fundamental conceptions are often contrasted with the vagueness of the Common Law. But all this needs careful qualification. There is, in truth, no lack of precision in the theories of learned civilians, but the theory of one learned civilian will be precisely opposite to that of another. There will often be a multitude of writers, no two agreeing with each other, and without any common arbiter.

Take, for instance, the leading topic of possession. Before 1803, when Savigny first published his treatise, not including the glossators, nor the other commentators down to the end of the fifteenth century, and excluding also a great number of writings to which Savigny says it would be paying far too high honor to say of each separately that it was good for nothing, thirty-three authors had written on the subject. In the following sixty-two years, down to 1865, when the seventh and last edition of Savigny's book was published, one hundred and twenty

whole library of works on testamentary succession, to find therein numbers of clever and sagacious rules of construction but not a word to show what sort of wills *are* commonly drawn at the present time." Eugen Ehrlich, Freie Rechtsfindung (Freedom of Judicial Decision), Ch. II, § 22 at end. Transl. in Science of Legal Method, p. 79. (Modern Legal Philosophy Series.)

[1] Story, Bailm. §§ 245-247, 285.

more books and articles had been added to the list;[1] and before the beginning of this century there had been published over thirty more separate treatises on the subject, not including the discussions in the general works or the articles in the legal periodicals.[2] More than forty years ago, Ihering was able to enumerate eight different theories on the reason for the protection of possession, to which eight theories he proceeded to add a ninth.[3] Whether it is better to protect possession with nine inconsistent theories, or without any theory at all, is a question not to be answered offhand in favor of the civilian position.

Advantages of judicial decisions as authorities

On another matter, I may perhaps be allowed to quote my own words from the same article which I have just cited: "As to the comparative fair-mindedness of the judge and the jurist, there is something to be said on either side. Cases present themselves to the legal writer in a more impersonal manner. The parties are mere names to him. But, on the other hand, the useful conventionalities of a judge's position and of the judicial style, as well as the rapid succession of different questions which pass before him, indispose him from identifying himself personally with a pet theory, and brooding over it until it becomes distorted into an altogether undue importance, a tendency to which the solitary student or writer is in danger of yielding. Compare the general tone of our courts in dealing with the opinions of other tribunals, and that of the German jurists who, as has been said, seem to write mainly for the purpose of refuting and reviling each other, and one will be inclined to believe the atmosphere

[1] Savigny, Das Recht des Besitzes, Einleitung II.
[2] See bibliography, *e.g.*, in Cornil, Possession dans le droit Romain.
[3] Ihering, Grund des Besitzesschutzes, §§ 1-5.

of a court room quite as favorable to unbiassed consideration of legal questions as that of the study.

"One thing more, judges, as a class, have brought to their tasks higher conscientiousness. The knowledge that a decision will have direct consequences, often of the most serious character, to actual human beings is a tremendous sanction for rendering right judgment. It is true that a feeling of the consequences sometimes unduly deflects the decision of a court; but in a vastly greater number of cases it furnishes a motive for just judgment which the most light-minded man must feel. There is no such direct and impressive presence before the legal writer; the careless statement, the hasty conclusion, the unverified authority, are apt to sit too lightly on the consciences of the writers of text-books."

If hard cases make bad law, bad law makes hard cases. The temptation of professional men, judges and jurists alike, is to subordinate the welfare of persons subject to a system of Law to the logical coherency of the system itself, and there is more danger of yielding to this temptation when the question is whether an imaginary Numerius Negidius shall be condemned in a sum of imaginary sesterces, than when it is whether a real John Jones shall be mulcted so many real dollars.

Increasing importance of the jurist

The enormous number of judicial decisions, and the rapidity in their rate of increase, has been so great as to indicate that the function of the jurist will rise more and more in importance in the Common Law, from the mere fact that the mass of material will become too great for any one to cope with it all, and that it can be dealt with only by systematic study directed to particular parts. At the end of the eighteenth century the total number of printed volumes of reported cases in England, Ireland, the English colonies, and the United States of America was two hundred and sixty. At the end of the year 1865 they had increased more than twelve fold to over three thousand, not including the Indian Reports, and at the end of the nineteenth century the published reports of decisions in the United States alone were contained in about six thousand volumes.

The work of the jurist is therefore likely to rise in importance during the coming years, and a corresponding improvement in the quality of treatises on the Law may be confidently expected. If the Common Law has been wise in attaching great weight to precedents, it has certainly not held out sufficient welcome, I do not say to actual, but to possible, jurists.

Notwithstanding the difference in the comparative weight attached to the opinions of judges and of jurists in the Common and in the Civil Law, it is a matter of prime importance to observe that in both systems alike the development of the Law has been mainly due, neither to the legislatures on the one hand, nor to the people on the other, but to learned men, whether occupying judicial position or not. This is well brought out by Professor Munroe Smith in his valuable and interesting article on Problems of Roman Legal History, 4 Columbia Law Rev. 523.

CHAPTER XII

CUSTOM

Custom as a source of Law

CUSTOM is another of the sources of the Law. The courts have adopted certain rules, not because any statutes have required them to do so, not because there were any precedents for such rules in the reports of decided cases, not because they found any doctrine calling for the laying down of the rules in the writings of jurists, not because the rules recommended themselves to their moral sense, but because they found them followed, in society at large, or in some parts of it, in the intercourse of the members of the society with each other. Thus, in the Common Law, three days' delay in payment, called days of grace, are allowed on bills of exchange. The judges found this custom existing among merchants, and adopted it.

Custom has often been declared to be the source of all Law, except what rests upon statutes. Indeed, this may be said to be the commonest form of expression. Thus Blackstone: "This unwritten or common law is properly distinguishable into three kinds: 1. General customs; which are the universal rule of the whole kingdom, and form the common law, in its stricter and more usual signification. 2. Particular customs; which for the most part affect only the inhabitants of particular districts. 3. Certain particular laws; which by custom are adapted and used by some particular courts, of pretty general and extensive jurisdiction." He then refers to many doctrines of Law and says: "All these doctrines that are not set down in any written statute or ordinance, but depend merely upon immemorial usage, that is, upon common law, for their support." [1]

Mr. Carter's view

And now I must return to Mr. James C. Carter's posthumous book. I have before spoken of it in connection with the question whether judges make Law.[2] Mr. Carter denies that judges make Law; he says that they merely declare or discover Law already existing. I have tried to maintain the contrary, and to test the correctness of Mr. Carter's theory. But Mr. Carter goes further and denies that custom is only one of the sources of non-statutory Law. He says it *is* the non-statutory Law itself, that it is the whole non-statutory Law. This view he presses with great energy. We must consider whether it is correct.

I have spoken of Mr. Carter's fight, his successful fight, against the introduction of Mr. Field's Civil Code into New York, and how it led him to combat Austin's theory that all Law is the command of the Sovereign. Austin recognized that judges make Law, but he said that in making it they are obeying the command of the Sovereign, because whatever the Sovereign permits, he commands.[3]

The true view, as I submit, is that the Law is what the judges declare; that statutes, precedents, the opinions of learned experts, customs, and morality are the sources of

[1] 1 Bl. Com. 67, 68.
[2] Pp. 93 *et seq.;* 233 *et seq. ante.*
[3] P. 85, *ante.*

the Law; that back of everything lie the opinions of the ruling spirits of the community, who have the power to close any of these sources;[1] but that so long as they do not interfere, the judges, in establishing Law, have recourse to these sources. Custom is one of them, but to make it not only one source but the sole source, the Law itself, requires a theory which is as little to be trusted as that of Austin.

You will have observed a difference between the language used by Blackstone and Mr. Carter, and there is a difference in their theories. According to Blackstone, ancient custom is a source of the Law, but on this Mr. Carter says: "Such a limitation of custom in the making of law seems to me to be without foundation, . . . *present* custom, provided it is established, is as efficient as if it were centuries old."[2] And again Mr. Carter points out the novelty of his theory: "*Ancient* customs," he says, "they [legal writers] have indeed regarded as having the force of law, but this quality they impute, not to the custom, *qua* custom, but to its *antiquity,* whereas the conclusion at which I arrive erects *present existing* custom as the standard of law."[3]

And on this point Mr. Carter's theory seems an improvement on Blackstone's. Law may rest now on statutes or precedents, and to the making of the statutes and precedents ancient customs may have contributed, but so far as custom is a source of the Law as it now exists, it is present custom.

But waiving this point, let us consider whether cus-

[1] Pp. 123-124, *ante.*
[2] Carter, 71.
[3] P. 121.

tom, and custom alone, is the Law. We shall all agree that Law is made up of those rules to govern the conduct of men, which the State will enforce, whether those rules be made by the judges or by custom or by anything else.

Custom is not opinion

Now custom is not *opinion*, it is *practice*, and the neglect to clearly grasp this fact seems to me to lie at the root of Mr. Carter's theory. *Customary opinion* is an incorrect expression. Custom is what men *do*, not what they *think*. Mr. Carter sometimes recognizes this explicitly. Thus, he says:[1] "The simplest definition of custom is that it is *the uniformity of conduct* of all persons under like circumstances. . . . *Conduct* is some *physical movement* of the body." To put it in somewhat different words, the opinion of a community as to what a man *ought* to do is not based on custom, unless there is a general practice.

"Custom is effectual only when it is universal, or nearly so. In the absence of unanimity of opinion, custom becomes powerless, or rather does not exist." This is the language of Mr. Carter.[2] But at a later page he says: "The characteristic in early and rude societies—it is so to a much less extent in enlightened society—is that customs, in many respects, are not settled and are in conflict."[3] Here seems at once a contradiction. If customs are not settled, and are in conflict, they are not universal, and are, therefore, not customs. How does Mr. Carter escape from this contradiction?

If I understand him, and I think I do, it is in this way. Custom, he says, is universal conduct. But a question now arises which, in its present form, has never come

[1] Pp. 122, 123.
[2] P. 38.
[3] P. 66.

up before. There is no actual practice, for the question, in its present form, is new, but there are principles of morality, chief among which are these,—that a man should get from another what he has a right to expect, and that conduct should be judged by its consequences,—and that these principles of morality are put in general practice in the community, though not in the particular form that has arisen; that it is the custom to act upon these principles, and that therefore a judge, deciding in accordance with these principles, is really basing his decision on custom.

He illustrates this by a case: A man who has insured his ship did not disclose to the insurer a fact materially affecting the risk; the fact, however, was notorious. Mr. Carter supposes a suit by the owner of the ship to be decided against the underwriter. This is what he says: "Was this case decided by custom? Some would say it was not, because, avowedly, there was no precedent, which is authenticated custom, nor any evidence of actual custom not to make disclosure of notorious information, and they would declare that it was a clear case where the judges had *made* the law out of their own heads, upon a simple consideration of whether the failure to disclose was right or wrong. That the decision was based upon the consideration whether that action was right or wrong is, in a sense, true; but whose notion of right and wrong was it? It did not come from on High. It was not sought for in the Scriptures, or in any book on ethics. The judges in considering whether the act was right or wrong applied to it the method universally adopted by all men; they judged it by its *consequences;* they considered that the underwriter, in all probability, and therefore presumably, knew of the special peril, unless he was utterly negligent of his business, which could not be supposed; that therefore he had lost nothing by the act, nor in any manner changed his position. If we went no further it would be manifest that custom decided the case, for to determine whether it was right or wrong by the *customary modes* of determining right and wrong is to determine it according to custom. The court, indeed, declared that its decision was made upon *principle;* but what is meant by this? What is the import of this word 'principle'? It has various meanings, but as here employed it denotes a proposition very widely true, and the truth of which is universally admitted. The court in this case judged of the character of the act of concealment as we all, from the very constitution of our nature, judge of all conduct, *by its consequences.* It found that the underwriter had suffered no harm in consequence of the concealment, because he would have taken the risk, even if the knowledge had been disclosed, and that it was a principle of law that a man could not fairly complain of the act of another unless he had suffered injury from it; but this was a principle of law only because it accorded with the universal custom of men."[1]

Morality rather than custom the guide

I accept the question of Mr. Carter's: "Whose notion of right and wrong was it?" as bringing matters to a test. We all agree that many cases should be decided by the courts on notions of right and wrong, and of course every one will agree that a judge is likely to share the notions of right and wrong prevalent in the community in which he lives; but suppose in a case where there is nothing to guide him but notions of right and wrong, that his notions

[1] P. 72.

of right and wrong differ from those of the community,—which ought he to follow—his own notions, or the notions of the community? Mr. Carter's theory requires him to say that the judge must follow the notions of the community. I believe that he should follow his own notions.

To adopt Mr. Carter's theory, and to say that the Law in such cases is based on custom, seems to me to overlook the fact that custom is conduct, not opinions or notions, and that Mr. Carter's view is fully as objectionable as Austin's that Law is the command of the Sovereign; but, for the purposes of the discussion, I will assume that Mr. Carter's theory that the judge should follow the ideas of right and wrong prevalent in the community in which he lives, rather than his own, does lead logically and properly to the result that Law is custom,—is that theory correct?

A judge often decides, and properly decides, against his own opinion of right and wrong; for instance, when he is compelled by the precise words of a statute. Let us see how a judge's mind works, and ought to work, when he has to pass on the question whether an act was right or wrong, and we will suppose his own opinion to be that it was wrong.

He will first say to himself:—"Is there any statute of the State whose judge I am which declares that the act in question may be done? If there is, however foolish and wicked such legislation appears to me, I must follow the statute, and abstain from deciding that the act was wrong. But I find no such statute."

He will next say:—"Is there any judicial precedent in favor of the act? If there is, however much I may regret that my predecessors decided as they did, and although had I been in their place I should have held otherwise, yet I will follow the precedent. But I find no such precedent."

"Although there is no precedent on the point, yet there may be a *consensus* of judges in their *dicta* and of jurists in their writings against my notion. In face of the opinions of so many learned men, I ought to distrust my own judgment, I do distrust it, I should be slow to rely on it against theirs. But I find no such *dicta* of judges or writings of jurists."

"Is there any actual practice in the community against my opinion? If there is, may not my insisting on my opinion produce worse evils, by introducing change and confusion into daily life, than would be caused by a continuance of the practice? For instance, although there be no statute or precedent as to the rule of the road, the universal practice, in most of the United States, is to drive to the right, and though I should think, adopting Mr. Carter's expression, that there would be better consequences if people drove to the left, as they do in England; that the English practice is more in accord with the principles of utility, tends to produce the greatest happiness of the greatest number, is in short more moral; yet the contrary practice having been thoroughly established here and forming part of the daily conduct of life, I should do more harm than good by interference. But in this case before me, I find no actual practice."

"Although on this question I find no statutes, no judicial precedent, no opinions of learned men, no actual practice against my notion, yet I do recognize that the prevalent, perhaps the universal, opinion of right and wrong in the community on this matter is against me."

Now what ought the judge to do? Should he follow his own sense of right and wrong? Suppose that the general opinion in his community is that a harlot has a right to kill a man who has become tired of her company,—should he so decide?

Of course, the motive of a judge's opinion may be almost anything,—a bribe, a woman's blandishments, the desire to favor the administration or his political party, or to gain popular favor or influence; but these are not sources which Jurisprudence can recognize as legitimate. Is the opinion of his community on a question of morality, of right and wrong, not yet embodied in practice, a legitimate source of Law to which a judge ought to subordinate his own opinion? I know of no moralist or jurist who has answered this question in the affirmative.[1] I do not believe Mr. Carter would have answered it in the affirmative, yet it seems the unavoidable result of his theory. Perhaps he would have said that the judge is appealing from Philip drunk to Philip sober, but, even assuming that custom embraces opinion and not merely practice, it is *present* actual custom which Mr. Carter declares to be the Law, not what *ought* to be custom, nor what *will* be custom.

Mr. Carter's view seems to amount to this: there are two or three general notions of popular positive morality with which the rules laid down by the judges (and legislators) are usually not inconsistent. His conclusion is that all Law (statutory as well as non-statutory) is custom. I submit that his conclusion is not justified by his premise.

[1] See pp. 10, 92, *ante*. For instances where the law has been developed without regard to the prevailing opinion in the community, see article by Professor Pound, 25 Harvard Law Rev. 140, 166-167.

Adjective Law independent of custom

Although custom is not the Law, nor even the sole source of Law, it is undoubtedly one of the sources, and a very important source, of part of the Law. The Law is divided into substantive and adjective. Adjective Law, or, as it is technically called, procedure, embraces all that is necessary to enforce the substantive Law in the courts. It includes the forms of action, the written statements of the parties, the rules of evidence, the modes of appeal, and the enforcement of the judgments of the courts. I suppose that no laymen, and few lawyers whose attention has not been drawn to the subject, realize how large a part of the whole domain of the Law is occupied by procedure. Especially when we take into account how great has been the development and extent of the Law of evidence in the United States, a very large part of the rules laid down by the courts concern matters of procedure, and with procedure custom has had nothing to do; except so far as it has been affected by statute, the adjective Law has undeniably been made by the judges. Mr. Carter himself admits this in the most explicit manner. He says of the Law of Procedure that it is a "quite distinct and very noticeable branch of law, one which is involved in the daily work of the lawyers more than any other. . . . But it has no direct connection with conduct. Its rules are not rules of conduct. . . . The law of procedure cannot be created by general custom. . . . The actual work of shaping and adapting it should, for obvious reasons, not be undertaken by the Legislature itself, but should be delegated to the body best capable of performing it. This is the judges whose duty it is to apply it. . . . In all this body of contrivance, with its multitude of officers, many commands are prescribed concerning the duties of the officers and of the members of the community in relation to the public establishment, and a vast quantity of legal obligation and, therefore, of law is created; but the nature of it is widely different from the law of custom which governs the private transactions of men." [1]

In considering, therefore, how far custom is a source of Law, we are confined to the substantive Law. In what ways is custom a source of the substantive Law? I have denied the claim of custom to be the only source of the Law, but it is a very important source, nevertheless.

Custom important: in interpretation

The part of the Law in which custom has the most influence is in the sphere of interpretation. The judges determine the construction of contracts; they base the construction upon the meaning of words; and the meaning of words, except when they are used technically or the parties to the contract are shown to have given them a special meaning, is established by general practice, that is custom, *quem penes arbitrium est et jus et norma loquendi.*[2]

Perhaps I ought to refer, in passing, to the doctrine put forth by the late learned chief justice of New Hampshire, Chief Justice Doe. He declared that the question of the meaning of a contract was a question of fact, not of Law. Of course he did not deny that it was a question upon which the judges must pass, but he said it was not Law but fact that they were passing upon.[3] To discuss what element of truth there is in this doctrine would lead us too far afield. Suffice it to say that in the domain

[1] Pp. 238-240.

[2] "whose arbitrary sway"
"words, and the forms of language, must obey."
Horace, *Ars Poetica*, 72, Francis's trans.

[3] *E.g. Kendall* v. *Green*, 67 N. H. 557, 561.

of interpretation, so far as the judge is laying down a rule of Law, except where there is a statute or precedent to bind him, he is basing the rule on custom.

In questions of negligence

Another part of the Law in which custom plays an important part is in cases of negligence, cases which are occupying the courts to an alarming extent, threatening their efficiency in the administration of justice generally. In determining whether a man has been reckless or negligent in doing or not doing an act, we do not inquire whether he has taken every possible precaution. The test is whether he has acted as a reasonable man, and this must be settled largely upon whether he has acted in accordance with general practice; that is, custom.

Sometimes the courts undertake to lay down a rule that certain acts or omissions to act amount, as matter of Law, to negligence. Thus in some jurisdictions, a man who, in crossing a railroad track, fails to stop, look, and listen, is, as matter of Law, negligent; and some courts have held that if a man riding in a railroad car puts his arm out of the window, he is, as matter of Law, guilty of negligence. When such a decision is first made, it is often based on general practice; that is, on custom.

In most cases, however, the court instructs the jury that the party who is alleged to have been negligent was bound to act as a reasonable man, and leaves it to them to determine whether he has so acted. Here it is, perhaps, inexact to say that custom is a source of the Law, and it would be better to say that it is a ground of the decision.

It is to be borne in mind that in all cases where custom is correctly claimed to be a source of Law, this may be true only of the first case in which a court lays down a rule, and that subsequent decisions may rest on precedent rather than on custom.

Judicial decisions most frequently lie at origin of Law

Aside from the classes which I have mentioned, it is probable that the part which custom has in truth played as a source of Law has been much exaggerated. The contrary belief rests largely on a fiction. There is every reason to suppose that hundreds of rules in the substantive Law originated in the courts, and that the bulk of the community had nothing to do with them and knew nothing about them. How can we believe that the Rule in Shelley's Case,[1] for instance, had its origin in popular custom? Indeed, with many rules, such as the Rule against Perpetuities, we know the history of their origin and development and that they were the creatures of the judges.[2]

In a matter where the intention of the parties is the principal factor, they may have intended to contract with reference to a practice in the community at large, or in a particular trade or occupation or locality. This is usually a question of fact. But sometimes when such a practice has become universal in the community, or in the trade, occupation, or locality, the courts have laid down a rule that the custom shall be imported into the contract unless the contrary is proved. Here custom is a source of Law. But in cases not of contract the influence of custom upon the making of the Law is much less than has been sometimes supposed.

Mr. Greer[3] has some remarks on this point. He says:—"It is obvious that there is in principle a great

[1] See p. 142, *ante*.
[2] See pp. 236-238, *ante*.
[3] 9 Law Quart. Rev. 153.

difference between customs which create rights and obligations through the medium of a contract on the one hand, and customs which create rights and obligations, as it were directly, and independently of any contract, on the other. Whether or not a custom should be treated as an implied term in a contract is, properly speaking, a question of fact in each case, part of the larger question,—What was the contract between the parties? Except that the decisions have established certain presumptions in favor of customs of the trade, the effect of custom on contract is not a subject for general rules of law, but for decision, according to the particular facts of each case. On the other hand the rules which regulate the effect of custom in creating rights and liabilities between people independently of any contractual relationship are entirely matter of law and not of fact. It follows that the considerations which apply to the solution of the question,—When should a custom be deemed part of the Common Law? are very different from those that are applicable when the question is whether a given custom is to be held to be part of a particular contract."

In other words, a great part of the duty of the courts is to determine the meaning of a party to an agreement, and to do this the customs of the community of which the party is a member, or of the class, as stock-brokers, to which he belongs or with which he is dealing, are facts to be taken into account like other facts. Sometimes a custom is so universal that the courts frame a rule of Law that certain agreements shall be presumed to have been made in accordance with it; and, as different forms of business arise, as undoubtedly they will arise, especially with reference to the use of new mechanical devices, such as telephones or wireless telegraphs, customs will, as rules for determining the meaning of agreements, be taken up into the Law.

But when questions come up of giving rights or imposing duties apart from contract, then we have a different state of things. Aside from the question of negligence, of which I have spoken, it would not be easy to find an instance where courts at the present day (at least in Common Law countries) have had recourse to a custom to fasten a liability upon a man.

Miners' customs

One remarkable instance, however, in late years of the use of custom as a source of Law in matters non-contractual can be found—it is the introduction of the miners' customs in California. The discovery of gold brought, in 1849, a large and turbulent population into an almost uninhabited country; the civil authority could be but feebly enforced, and the miners made rules for themselves. These rules related not only to matters of contract, but also to questions of property and possession. They prescribed how possession was to be taken, how much could be taken into possession (four hundred feet by a discoverer and two hundred by a subsequent locator on a lode), and how possession was lost. These rules were adopted into the Law, and, though not formally enacted, they were recognized by the legislature and thus received a statutory sanction as sources of Law. By the Civil Practice Act of California of 1851,[1] it is provided that, "in actions respecting 'mining claims,' proof shall be admitted of the customs, usages, or regulations established and in force at the bar, or diggings, embracing such claim; and such customs, usages, or regulations,

[1] See 621; re-enacted, Code of Civil Procedure, 1872, sec. 748.

when not in conflict with the constitution and laws of this State, shall govern the decision of the action." In Yale's Legal Titles to Mining Claims and Water Rights in California, San Francisco, 1867, will be found an interesting account of these mining customs and their becoming Law.

Custom often arises from judicial decisions

Not only does custom play a small part, at the present day, as a source of non-contractual Law, but it is doubtful if it ever did, doubtful whether, at all stages of legal history, rules laid down by judges have not generated custom, rather than custom generated the rules. It has often been assumed, almost as a matter of course, that legal customs preceded judicial decisions, and that the latter have but served to give expression to the former, but of this there appears to be little proof. It seems at least as probable that customs arose from judicial decisions. Such was the opinion of Maine. In his Ancient Law he says:—"Custom [is] a conception posterior to that of Themistes or judgments. However strongly we, with our modern associations, may be inclined to lay down *a priori* that the notion of a custom must precede that of a judicial sentence, and that a judgment must affirm a custom or punish its breach, it seems quite certain that the historical order of the ideas is that in which I have placed them. The Homeric word for a custom in the embryo is sometimes 'Themis' in the singular,—more often 'Dike,' the meaning of which visibly fluctuates between a 'judgment' and a 'custom' or 'usage'." [1]

Ihering, in his *Kampf um's Recht*,[2] has pointed out how fallacious is the comparison between the growth of

[1] Ancient Law (Pollock's ed.), 4, 5. On Themis and Dike, cf. E. C. Clark, Jurisprudence, c. 4.

[2] (10th ed.) 5 *et seq.*

language and the growth of the Law,—the supposition that in old Rome the Law that a creditor could sell his debtor into slavery was formed in no other fashion than the rule that *cum* governs the ablative. To have a right by Law or custom means that by Law or custom another man's freedom of action is restricted, that he must act or refrain from acting, not as he wishes, but as another wishes; and it is probable that this abnegation of self did not arise quietly, but, on the contrary, that the assertion of superiority had to be made good by the forces of society being brought to bear. It does not seem likely that the part of the Law which does not merely give expression to principles for the interpretation of agreements, but which imposes duties as the consequence of occupying certain relations or doing certain acts, could have arisen from custom alone, without the aid of judicial decision. Take, for instance, the liability of innkeepers for goods stolen from their inns. This is said to rest on a custom, but it does not seem likely that innkeepers would voluntarily subject themselves to such a liability; nor, to take another instance, that a man who had assaulted another or converted his chattels would make compensation, unless compelled by the courts.

What has been said of customs in general may be true even of many of the local customs which are so common in England. They may also have had their origin in decisions of the local courts. Thus, the custom of borough English that the youngest son should inherit,[1] or the custom of London that if a horse left with an innkeeper had eaten off his head, the innkeeper might sell him,[2] or the

[1] Litt. § 165; 2 Pollock & Maitland, Hist. Eng. Law (2d ed.), 279.
[2] *Moss* v. *Townsend*. 1 Buls. 207.

custom in the forest of Hardwicke that any one stealing any commodity of the value of thirteen pence halfpenny "either hand-habend, back-berand or confessand," instead of being hanged, should be beheaded in the town of Halifax,[1] are all likely to have had their origin in judicial decisions.

In the Common Law, as has been said, custom has been deemed a more copious source of Law than the facts will warrant, but, back of custom, the courts and writers have not felt called upon to go; in Germany, however, there has been much discussion whether custom is a source of Law or whether it is only evidence of previously existing Law.

Custom as evidence of the Law

A theory which has widely prevailed in Germany is that custom is not a source of Law, but is only evidence or the means of acquiring knowledge of what the Law is; that it is the conviction of the *Volksgeist* that it is necessary that a certain thing should be Law which makes it Law; that custom is only evidence that there is such a conviction of the *Volksgeist*. This theory was first propounded by Savigny, and afterwards by Puchta, and the great reputation of these men and, at least in the case of Savigny, the deservedly great reputation, has caused the theory to find wide acceptance, not only in Germany but in other countries.[2]

One objection to this theory is that it rests on a fiction. There is no such thing *in rerum natura* as a *Volksgeist* having real consciousness and convictions. The fact is that certain individuals, exercising their separate wills,

[1] Halifax and its Gibbet Law placed in a true light. Halifax (1708). (By Samuel Midgley.) Reprint, 1886, p. 13.

[2] P. 89, *ante*.

repeatedly do certain acts, and judges may consider with favor these modes of action and apply them as rules; but the matter is not made easier by saying that such repeated acts are the means of knowing the necessary convictions of a non-existent entity.

As the views of the German philosophers which exercised an overmastering influence, even on such minds as that of Savigny, are becoming antiquated and are losing their following in their native country, the later German jurists are going back to the theory which prevailed before the rise of the so-called Historic School and are holding that it is custom which is a source of Law and not the *Ueberzeugung* (conviction) of the *Volksgeist*.[1] It must be said, however, that the Imperial Court seems to have a leaning for the Savigny-Puchta theory.[2]

Decisions often independent of custom

Customs, it is very probable, owed their origin in many cases to judicial decisions, but even in those cases in which customs may have preceded the decisions, they were often, in earlier days, taken up into the Law by the courts, not simply because they were the customs of the community, but because they commended themselves to the judges' own sense of right or policy, or frequently because the judges believed or feigned to believe that they were of supernatural origin. But, more than this, in early times it was the same privileged class, generally sacerdotal in its character, which furnished both legislators and judges, and from the accounts that we have of the Hebrews, it is clear that it was not what was believed

[1] See 1 Windscheid, Pand. § 16, note 1; Zitelmann, 66 Arch. f. civ. Pr. 323; Rümelin, 27 Jahrb. f. Dogm. 153.

[2] See Zitelmann, *ubi sup.* and also 12 Entsch. des Reichsg. Civ. 294; 26 Entsch. Civ. 193.

to be the customs of the people, but what was believed to be the expressed will of God, that was taken up into the Law; and, indeed, that the Law was antagonistic in the extreme to the beliefs and customs of the nation.[1]

[1] Compare p. 92, *ante*.

CHAPTER XIII

MORALITY AND EQUITY

Morality a necessary source of Law

WHEN a case comes before a court for decision, it may be that nothing can be drawn from the sources heretofore mentioned; there may be no statute, no judicial precedent, no professional opinion, no custom, bearing on the question involved, and yet the court must decide the case somehow; the decision of cases is what courts are for. The French Code Civil says: *"Le juge qui refusera de juger sous prétexte du silence, de l'obscurité ou de l'insuffisance de la loi, pourra être poursuivi comme coupable de déni de justice."*[1] And I do not know of any system of Law where a judge is held to be justified in refusing to pass upon a controversy because there is no person or book or custom to tell him how to decide it. He must find out for himself; he must determine what the Law ought to be; he must have recourse to the principles of morality.

In organized communities, political or other, the courts, in laying down rules for the decision of cases, are hemmed in and limited in many ways; the duty and responsibility of considering what rules they ought to apply is largely taken away from them, and there is imposed upon them, or they impose upon themselves, by reason of statutes, precedents, professional opinion or custom, lines of con-

[1] Art. 4.

duct to be followed without regard to their moral character; but where these limitations have not been imposed, then it is safe to say that in all civilized societies the courts are impliedly directed to decide in accordance with the precepts of morality.

Scope of term "morality"

Of course, I take morality in its largest sense, and mean by moral conduct, right conduct. In many, perhaps in most, of the questions, which are raised in the Law, morality presents itself in the guise of public policy. But even when the motive of the judge is simply to bring one doctrine into harmony with another doctrine, or to extend a doctrine by analogy, he is acting in an ethical way, for it is a good thing in itself that the rules of the Law should be harmonious, and should be extended harmoniously.

It is from this source that a great amount of our Law is drawn. In fact it is the way in which most new Law is now brought in, except what is due to the statute-book; and it should be observed that this source not only works alone when the others fail, but that when the others are in operation, this mingles with them and largely influences their direction and effect. Whether a statute shall be interpreted one way or another is often determined by the moral character which the one or the other interpretation will give to it; and there are few judicial precedents or professional opinions or customs whose position as sources of Law is not strengthened or weakened by the fact of their agreeing or disagreeing with sound ethical principles. In fact, in a large number of cases, the sources of the Law are indistinguishably joined.

Morality as a topic for Jurisprudence

Austin, in his Province of Jurisprudence Determined, having devoted the first lecture to a consideration of the

Nature of Law, takes up in the second the question of the index to the unrevealed Divine Law, and discusses it at great length through three lectures; as is well known, he arrives at the conclusion that utility is the index of the Divine Law and the test of morality.

It is hard to defend Austin's consistency in thus giving up so large a part of the volume to a discussion on the test of morality. The main thesis of the book is to show that positive Law is the command of the Sovereign; that its existence and force are in no way dependent upon the ethics of its contents; and that positive Law is the subject-matter of Jurisprudence as compared with the Science of Legislation. And this has often been remarked upon. Thus Sir Henry Maine:[1]—"The truth is that Austin's system is consistent with *any* ethical theory; and, if Austin seems to assert the contrary, I think the cause is to be sought in his firm conviction of the truth of his own ethical creed, which, I need not say, was Utilitarianism in its earlier shape. . . . Devotion to this philosophy, coupled with what I hold to be a faulty arrangement, has produced the most serious blemish in the 'Province of Jurisprudence Determined.' The second, third, and fourth lectures are occupied with an attempt to identify the law of God and the law of Nature (so far as these last words can be allowed to have any meaning) with the rules required by the theory of utility. . . . Taken at its best, it is a discussion belonging not to the philosophy of law, but to the philosophy of legislation. The jurist, properly so called, has nothing to do with any ideal standard of law or morals."

[1] Early Hist. of Inst. 368-370.

From Austin's point of view, his discussion of the test of morality may not be justifiable, but when we believe the doctrines of morality to be a source, and one of the main sources, from which the Law is drawn, they are as appropriate for the consideration of Jurisprudence as are the statutes, precedents, professional opinions, or customs to which the courts have recourse for their rules.

Indeed, if Jurisprudence is to be a progressive science, it must take cognizance of the changes which knowledge or ignorance has produced in human beliefs and ideals. Take three communities, let them have the same statutes and the other sources of Law the same, but let the courts of one of them adopt the Koran as its index of morality, another the Bible as interpreted in England one hundred and fifty years ago, and another the scheme of morals, whatever it may be, which prevails, say in France, at the present day, the Laws of those three communities will show before long a varying development.[1]

The test of morality

What is the true test of morality is not a question

[1] "Now for what I have called the deontological method of dealing with the Law, the consideration of its fitness or unfitness to meet the needs of society. This is for legislators and the advisers of legislators. How far is it a method to be followed by judges and jurists? The opinions of judges in the Common Law and of jurists in the Civil Law on what society needs have profoundly influenced the Law, and for the better. And what could be a happier state of affairs than that judges and jurists should approach the Law from the side of the public welfare and seek to adapt it to the promotion of the common good? And yet we must use caution here. Nothing would be more to be desired than that judges and jurists should mould and guide the Law to make it correspond to the needs of society, *if* they know what the needs of society are. But this is a tremendous *if;* they probably do not know; there is little in their calling and life to have given them that knowledge. Judges and jurists are men of their time; they are swayed, like the rest of us, by the *Zeitgeist*, and it is well that they are; but that they should consciously set about developing the Law, say in a socialistic or anti-socialistic manner, is not well." (Nature and Sources of the Law, 1st ed., sections 7 and 8.) See also pp. 139-144, *ante.*

which can be answered here. It is obvious that it is very important for the theory of the Law. To take an instance: In many of the States, the question of the liability of the Pullman Car Company for the loss by theft from a sleeping car of a commercial traveller's bag containing samples of hat pins, is a novel one, and the judges are or will be called on to make Law upon it. What question should a judge ask? Should it be, "What protection of a sample bag is desirable to secure the greatest happiness of the greatest number?" or should it be, "What is my intuitive moral sense on the subject of Pullman cars?" or again, should it be, "What is God's revealed or unrevealed will touching bagmen?" or again, "What dealing with drummers is most in accordance with the Freedom of the Will?" or, "What protection to hat pins is most according to Nature?" or is it a mixed affair to which two or more of these tests should be applied? It is conceivable that application of these different tests might lead to different results.

But although the test selected for determining the morality of a course of conduct and, therefore, the propriety of a decision, is theoretically of the first importance, yet it must be admitted that the conscious adoption of one test rather than another by a judge is not of so much practical consequence as might at first be supposed, for, by a familiar principle of human nature, when a man thinks that a thing ought to be done, he will not find it difficult to make it stand all the tests of morality that may be applied to it, and he will come to the conclusion that the greatest happiness of the greatest number, the dictates of conscience, the will of God, the Freedom of the Will, and Nature, unite in demanding it.[1]

Whatever may be the test to establish the ultimate principles of morality, the doctrine of utility must be all-important in working out details. But whose good should a court seek, the good of the community whose organ it is, or the good of the world at large? Should it, for instance, give preference to the domestic over the foreign creditors of a bankrupt? The true doctrine, though I advance this with some diffidence, would seem to be that the position of the courts should be much the same as that of a private individual. With an individual, regard for himself, for his family, and for others, all go to make up a complete morality; so, with a judge, as an organ of the State, regard for the members of the State and for persons not members of the State should be joined. The science of ethics, whatever it may do in the future, has as yet made trifling progress in settling any practical rules for the decision of such questions.

Equity is sometimes spoken of as one of the sources of Law, but it seems neither desirable nor possible to differentiate "equitable" considerations from other considerations looking to the general weal out of which the courts frame rules. **Equity**

Equity with us consists of the rules that were brought into the English Law by the special court held by the Chancellor. Austin[2] and Maine[3] take *æquitas* in the

[1] It should be observed as an excuse, if not a justification, for much of the talk about the Law of Nature, that if accordance with Nature be the test of morality, then it is not wrong to speak of Nature as a source of the Law.

[2] 2 Jur. (4th ed.) 577.

[3] Ancient Law, chap. 3.

Roman Law as having an analogous meaning; they apply the term to those rules which the prætors introduced through the Edict in modification of the *jus civile.* The analogy between the prætor and chancellor is certainly striking and had often been remarked before, as by Gilbert in his *Lex Prætoria,*[1] but it seems to be an error to suppose that *æquitas* had this sense in the Roman Law. Professor Clark doubts "whether *æquitas* is ever clearly used by the Roman jurists to indicate simply a *department* of law;"[2] and an examination of the authorities more than justifies his doubt; *æquitas* is opposed to *strictum jus,* and, as Professor Clark says, varies in meaning "between reasonable modification of the letter, and substantial justice"; and Krüger appears to be right in taking *æquitas* as a frame of mind in dealing with legal questions and not as a source of Law.[3] It is true that the prætor's Edict was a field favorable for the exercise of this "sweet reasonableness," but it was not the only one, and in the constitution of Severus and Antoninus (A.D. 202), concerning the amendment of pleadings, *æquitas* is given as a reason for going outside the provisions of the Edict in allowing amendments, *"prout edicti perpetui monet auctoritas vel jus reddentis decernit æquitas."*[4]

Relation of Law to Morality

A chief object in these lectures has been an attempt to show that one of the main difficulties and causes of confusion in Jurisprudence has been the failure to distinguish between Law and the sources of Law. The Law of a

[1] History and Practice of the High Court of Chancery, chap. 2, *et passim.*

[2] E. C. Clark, Jurisprudence, 367.

[3] Krüger, Geschichte d. Quellen, § 17, pp. 125, 126.

[4] "Accordingly as the authority of the perpetual edict prescribes, or the equity of him who is rendering justice determines." Cod. II, 1, 3. On the Edict, see p. 199, *ante.*

country or other organized body of men is composed of the rules for conduct that its courts follow and that it holds itself out as ready to enforce; no ideas, however just, that its courts refuse to follow are Law, and all rules which they follow and to which it enforces obedience are Law; and to introduce any notion of the Law of Nature or of *nicht positivisches Recht* into the conception of the Law is to take a step backward in Jurisprudence. It is depressing to see a recent writer like Mr. George H. Smith [1] taking up this exploded superstition, when the Germans who have so long labored under it are throwing off the burden.[2]

On the other hand, it is the failing of many advocates of codification to regard the Law too much as a fixed product of statutes, precedents, and customs, and not to take into sufficient account the growth and change of the Law. This growth and change is not a mere weaving of spider webs out of the bowels of the present rules of Law; a source of the Law, not the only source, but a source and a main source, is found in the principles of ethics. These principles, therefore, are legitimately a part of Jurisprudence, and the more the bounds of Comparative Jurisprudence are extended, the greater part will they play.[3]

[1] In his book cited above, p. 15.

[2] See Bergbohm, *Jurisprudenz und Rechtsphilosophie, passim.* See also pp. 94-96, *ante.*

[3] See pp. 141-144, *ante.*

APPENDIX I

PII USUS IN THE LATER ROMAN EMPIRE[1]

Of the *Pii usus* in the later Roman Empire and their legal position, we derive most of our knowledge from passages in the Code and Novels of the *Corpus Juris*; the provisions of the Code touching the matter which antedate Justinian are few.

Constantine (A.D. 321), at or soon after his conversion, issued a proclamation *"ad Populum,"* declaring that any one might leave property *"sanctissimæ catholicæ* [*ecclesiæ*] *venerabilique concilio."*[2] The council seems to have been regarded as the corporate body of the church. This view, however, did not prevail. I am not aware of any other passage which indicates that the Church Universal was regarded, in the eye of the Civil Law, as a juristic person.

The Emperors Honorius and Theodosius enacted (A.D. 409) that not over nine hundred and fifty deacons should be assigned to the Church of Constantinople and that *"nulli alii corporatorum"* beyond that number should any immunities be granted,[3]—thus apparently recognizing the deacons as members of a corporation.[4] Later, the same Emperors (A.D. 423) spoke of *"divinæ domi*

[1] See p. 59, *ante.*
[2] Cod. I, 2, 1.
[3] Cod. I, 2, 4.
[4] See Cod. I, 2, 14.

et venerabiles ecclesiæ" as charged with the duty of repairing roads and bridges.[1] The particular church or other ecclesiastical body appears to have been regularly considered as the corporate unit,[2] and (A.D. 434) the Emperors Theodosius and Valentinian issued an edict permitting the clergy, or monks, or nuns to bequeath property to their church or monastery, and giving the church or monastery its action to recover the property,[3] thus recognizing it fully as a juristic person; and it was enacted (A.D. 455) by the Emperors Valentinian and Marcian that any widow or deaconess or virgin dedicated to God, or *"sanctimonialis mulier,"* might leave property by will, *"ecclesiæ vel martyrio vel clerico vel monacho vel pauperibus,"* [4] and two days later, the objection having apparently been made that a gift *pauperibus* might be held bad as *incertis personis,* it was enacted: *"Id quod pauperibus testamento vel codicillis relinquitur, non ut incertis personis relictum evanescat, sed modis omnibus ratum firmumque consistat."* [5]

The difficulty of administering a gift to an uncertain class who could not be considered as constituting a juristic person seems to have been first felt in the case of gifts for the redemption of captives. The Emperor Leo enacted (A.D. 468) [6] that if a testator gave a legacy for the redemption of captives and named a person through whom the redemption should be made, such person should have

[1] Cod. I, 2, 7.
[2] See Cod. I, 2, 12.
[3] Cod. I, 3, 20.
[4] Cod. I, 2, 13.
[5] "A legacy left to the poor by a will or codicils is not to fail as being left to uncertain persons, but is in every way to stand approved and established." Cod. I, 3, 24.
[6] Cod. I, 3, 28.

the right to get the legacy; but that if the testator had not named any one to take it, then the bishop should have the right to exact it from the heirs and should carry out the intent of the testator and render an account to the governor of the province. This *"facultas exigendi"* gave legal personality to the bishop in his official character.[1]

In the year 472, in the reign of the Emperors Leo and Anthemius, we find, for the first time, mention of *xenodochia* and *ptochia*, or guest houses and almshouses, and of the privileges awarded to them.[2] And in the same year, all the privileges granted *"orphanotrophio sive asceteriis vel ecclesiis aut ptochiis seu xenodochiis aut monasteriis atque ceteris hominibus etiam ac rebus juris eorum,"* were put under the charge of Nico, a priest and *orphanotrophus,* and his successors.[3] This brings us down to the time of Justinian.

There was a great deal of legislation by Justinian on matters concerning the Church, much of it with reference to the alienation of ecclesiastical property, which was in general prohibited. This legislation is contained both in the Code and in the Novels. The first edition of the Code was published A.D. 529, and the second, *repetitæ prælectionis,* A.D. 534. The provisions of the Code concerning eleemosynary institutions are contained mainly in the second and third chapters of the first book. Gifts for ecclesiastical or eleemosynary purposes are said to be *super piis causis,*[4] εἰς εὐσεβεῖς χρείας,[5] and besides the objects that were enumerated in the edicts of Jus-

[1] Cf. Cod. I, 3, 48 (49); Nov. 131, 11.

[2] Cod. I, 3, 32 (33), 7.

[3] "To an orphanage or hermitages or churches or almshouses or guest houses or monasteries, or to other persons [*i.e.* slaves] or things belonging to them." Cod. I, 3, 34 (35).

[4] Cod. I, 2, 19.

[5] Cod. I, 3, 41 (42), 1.

tinian's predecessors, *ecclesiæ, divinæ domi, martyria, orphanotrophia, asceteria, ptochia, xenodochia, monasteria,* we now find also *noscomia, ptochotrophia,*[1] *xenones, brephotrophia, gerontocomia.*[2]

Where the remains are so scanty, it is dangerous to speak with certainty, but it seems as if these various institutions were corporations with members, like those of the Common Law and the secular corporations of the Romans, and not mere abstract conceptions, without individual members, like the modern German *Stiftungen.* Thus, after enumerating several of these eleemosynary institutions, Justinian adds, *"vel siquid aliud tale consortium";* and later in the same edict, he speaks of *"domuum quæ piis consortiis deputatæ sunt,"* [3] and in another edict, after speaking of gifts and legacies, *ecclesiis, xenonibus,* etc., he goes on: *"Sive itaque memoratis religiossimis locis vel civitatibus hereditas sive legatum sive fideicommissum fuerit relictum."* [4] And in a law passed A.D. 530, after speaking of gifts to several kinds of eleemosynary institutions which he specifies, he goes on: "Ἢ ἁπλῶς συστήμασί τισιν εὐαγέσιν ἢ ὅλως οὐκ ἀπηγορευμένοις τῶν ἐκ πλήθους ἠθροισμένων." [5] And in a new law, A.D. 534, he speaks of property granted in perpetuity "τοῖς εὐαγέσιν οἴκοις καὶ ταῖς αὐτῶν συστάσεσιν." [6]

We have seen that it had been declared in 455 that a gift to the poor should not be deemed bad as made

[1] "Infirmaries, almshouses." Cod. I, 2, 19.

[2] "Guest houses, foundling hospitals, homes for the aged." Cod. I, 2, 22.

[3] "Or any other such association," "of the houses allotted to religious associations." Cod. I, 2, 22.

[4] "And so if an inheritance or a legacy or a trust shall be left to renowned holy places or cities." Cod. I, 2, 23. Cf. Cod. I, 2, 19.

[5] "Either simply to any religious congregations or to societies not in any way prohibited by law." Cod. I, 3, 45 (46), 9.

[6] "To the holy houses and their congregations." Cod. I, 3, 55 (57), 3.

incertis personis, but that nothing was done by way of creating a right to have such a gift enforced. This defect Justinian cured. By an edict (A.D. 531), after dealing with some special cases, he declared that if "the poor" simply were made heirs, the inheritance should go to the xenon of the city—"*xenonem ejus civitatis omnimodo hereditatem nancisci*";[1] and an even more striking rule had been established in the preceding year, that if any one should make Christ his heir, the church of the testator's domicil should be the heir; and if any archangel or martyr was named as heir, his oratory should be deemed the heir.[2]

If the heirs of a testator did not carry out the will of the testator, for instance, in building a church or a *xenodochium,* it was made the business of the bishop to bring them before the court (ἀπαιτεῖν) and compel them to perform the will of the deceased.[3]

The Novels add but little to our knowledge of the constitution of eleemosynary institutions. We find the word *collegium* used to indicate such a body;[4] an action is given to a church against its *œconomi* or administrators;[5] and for certain transactions the consent is required, not only of the rulers of every "*venerabilis domus,*" but also of the "*amplior pars in eis deservientium.*"[6]

These eleemosynary institutions were, therefore, probably regarded in the later Roman Empire as corporations.

[1] "The guest house of that city shall surely obtain the inheritance." Cod. I, 3, 48 (49).

[2] Cod. I, 2, 25 (26). Cf. Nov. 131, 9.

[3] Cod. I, 3, 45 (46). Cf. Nov. 131, 10.

[4] Nov. 7, *passim.*

[5] Nov. 7.

[6] "The greater part of those attached to their service." Nov. 120, 6 *et* 7.

APPENDIX II

HEREDITAS JACENS[1]

THERE are few Common Law lawyers who have nibbled ever so little in the pastures of the Civil Law who have not been fascinated with the conception of the *hereditas jacens.* Beside the clumsy machinery of our Law for getting the property which has belonged to a deceased person home to those who are to have the beneficial interest in it, the conception of an entity which can continue the legal relations of the deceased towards persons and things until new relations of the living are established in their place, seems one of the most philosophical and practically useful of legal conceptions, to have all of the advantages and few of the disadvantages that spring from making an abstraction into a legal person. But a slight examination shows that the Civil Law is no better off than ours, and that *hereditas jacens* has but a limited scope.

Let me first call attention to what becomes of a man's rights at Common Law upon his death. There is a great difference between real and personal property.

And first as to land. If a man dies intestate, there is no interval in the ownership of land; the heir is at once seised of the land, he has seisin in law, he is the

[1] See p. 56, *ante*.

owner. The succession is not that of a universal successor;[1] the heir takes each parcel of land as a singular successor.[2] It is true that until the heir entered into actual possession of the land, he did not, at Common Law, become a stock of descent, and on his death the estate in the land passed not to his heir, but to the heir of the ancestor last seised in fact, and if a stranger entered upon the land before the heir, there was said to be an abatement, and not a disseisin;[3] but, in general, the heir's rights and remedies are the same whether he has entered or not.[4]

The devisee of land is also a singular successor. A devisee need not accept a devise. Whether acceptance of a devise is a condition precedent to the seisin passing to the devise is, perhaps, not entirely clear; but even if it is necessary, yet there is no vacancy in the seisin; if it is not in the devisee, it is in the heir.

As to personal property. Until the executor assented or intermeddled, or, in case of intestacy, until the administrator was appointed, the ordinary (*i.e.* the bishop) in England succeeded to the rights of the deceased,[5] and now, by statute, the Judge of the Probate Court takes what the ordinary did formerly (21 & 22 Vict. c. 95,

[1] One who acquires all the rights and duties of the person to whom he succeeds.

[2] One who takes only particular property, and is not liable for the former owner's debts.

[3] 2 Bl. Com. 209.

[4] There seems to be a real vacancy in the possession, on the death of an individual who is a corporation sole (see p. 57, *ante*), until the successor is appointed (Litt. § 647); and so, also, upon the death of a tenant *pur auter vie*, until the general occupant enters. (At common law, when a person, who held land during the life of another person, died during the life of that other person, the remainder of the term was enjoyed by whoever first took possession of the land. He was called the general occupant. See 2 Bl. Com. 258.)

[5] 2 Bl. Com. 494; 2 Pollock & Maitland, Hist. of Eng. (2d ed.) 356 *et seq.*

§ 19). The question seems never to have been discussed in the United States.

A difficulty under which we lie at the Common Law from not having a legal entity corresponding to the popular idea of the "estate" of a deceased person appears after the legal title has become vested in the executor or administrator, from the circumstance that there is no way in which the "estate" can be bound, otherwise than by a mortgage or pledge of the assets. For instance, suppose it is desirable that goods should be cared for, there is no way of binding the estate to pay for it, the suit must be against the executor. It is true the executor has a right to compensate himself out of the assets of the estate, and that the warehouse-keeper can be subrogated to the right of the executor, but if the balance of the accounts between the estate and the executor is against the latter, there is nothing to which the creditor can be subrogated.

Perhaps when it came to be applied, it would be found that the idea of an abstract entity in which resided the rights and obligations of the deceased, and of which the executor was the agent, however attractive in theory, might not work well in practice. Certain it is that the Roman Law did not rise to such a conception.

If the Law of Succession is one of the least admirable parts of our Jurisprudence, it is also not one of those parts of the Roman Law which are entitled to much praise. It was not till the time of Justinian, long after the period of the classical jurists, that an heir could accept an inheritance without making himself personally liable for all the debts of the deceased. As soon as he accepted the inheritance, he immediately owned the property, he was the one who sued to enforce all claims that the deceased had, and every claim of a creditor or legatee was a claim against him personally, which he had to satisfy in the same way as a debt which he had himself incurred. And yet the settlement of the estate could be worked out only through the instrumentality of the heir.

In the interval, as I have said, between the death of the ancestor and the moment when the heir accepted the inheritance, the Romans placed the *hereditas jacens,*— an expression, by the way, which does not occur in the *Corpus Juris,* but is taken from the language of D. XVIII, 24, 13, 5, *"puta hereditas jacebat."* [1]

Whether the *hereditas jacens* is or is not a juristic person, yet in the sense common among the Romans, of *persona* as character, office, function, the *hereditas jacens* has a *persona.* Whether it represents the *persona* of the ancestor or of the heir, has been disputed. If it is the latter, then the title of the heir relates back to the death of the ancestor, and the property passes immediately from the ancestor to the heir. If, on the other hand, the *hereditas* continues the person of the ancestor, then the succession passes, not directly from the ancestor to the heir, but through the *hereditas.* According to Ihering's view,[2] which I am inclined to accept, the original doctrine was that the title of the heir related back to the death of the ancestor, but subsequently the theory that the *hereditas jacens* represented the ancestor was adopted and prevailed, some survivals of the older view remaining to mar the symmetry of his new doctrine.

To come back to the question whether the *hereditas jacens* is a juristic person, the subject of rights and duties. It has no organs through which it can express

[1] "Suppose, the inheritance lies (vacant)"
[2] Abhandlungen aus d. röm. R. p. 149 *et seq.*

volition; no action seems to have been given to it; nor does it appear to have been the subject of legal duties, to have ever been recognized as bound to do or forbear, or as an object of compulsion. By a *missio in bona* (delivery of possession of the goods), the goods of a deceased person were sold and the purchaser became the universal successor of the deceased, but the *hereditas jacens* never seems to have been a party to the proceeding, nor to have been called upon for any action. Savigny [1] and Sohm [2] agree in denying that the *hereditas jacens* is a juristic person. But it must be admitted that it is often called so. As by Florentinus: "*Hereditas personæ vice fungitur, sicut municipium et decuria et societas*"; [3] and frequently by modern civilians; [4] and although it could not sue or be sued, it must, I suppose, have had a right to police protection like that awarded to the property of new-born children and infants,[5] and so must be considered as having some legal rights and as being, therefore, though to a very limited extent, a juristic person.

In Scotland, which derives its Jurisprudence from the Roman Law, the *hereditas jacens,* besides having the right to police protection, of which I have just spoken, seems to be the subject of a legal duty, for, in that country, when the heir renounces, a decreet issues at the suit of a creditor of the deceased, *cognitionis causa, contra hereditatem jacentem et bona immobilia* and other goods and gear appertaining to the defunct.[6]

[1] 2 Heut. röm. Recht, § 102.

[2] Inst. § 96.

[3] "The inheritance takes the place of a person, just like a municipality or a board or an association." D. XLVI, 1, 22.

[4] See 3 Windscheid, Pand. § 531.

[5] See p. 22, *ante*.

[6] "To make inquest, against the vacant inheritance and the landed property." 1 Erskine, Inst. Book II, tit. 12, §§ 47 *et seq.;* Dallas, Styles (ed. 1697) 214.

APPENDIX III

RECEPTION OF THE ROMAN LAW[1]

ALTHOUGH the claim of the Emperors of Germany to continue the succession of the Roman Emperors naturally made them think and speak of the Roman Law as their law;[2] although, in the second half of the twelfth century, Frederick Barbarossa, in deciding disputes in Germany, relied on rules of the Roman Law;[3] and although, in course of time, there was formed a conception of imperial law (which, however, embraced not only the *Corpus Juris* of Justinian, but also the laws of the German Empire); yet very much was wanting to the practical operation of these views, and throughout the whole of the Middle Ages there are but rare traces in Germany of the application of Roman legal doctrines in life and in the courts.

About the middle of the fifteenth century, however,

[1] See p. 93, *ante*.

[2] Thus, at the beginning of the eleventh century, Otto III, during his stay at Rome, provided thus for the investiture of a judge: "*Tunc dicat imperator judici: 'Cave ne aliqua occasione Justiniani sanctissimi antecessoris nostri legem subvertas.' Tunc imperator . . . det ei in manum librum codicum et dicat: 'Secundum hunc librum judica Romam et Leoninam orbemque universum.*" "Then let the emperor say to the judge: 'Take care lest on any occasion you subvert the law of Justinian our most holy predecessor.' Then let the emperor . . . give into his hand the book of the codes and say: 'According to this book judge Rome, and the Leonine city, and the whole world.'" (The Leonine city was a part of Rome fortified by Pope Leo IV.) Cited 1 Stobbe, Geschichte der deutschen Rechtsquellen, § 59, p. 613.

[3] See 1 Stobbe, pp. 616-618.

the German universities began to teach the Roman Law, at first in a sufficiently stupid manner, but afterwards, following the lead of Italy, more intelligently; and in the great and, indeed, extravagant admiration of learning, characteristic of the time, men who had been educated at German or foreign universities, and who were imbued with the doctrines of the Civil Law, came by rapid degrees to acquire Court favor, power and judicial position, and introduced into the practice of the tribunals elements of an entirely novel and foreign character.

There is much to explain this. The German people were split up into a great number of States, many of them very petty, each with its own separate system of Law. Undoubtedly there was much unity of spirit in those systems, but this unity has been rather a discovery of modern times than what was then obvious. The philologist can trace the close grammatical connection between the languages of two countries, and yet the inhabitants of one of the countries may be totally unable to understand those of the other. The like is true as to the Law. And further, in the rapid growth from barbarism to civilization, it was natural and laudable that aid should be sought from the only system of law of which anything was known that had prevailed among a civilized people.

But, none the less, the introduction of the Roman Law, instead of carrying out the convictions of the people, was extremely distasteful to them. To quote from Stobbe: "This law was and continued to be a foreign law; the people did not know or understand it; it was centuries before the want of harmony which necessarily resulted from the mixture of heterogeneous elements was overcome. With nothing less than violence was the foreign law brought in. While in the court and city tribunals it obtained an almost unlimited control, customary law and ancient usages held their own for centuries yet in the peasant's courts. . . . By degrees only was the foreign law assimiliated to the domestic, and not even to-day have many legal principles, taken over from foreign law, become popular, that is, corresponding to a general legal feeling. . . . The jurists disputed over the interpretation of this or that passage, and over the decision of controversies; the people, without exception, had no interest and no understanding for these moot questions and gave up all influence on the definition and development of its law." [1]

Stobbe gives many instances of the dislike, and indeed hatred, of the Roman Law and its professors. As an instance, here is one more moderate in its tone than several others. "*Cum jus municipale servandum sit et antiquæ consuetudines pro legibus habendæ sint, fit, ut multa his contraria fiant, unde deceptiones, errores et turbæ oriuntur. Illi enim juris professores nostrum morem ignorant, nec etiam si sciant, illis nostris consuetudinibus quicquam tribuere volunt.*" [2]

Nothing could be more unlike what is styled customary law than the Roman Law as it was received by the jurists. Customary law so called is built up of practical rules taught by experience, but the Roman Law was accepted

[1] 2 Stobbe, § 65, pp. 137, 139.

[2] "Although the local law should be observed, and the ancient customs should be considered as taking the place of written statutes, it comes to pass that many things are done contrary to them, whence frauds, mistakes and disturbances arise. For those professors of law are ignorant of our usages; and even if they know them, they will not make any concessions to those customs of ours." 2 Stobbe, § 64, p. 95.

as a whole by persons who were utterly ignorant of many things, if not of most things, that it contained. It was accepted as a whole by men who had yet to learn the rules which it comprised, while in customary law the rules come first and the system to unite them comes afterwards.

The view of the jurists themselves was not at all that they were the representatives of the people, to give effect to its legal customs by aid of their superior intelligence and training; on the contrary they regarded the Roman Law as the only true Law and the customs as irregularities to be regretted. To quote Stobbe once more: "In many writings and sayings they [the jurists] express the liveliest joy that they possess the *Leges,* and that by them, with a bound, they have risen from the deepest barbarism to civilization. But no one ever thought to ask the question how they got the *Leges* and whether they had a right to apply them. . . . In consequence of their measureless veneration for the foreign law, the jurists had utterly departed from the idea that the domestic German Law, which was expressed in general and particular customs and statutes, was the original law, and that the Roman Law came to it in later times as an auxiliary law; they had no feeling of the equal importance of the German Law. On the contrary, they argued as if the Roman Law, which was certainly older but which only at a late period had had any practical value for Germany, was the original, which, through particular German doctrines, had been modified or put out of use. Instead of saying that a Roman provision stood in contradiction with the German legal consciousness, so that its application was excluded through German rules of Law, they completely reversed the relation; it was the rule of the foreign law which, through a German custom or a German statute, had fallen into disuse. They spoke as if, before the reception of the Roman Law, there had been no law at all in Germany, and as if everything of German Law which prevailed in practice and was not abandoned had to be treated as a mere irregularity. A consequence of these views was that they despised the unwritten law, the German customs, and regarded them, so far as they did not agree with the Roman Law, as evil customs." [1]

[1] Stobbe, § 65, pp. 112, 115-117.

APPENDIX IV

AUTONOMY

It is said in the text[1] that the Germans do not attribute autonomy to ordinary private corporations; but there is a class of corporations, *öffentlichrechtlichen Corporationen* (public law corporations), to which autonomy has been attributed. Guilds (*Zünfte*) and the Universities belong to this class.[2] The power of independent self-government which bodies of this class possessed when they were originally formed and the slenderness of the tie between them and the State appears to have been the cause why they have been considered as having autonomy.[3] Such corporations, if now formed for the first time, would probably be relegated to the class of private corporations and all autonomy denied them. It is difficult to see at the present day how the rules made by such a body differ from the by-laws of the latest telephone company, and why one should have autonomy and the other not.[4]

The question which has been most discussed is whether the higher German nobility have autonomy; that is, whether the power given to the heads of the families of

[1] Pp. 158-159, *ante*.

[2] 1 Stobbe, Handb. d. deutsch. Privatr. § 20, pp. 124, 125.

[3] See Schröder, Lehrb. d. deutsch. Rechtsgeschichte (6th ed.) § 51, pp. 703-705.

[4] See pp. 107-109, *ante*.

the higher nobility, sometimes with, sometimes without, the consent of the other members of the family, to settle the order of devolution of the family property, is to be considered as the offspring of their autonomy, or whether it is merely an instance of authority given by the State to a certain class to deal with property in a certain way.

Gerber has denied the existence of autonomy altogether, and although his remarks are aimed principally at the claim to it by the higher nobility, he seems to deny it also to any corporations. Most of the writers, however, allow autonomy to the higher nobility, but differ greatly among themselves whether a family of that nobility is a corporation, some thinking autonomy to be a privilege which can be given only to a corporation, others denying this. Gerber, although apparently without much following in Germany, seems to a common-law lawyer to have the best of the argument.

The modern German writers, both those who admit autonomy to a greater or less extent, and those who deny it altogether, agree upon the test to be adopted. "The essential mark of the autonomic institution" (*Satzung*) is "that it has not the application of the Law, but the making of the Law for its object; that it establishes not legal relations but legal principles, and is not a legal transaction but an institution."[1] But this does not help us forward much.

The fact is that in early times there were bodies within the territorial limits of a State which, through their tribunals, exercised compulsion over persons, and yet these bodies were not the creatures of the State, and did not owe their authority to it. In the course of time,

[1] 1 Holtzendorff, Rechtslex. *Autonomie.*

as civilization has progressed, these bodies have lost their power of compulsion, except as they derive it from the State. If autonomy still exists in the higher German nobility, it is only a survival of early barbarism.

Neither the Roman Law, nor the English Common Law, nor, so far as I am aware, the Law of any country on the continent of Europe, except Germany, knows anything of autonomy.[1]

There does, however, seem to be one case of real autonomy, though I am not aware that the word has been used in connection with it, a case where general rules in an express form are sources of Law to the courts of an organization, although they are made by the legislative department of another organization. I refer to a church which, while not being an organ of the State, is yet recognized by the State as the only true Church. This, of course, is not so in the case of a State Church like the English, whose courts are His Majesty's Ecclesiastical Courts, which are at the mercy of Parliament, and which Parliament does not hesitate to alter in the most thoroughgoing manner; witness the establishment of the Judicial Committee of the Privy Council as the supreme ecclesiastical tribunal.[2]

[1] If autonomic Law has not been reduced to writing, it is usual to speak of *observance*, not of autonomy.

On autonomy see Gerber, Ueber den Begriff der Autonomie (1854) 37 Arch. für d. civ. Pr. 35-62; Nachträgliche Erörterungen (1859) 3 Jahrb. für Dogm., 411-448 (these two articles are also to be found in Gerber, Juristische Abhandlungen, 36, 64); Maurer, Ueber den Begriff der Autonomie (1855) 2 Kritische Ueberschau, 229-269; Jolly, Das Hausgesetz der Grafen von Giech (1859) 6 Kritische Ueberschau, 330-384; 1 Stobbe, Handb. d. deutsch. Privatr. §§ 19, 20, pp. 129-143; 1 Winscheid, Pand. § 19; Holtzendorff, Encyclopädie (5th ed.) 570. On the question whether a family of the upper German nobility is a juristic person, see Mejer, 5 Grünhut, Zeitschr. 229-269; in answer to Mejer, Beseler, *Ib.* 540-556; and Gierke, *Ib.* 557-599; and Mejer's reply, 6 Grünhut, Zeitschr. 201-210.

[2] See p. 109, note, *ante*.

An instance of what I have in mind is the Catholic Church in Spain,[1] or the Mohammedan Church or Synagogue, or whatever be the proper designation for the body of Moslem believers, in Turkey.[2] The canons of such a body are binding on the State courts, and yet the ecclesiastical council or the assembly of the Ulema is not an organ of the State. We may say of these rules, as Austin says of all Law, that inasmuch as the State could, if it would, forbid its courts to follow them, they must be considered as established by the State, but this mode of expression does not correspond to what is the opinion of the judges of the State, or of those to whom it administers justice.[3]

[1] *E.g.* Spanish Civil Code, Art. 42, 75, 80. I Lehr, Droit Civil Espagnol, 54 *et seq.* See also *Parapano* v. *Happaz*, [1894] A. C. 165.

[2] In India, the British courts recognize the Mohammedan religious law as binding on Mohammedan subjects, in certain matters. Sir R. K. Wilson, Anglo-Muhammedan Law (4th ed.) pp. 3, 83. It seems, however, that there exists nowhere within the Mohammedan Church any power to change or add to that law by legislation. *Ib.* 19, 23.

[3] See p. 85, *ante.*

APPENDIX V

DESUETUDE OF STATUTES IN THE UNITED STATES[1]

South Carolina. In South Carolina, as is said in the text,[2] certain Acts of the English Parliament were reënacted (1712) in terms and made expressly statutes of the Province; among these was the St. of 4 & 5 Ph. & M. *c.* 8, for the Punishment of such as shall take away maidens within the age of sixteen years. In 1802 an indictment under this statute was sustained. The reporter of the case remarks that this was the first conviction in South Carolina under the statute, and adds: "It may not be amiss here to observe that it does not follow that because a statute has been a long time dormant, it is, therefore, to be considered as obsolete."[3]

In 1818, the Constitutional Court of South Carolina held that a statute of 1706, giving a *qui tam* action[4] against a magistrate, being a layman, for presuming to marry any persons, was not in force. The court said that the statute was intended as one of the means of establishing the Episcopal Church, "but since the establish-

[1] P. 197, *ante.*

[2] P. 197, *ante.*

[3] *State* v. *Findlay*, 2 Bay, 418. See also *State* v. *O'Bannon*, 1 Bail. 144; *State* v. *Tidwell*, 5 Strob. 1.

[4] *Qui tam* actions are instituted by a person under a statute which imposes a penalty and gives a share to the informer, "*qui tam pro domino rege quam pro se ipso sequitur*," *i.e.*, "sues as well for the king as for himself."

ment of our free Constitution, the Act is totally inapplicable to our change and situation, and must, therefore, be considered as obsolete."[1] This would seem to have been a case of repeal by implication rather than of abrogation by desuetude, but Chancellor Wardlaw[2] spoke of it as "the only instance in our judicial history, in which courts have ventured to declare an Act of the Legislature inoperative from mere *non user.*"

All of the statutes passed by the Province of South Carolina before 1694 are said[3] to have been regarded by Judge Grimke, who compiled the Laws of South Carolina in 1790, as not in force.[4] On what this theory was based I do not know. It was adopted by the Court of Appeals, in reference to an Act passed in 1691 providing that any person guilty of "the odious and loathsome sin of drunkenness" might be punished *inter alia* by sitting in the stocks. The court say, "We would hesitate, even with some authority to sustain us, before we declared an Act found on our statute book obsolete from desuetude. But when that declaration has been made more than a century by an eminent jurist and the earliest compiler of our statute law, we may safely adopt his conclusion, especially in reference to the provisions of an Act so inapplicable at the present day."

Pennsylvania. In two cases in 1805[5] it was held that no statute can be repealed by *non user.* But in 1824, in a case[6] in which it was held that in Pennsylvania a com-

[1] *Watson* v. *Blaylock*, 2 Mill, 351.
[2] *Canady* v. *George*, 6 Rich. Eq. 103, 106 (1853).
[3] *O'Hanlon* v. *Myers*, 10 Rich. 128, 131 (1856).
[4] But see 2 Cooper, Sts. of So. Car., p. 1.
[5] *Respublica* v. *Commissioners of Philadelphia*, 4 Yeates, 181, 183; and *Glancey* v. *Jones*, *Id.* 212, 215.
[6] *James* v. *Commonwealth*, 12 S. & R. 220, 228.

mon scold could not be punished by being "placed in a certain engine of correction, called a cucking or ducking stool," Duncan, J., said: "As to the abrogation of statutes by '*non user*,' there may rest some doubt; for myself, I own my opinion is, that '*non user*' may be such as to render them obsolete, when their objects vanish or their reason ceases."

In 1826 [1] the court refused to declare obsolete a statute passed in 1722. Tilghman, C. J., said: "It must be a very strong case, to justify the court in deciding that an act standing in the statue book, unrepealed, is obsolete and invalid. I will not say that such a case may not exist—where there has been a *non user* for a great number of years—where, from a change of times and manners, an ancient sleeping statute would do great mischief, if suddenly brought into action—where a long practice, inconsistent with it, has prevailed, and especially where, from other and later statutes, it might fairly be inferred that, in the apprehension of the legislature, the old one was not in force. But this is not the case with the act of the year 1722. Its provisions are not unsuited to modern times."

In 1858 [2] it was sought to enforce a statute of 1819 limiting auditors' fees to $2 *per diem*. Woodward, J., delivering the opinion of the Supreme Court, said: "For many years this Act of Assembly was lost sight of—was omitted from our digests—and would seem to have been overlooked by this court in *Baldwin's Estate,* 4 Barr, 248, and perhaps in other cases. It is said, in view of these circumstances, that the Act is obsolete or repealed by *non*

[1] *Wright* v. *Crane,* 13 S. & R. 447, 452.
[2] *Porter's Appeals,* 30 Pa. 496, 498, 499.

user. On the other hand it is maintained that an Act of Assembly cannot be repealed by *non user.* Though I do not think this Act is repealed by *non user,* I cannot assent to the doctrine that the usages and customs of an advancing people are incapable of displacing an Act of Assembly that has become unfitted for modern use." The learned Judge then quoted Chief Justice Tilghman's language given above, and afterwards continued: "The notion that statutes are not repealable by *non user* is founded on two cases of not very high authority, 4 Yeates, 181, 212,[1] both of which depend on an *obiter dictum* in *White* v. *Boot,* 2 T.R. 275, a case that was overruled in *Leigh* v. *Kent,* 3 T.R. 364. A proposition no better supported cannot prevail against the clear reasoning of Chief Justice Tilghman in the case already cited from 13 S. & R.; but we quite agree with him, that it must be a very strong case in which we would set aside a statute on that ground, and we do not think this is such a case." The court, however, came to the conclusion that although the Act of 1819 was in force it did not apply to the case before it.

In 1882 [2] the court said of a statute of 1834: "So the law is written, and neither the overseers of the poor nor the courts can treat it as obsolete"; and in 1884 [3] a statute of 1721 forbidding any one to sell fireworks in Philadelphia "without the Governor's special license" was held to be in force. The court say: "It was long ago settled that an Act of Parliament cannot be repealed by *non user.* That this is also the rule in this State accords with reason and the absence of authority to the

[1] Cited p. 330, *ante.*
[2] *Kitchen* v. *Smith,* 101 Pa. 452, 456, 457.
[3] *Homer* v. *Commonwealth,* 106 Pa. 221, 226.

contrary. The settled rule is, that a statute can be repealed only by express provision of a subsequent law, or by necessary implication." [1]

Maryland. In 1829 [2] Bland, C., after referring to cases in England, where it was supposed that the doctrine of desuetude had been applied, and saying, "Our own act [1747, *c.* 3, § 10], which positively prohibits clerks and registers from suffering the papers and records to be taken out of their offices, appears to have been so long and so generally disregarded as to have fallen into oblivion," goes on thus: "These precedents would seem to sanction the position that a positive legislative enactment may be virtually repealed by a long, general, and uninterrupted course of practice. But they are precedents which I should feel a great repugnance to adopt and enlarge upon. . . . There can be no difference between the power to declare an act of Assembly obsolete, and the power to enact a new law. The power to repeal and to enact are of the same nature. I shall therefore always consider an express provision of a constitutional Act of Assembly as an authority superior to any usage or adjudged case whatever." [3]

Iowa. The Supreme Court of Iowa in 1887 [4] held that a provision in the Code of 1851, authorizing the proceeding against a distillery as a nuisance, was not to be considered repealed by *non user,* because no action had ever been taken under it, and, referring to an earlier case in Iowa,[5] which had been cited in support of the doctrine

[1] See also *Heidenwag* v. *Philadelphia,* 168 Pa. 72.
[2] *Snowden* v. *Snowden,* 1 Bland, 550.
[3] See *Tise* v. *Shaw,* 68 Md. 1, 8 (1887).
[4] *Pearson* v. *International Distillery,* 72 Iowa, 348, 357.
[5] *Hill* v. *Smith,* Morris, 70 (1840).

of repeal by *non user,* they say: "It is not said that the statute was repealed by *non user* alone, and it cannot be presumed that the court intended to present such a thought," and they declare that the repeal of the statute discussed in that case was by a later statute and not by mere *non user.*[1]

[1] See also p. 245, note, *ante.* for desuetude of a Kentucky statute.

TABLE OF CASES CITED

TABLE OF AUTHORS COMMENTED ON OR QUOTED

INDEX[1]

[1] See also Table of Authors Commented on.